Patterns in Java™, Volume 1

Patterns in Java™, Volume 1

A Catalog of Reusable Design Patterns Illustrated with UML

MARK GRAND

WILEY COMPUTER PUBLISHING

John Wiley & Sons, Inc.

New York • Chichester • Weinheim • Brisbane • Singapore • Toronto

Publisher: Robert Ipsen
Editor: Theresa Hudson
Assistant Editor: Kathryn A. Malm
Managing Editor: Angela Murphy
Electronic Products, Associate Editor: Mike Sosa
Text Design & Composition: North Market Street Graphics

This publication is designed to provide accurate and authoritative information in regard to the subject matter covered. It is sold with the understanding that the publisher is not engaged in professional services. If professional advice or other expert assistance is required, the services of a competent professional person should be sought.

Library of Congress Cataloging-in-Publication Data:
Grand, Mark.
    Patterns in Java : a catalog of reusable design patterns
illustrated with UML / Mark Grand.
      p. cm.
    "Wiley computer publishing."
    Includes bibliographical references and index.
    ISBN 0-471-25839-3 (v. i : pbk.)
     1. Java (Computer program language)   2. UML (Computer science)
   3. Software patterns. I. Title.
QA76.76.P37G73   1998
005. 13'3—dc21   98-29976

Printed in the United States of America.

10 9 8 7 6 5 4

C O N T E N T S

ACKNOWLEDGMENTS

This book would not have been possible without the inspiration, encouragement, and assistance of others. The largest share of that credit goes to my loving wife, Ginni, who is an amazing and wonderful person. She encouraged me to write this book and then put up with the long hours I spent writing it. I also want to thank my daughters, Rachel and Shana, for their patience.

I want to thank Craig Larman, my most conscientious reviewer. He convinced me of the importance of patterns. Craig also provided me with much invaluable feedback on the use of UML and the presentation of patterns. His valuable suggestions greatly improved the way that I present patterns in this book.

Jack Harich is another reviewer who made many useful suggestions about the organization of this book. He convinced me to expand my coverage of fundamental patterns. He also supplied the example I use for the State pattern.

Brad Appleton provided me with the most voluminous and detailed comments.

The UIUC patterns group provided insightful discussions of the patterns in this book. The participants in those discussions included Brian Foote, Ed Peters, Dragos Malonescu, Peter Hatch, Don Roberts, Joseph W. Yoder, Ralph Johnson, John Brant, James Overturf, Jean Pierre Briot, Eiji Nabika, Hiro Nakamura, and Ian Chai.

I also want to acknowledge some of my other reviewers, Michael Wheaton, Michael Pair, and Kyle Brown.

ABOUT THE AUTHOR

Mark Grand is a consultant specializing in Java and object-oriented topics with over 20 years of experience. In addition to authoring the *Patterns in Java* series for John Wiley & Sons, he is the author of two Java reference manuals from O'Reilly & Associates and numerous magazine articles. Mark has had a lengthy career as a software developer. In his role as a consultant, Mark has provided mentoring and training in Java and object-oriented techniques to numerous organizations. Mark has been involved in multiple, large-scale commercial Java projects as an architect, mentor, and technical lead. Prior to his involvement with Java, Mark spent over 11 years as a designer and implementor of 4GLs. His most recent role in this vein was as the architect and project manager for an electronic data interchange product. Mark has worked with a number of MIS organizations in such capacities as Oracle database architect, network designer and administrator, and Sun system administrator. He has been involved with object-oriented programming and design since 1982. Mark Grand has a B.S. degree in computer science from Syracuse University. He can be contacted through his Web page, at http://www.mindspring.com/~mgrand.

1

Introduction to Software Patterns

Software patterns are reusable solutions to recurring problems that occur during software development. Because this book is all about software patterns, they are simply referred to as *patterns* in the rest of this book.

What makes a bright, experienced programmer much more productive than a bright, but inexperienced, programmer is experience. Experience gives programmers a variety of wisdom. As programmers gain experience, they recognize the similarity of new problems to problems they have solved before. With even more experience, they recognize that solutions for similar problems follow recurring patterns. With knowledge of these patterns, experienced programmers recognize the situations to which patterns apply and immediately use the solution without having to stop, analyze the problem, and then pose possible strategies.

When a programmer discovers a pattern, it's just an insight. In most cases, to go from an unverbalized insight to a well-thought-out idea that the programmer can clearly articulate is surprisingly difficult. It's also an extremely valuable step. When we understand a pattern well enough to put it into words, we are able to intelligently combine it with other patterns. More important, once put into words, a pattern can be used in discussions among programmers who know the pattern. That allows programmers to more effectively collaborate and combine their wisdom. It can also help to avoid the situation in which programmers argue over different solutions to a problem, only to find out later that they were really thinking of the same solution but expressing it in different ways.

Putting a pattern into words has an additional benefit for less experienced programmers who have not yet discovered the pattern. Once a pattern has been put into words, more experienced programmers can teach it to programmers who aren't familiar with the pattern.

The intended value of this book is that it provide experienced programmers with a common vocabulary to discuss patterns. It should also allow programmers who have not yet discovered a pattern to learn about the pattern.

Though this book includes a substantial breadth of patterns, there are additional patterns that I'm aware of but did not have enough time to put in the book. Readers may discover some of these patterns. Some patterns may be highly specialized and of interest to only a small number of people. Other patterns may be of very broad interest and worthy of inclusion in a later volume of this work. Readers who wish to communicate such a pattern to me can drop me an e-mail at mgrand@mindspring.com.

The patterns cataloged in this book convey constructive ways of organizing parts of the software development cycle. There are other patterns that recur in programs that are not constructive. These types of patterns are called *AntiPatterns*. Because AntiPatterns can cancel out the benefits of patterns, this book does not attempt to catalog them.

Description of Patterns

Patterns are usually described using a format that includes the following information:

- A description of the problem that includes a concrete example and a solution specific to the concrete problem
- A summary of the considerations that lead to the formulation of a general solution
- A general solution
- The consequences, good and bad, of using the given solution to solve a problem
- A list of related patterns

Pattern books differ in how they present this information. The format used in this book varies with the phase of the software life cycle that the pattern addresses. The patterns in this volume are all related to the design phase of the software life cycle. The descriptions of design-phase-related patterns in the volume are organized with the following headings into sections.

Pattern Name

The heading of this section consists of the name of the pattern and a bibliography reference in brackets that indicates where the pattern came from. Most patterns don't have any additional text under this heading. For those that do, this section contains information about the derivation or general nature of the pattern.

Synopsis

This section contains a one- to two-sentence description of the pattern. The synopsis conveys the essence of the solution provided by the pattern. The synopsis is primarily directed at experienced programmers who may recognize the pattern as one they already know, but for which they may not have had a name. After recognizing the pattern from its name and synopsis, it may be sufficient to skim the rest of the pattern description.

Don't be discouraged if you don't recognize a pattern from its name and synopsis. Instead, carefully read through the rest of the pattern description to understand it.

Context

The Context section describes the problem that the pattern addresses. For most patterns, the problem is introduced in terms of a concrete example. After presenting the problem in the example, the Context section suggests a design solution to that problem.

Forces

The Forces section summarizes the considerations that lead to the general solution presented in the Solution section.

Solution

The Solution section is the core of the pattern. It describes a general-purpose solution to the problem that the pattern addresses.

Consequences

The Consequences section explains the implications, good and bad, of using the solution.

Implementation

The Implementation section describes the important considerations to be aware of when executing the solution. It may also describe some common variations or simplifications of the solution.

Java API Usage

Where there is an appropriate example of the pattern in the core Java API, it's pointed out in this section. Those patterns that are not used in the core Java API don't have this section in their description.

Code Example

This section contains a code example that shows a sample implementation for a design that uses the pattern. In most cases, this will be the design described in the Context section.

Related Patterns

This section contains a list of patterns that are related to the pattern described.

A Brief History of Patterns

The idea of software patterns originally came from the field of architecture. Christopher Alexander, an architect, wrote two revolutionary books that describe patterns in building architecture and urban planning: *A Pattern Language: Towns, Buildings, Construction* (Oxford University Press, 1977) and *The Timeless Way of Building* (Oxford University Press, 1979).

The ideas presented in these books are applicable to a number of fields outside of architecture, including software.

In 1987, Ward Cunningham and Kent Beck used some of Alexander's ideas to develop five patterns for user-interface (UI) design. They published a paper on the UI patterns at OOPSLA-87 entitled "Using Pattern Languages for Object-Oriented Programs."

In the early 1990s, Erich Gamma, Richard Helm, John Vlissides, and Ralph Johnson began work on one of the most influential computer books of this decade: *Design Patterns*. The book, published in 1994, popularized the idea of patterns. *Design Patterns* is often called the "Gang of Four" (or GoF) book.

Patterns in Java represents an evolution of patterns and objects since the GoF book was published. The GoF book used C++ and Smalltalk for its examples. This book uses Java and takes a rather Java-centric view of most things. When the GoF book was written, Unified Modeling Language (UML) did not exist. It is now widely accepted as the preferred notation for object-oriented analysis and design. Therefore, that is the notation this book uses.

Organization of This Book

The *Patterns in Java* series of books covers a wider range of patterns than is found in previously published works. Even with the goal of providing coverage of a broad selection of patterns, time constraints have limited the number of patterns that can be included. Current plans call for two volumes of this work. If there is sufficient interest, more volumes will follow.

This first volume focuses exclusively on design patterns; the second volume includes patterns used during the analysis, coding, and testing phases of the life cycle. Both volumes begin with a description of the subset of UML used in that volume. Chapter 2 contains an overview of the software life cycle, to provide the context in which the patterns are used. Chapter 2 also provides a case study that includes examples for using patterns in that particular volume. The remaining chapters describe different types of patterns.

The CD-ROM that accompanies this book contains all of the code examples that are found in this book. In some cases, the examples on the CD-ROM are more complete than the examples that appear in this book.

The Java examples that appear in this book are based on JDK 1.2. The UML diagrams in this book are based on version 1.0 of the Object Management Group's UML standard.

CHAPTER 2

Overview of UML

The *Unified Modeling Language* (UML) is a notation that you can use for object-oriented analysis and design. This chapter contains a brief overview of UML that introduces you to both the subset and extensions to UML used in this book. For a complete description of UML, see http://www .rational.com/uml/documentation.html.

Books that are specifically about UML call the pieces of information stored in instances of a class *attributes;* they call a class's encapsulations of behavior *operations.* Those terms, like UML, are not specific to any implementation language. This book is not language neutral. It assumes that you are using Java as your implementation language. This book also uses Java-specific terms in most places, rather than terms that are language neutral but less familiar to Java programmers. For example, this book uses the words *attribute* and *variable* interchangeably, with preference for the Java-specific term *variable*. This book also uses the words *operation* and *method* interchangeably, with preference for the Java-specific term *method*.

UML defines a number of different kinds of diagrams. The kinds of diagrams found in this book are *class diagrams, collaboration diagrams,* and *statechart diagrams.* The rest of this chapter is organized into sections

that describe each of these diagrams and the elements that appear
in them.

Class Diagram

A class diagram is a diagram that shows classes, interfaces, and their relationships. The most basic element of a class diagram is a *class*. Figure 2.1
provides an example of a class that shows many of the features that a class
can have within a class diagram.

Classes are drawn as rectangles. The rectangles can be divided into
two or three compartments. The class rectangle shown in Figure 2.1 has
three compartments. The top compartment contains the name of the class.
The middle compartment lists the class's variables. The bottom compartment lists the class's methods.

The symbols that precede each variable and method are *visibility
indicators*. There are three different types of visibility indicators, as shown
in Table 2.1. The variables in the middle compartment are shown as

```
visibilityIndicator name : type
```

Therefore, the two variables shown in the class are private variables. The
name of the first variable is `instance` and its type is `AudioClipManager`.
The name of the second variable is `prevClip` and its type is `AudioClip`.

Though not shown in Figure 2.1, an initial value can be indicated for
a variable by following the variable's type with an equal (=) sign and the
value like this:

```
ShutDown:boolean = false
```

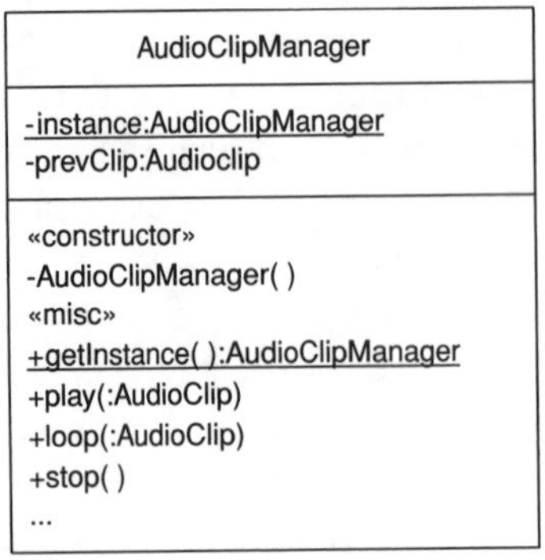

```
┌─────────────────────────────────────┐
│           AudioClipManager           │
├─────────────────────────────────────┤
│ -instance:AudioClipManager           │
│ -prevClip:Audioclip                  │
├─────────────────────────────────────┤
│ «constructor»                        │
│ -AudioClipManager( )                 │
│ «misc»                               │
│ +getInstance( ):AudioClipManager     │
│ +play(:AudioClip)                    │
│ +loop(:AudioClip)                    │
│ +stop( )                             │
│ ...                                  │
└─────────────────────────────────────┘
```

FIGURE 2.1 Basic class.

TABLE 2.1 Visibility Indicators

Visibility Indicators	Meaning
+	Public
#	Protected
−	Private

Notice that the first variable shown in the class is underlined. If a variable is underlined that means that it's a static variable. This applies to methods, too. Underlined methods are static methods.

The methods in the bottom compartment are shown as

```
visibilityIndicator name ( formalParameters ) : returnType
```

The `getInstance` method shown in the class found in Figure 2.1 returns an `AudioClipManager` object.

UML indicates a void method by leaving out the "`: returnType`" from a method to indicate that it doesn't return anything. Therefore, the `stop` method shown in Figure 2.1 does not return any result.

A method's formal parameters consist of a name and a type like this:

```
setLength(length:int)
```

If a method has multiple parameters, commas separate them like this:

```
setPosition(x:int, y:int)
```

Two of the methods in the aforementioned class are preceded by a word in guillemets, like this:

```
«constructor»
```

In a UML drawing, a word in guillemets is called a *stereotype*. A stereotype is used like an adjective to modify what comes after it. The `constructor` stereotype indicates that the methods that follow it are constructors. The `misc` stereotype indicates that the methods that come after it are regular methods. Additional uses for stereotypes are described later in this chapter.

One last element that appears in Figure 2.1 is an ellipsis (. . .). If an ellipsis appears in the bottom compartment of a class, it means that the class has additional methods that the diagram does not show. If an ellipsis appears in the middle compartment of a class, it means that the class has additional variables that the diagram does not show.

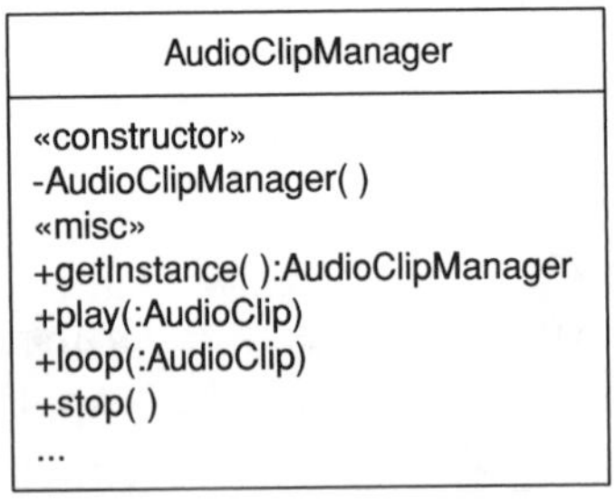

AudioClipManager
«constructor» -AudioClipManager( ) «misc» +getInstance( ):AudioClipManager +play(:AudioClip) +loop(:AudioClip) +stop( ) ...

FIGURE 2.2 Two-compartment class.

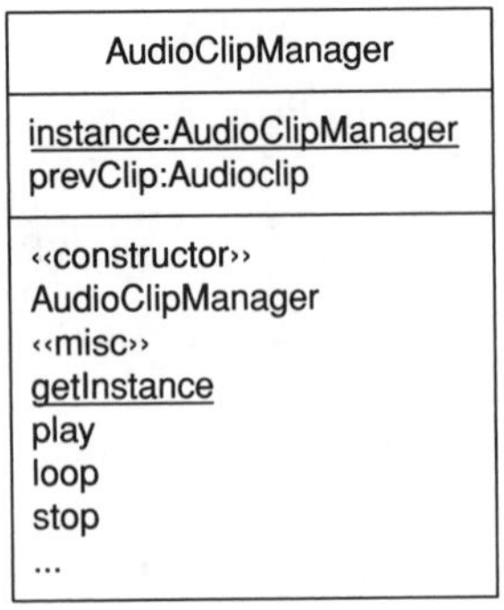

AudioClipManager
instance:AudioClipManager prevClip:Audioclip
‹‹constructor›› AudioClipManager ‹‹misc›› getInstance play loop stop ...

FIGURE 2.3 Simplified class.

Often, it's not necessary or helpful to show as many details of a class as were shown in Figure 2.1. A class can also be drawn with only two compartments, as shown in Figure 2.2.

When a class is drawn with only two compartments, its top compartment contains its name and its bottom compartment shows its methods. If a class is drawn with only two compartments, that just means that its variables are not shown. It does not mean that it has no variables.

The visibility indicators may be omitted from methods and variables. When a method or variable is shown without a visibility indicator, it means there is no indication of the method's or the variable's visibility. It does not imply that the methods or variables are public, protected, or private.

A method's parameters can be omitted if their return values are also omitted. For example, the visibility indicators and method parameters are omitted from the class shown in Figure 2.3.

Figure 2.4 shows the simplest form of a class, with just one compartment containing the class name. A one-compartment representation of a class merely identifies the class. It provides no indication about the variables or methods that the class has.

Interfaces

Interfaces are drawn in a manner similar to classes. The only difference is that the name in the top compartment is preceded by an «interface» stereotype. Figure 2.5 shows an example of an interface.

Classes and interfaces are important elements of class diagrams. The other elements of a class diagram show the relationships between classes and interfaces. Figure 2.6 is a typical class diagram.

AudioClipManager

FIGURE 2.4 One-compartment class.

The lines in Figure 2.6 indicate the relationship between the classes and the interface. A solid line with a closed arrowhead like the one in Figure 2.7 indicates the relationship with a subclass that inherits from a superclass. Figure 2.6 shows the abstract class `Product` as the superclass of the `ConcreteProduct` class. You can tell that it's abstract because its name is italicized. You can tell that its methods are abstract because they are also italicized.

A similar sort of line is used to indicate that a class implements an interface. It is represented with a dotted or dashed line with a closed head, like the one shown in Figure 2.8. In Figure 2.6 the `Factory` class implements the `FactoryIF` interface.

The other lines show the other types of relationships between the classes and the interface. UML calls these other types of relationships *associations*. There are a number of things that can appear with an association that provide information about the nature of an association. The following items are optional, but this book consistently uses them wherever it makes sense.

- **Association Name.**   Somewhere around the middle of an association there may be an association name. The name of an association is always capitalized. There may be a triangle at one end of the association name. The triangle suggests the direction in which you read the association. An example of this is found in Figure 2.6, where you see that the association between the `Factory` and `ConcreteProduct` classes has the name `Creates`.

«interface»
AddressIF

getAddress1
setAddress1
getAddress2
setAddress2
getCity
setCity
getState
setState
getPostalCode
setPostalCode

FIGURE 2.5 Interface.

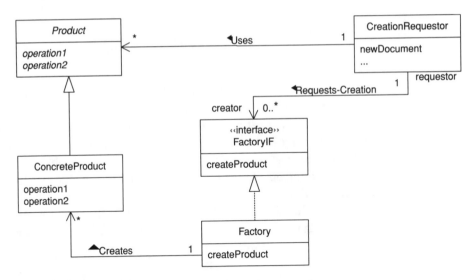

FIGURE 2.6 Class diagram.

- **Navigation Arrows.** Arrowheads that appear at the ends of an association are called *navigation arrows*. Navigation arrows indicate the direction in which you can navigate an association. Looking at the association named `Creates` in Figure 2.6, you see that it has a navigation arrow pointing from the `Factory` class to the `ConcreteProduct` class. That means `Factory` objects will have a reference that allows them to access `ConcreteProduct` objects, but not the other way around.

  Because of the nature of creation, it seems clear that this means the `Factory` class is responsible for creating instances of the `ConcreteProduct` class. The nature of some associations is less obvious. To clarify the nature of such associations, it may be necessary to supply additional information about the association. One common way to do this is to name the role that each class plays in the association.

- **Role Name.** To clarify the nature of an association, the name of the role that each class plays in the association can appear at each end of an association, next to the corresponding class. Role names are always lowercase. That makes them easier to distinguish from association names, which are always capitalized. The class diagram shown

◁─────────── **FIGURE 2.7** Subclass inherits from superclass.

◁------------------------ **FIGURE 2.8** Class implements an interface.

in Figure 2.6 shows the `CreationRequestor` class and the `FactoryIF` interface participating in an association named `Requests-Creation`. The `CreationRequestor` class participates in that association in a role called `requestor`. The `FactoryIF` interface participates in that association in a role called `creator`.

- **Multiplicity Indicator.** Another detail of an association that is usually supplied is how many instances of each class participate in an occurrence of an association. A multiplicity indicator may appear at each end of an association to provide that information. A multiplicity indicator can be a simple number like 0 or 1. It can be a range of numbers indicated like this:

```
0..2
```

An asterisk used as the high value of a range means an unlimited number of occurrences. The multiplicity indicator 1..* means at least one instance; 0..* means any number of instances. A simple * is equivalent to 0..*. Looking at the multiplicity indicators in Figure 2.6, you see that each one of the associations in the drawing is a one-to-many relationship.

Figure 2.9 is a class diagram that shows a class with multiple subclasses.

Figure 2.9 is perfectly valid. However, UML provides a more aesthetically pleasing way to draw a class with multiple subclasses. You can combine the arrowheads, as shown in Figure 2.10. Figure 2.10 is identical in meaning to the diagram shown in Figure 2.9.

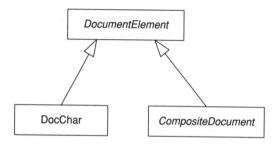

FIGURE 2.9 Multiple inheritance arrows.

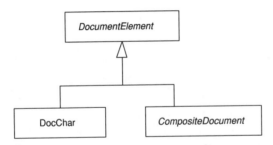

FIGURE 2.10 Single inheritance arrow.

Occasionally there is a need to convey more structure than is implied by a simple one-to-many relationship. The type of one-to-many relationship in which one object contains a collection of other objects is called an *aggregation*. A hollow diamond at the end of an association indicates aggregation. The hollow diamond appears at the end of the association attached to the class that contains instances of the other class. The class diagram in Figure 2.11 shows an aggregation.

Figure 2.11 shows a class named `MessageManager`. Each of its instances contains zero or more instances of a class named `MIMEMsg`.

UML has another notation that indicates a stronger relationship than aggregation. This relationship is called *composite aggregation*. For an aggregation to be composite:

- Aggregated instances must belong to only one composite at a time.
- Some operations must propagate from the composite to its aggregated instances. For example, when a composite object is cloned, its clone method typically clones the aggregated instances so that the cloned composite owns clones of the original aggregated instances.

Figure 2.12 shows a class diagram that contains composite aggregations.

Figure 2.12 shows a `Document` class. `Document` objects can contain `Paragraph` objects. `Paragraph` objects can contain `DocChar` objects. Because of the composite aggregation, you know that `Paragraph` objects do not share `DocChar` objects and `Document` objects do not share `Paragraph` objects.

FIGURE 2.11 Aggregation.

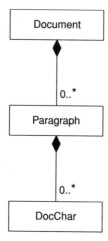

FIGURE 2.12 Composite aggregation.

Some associations are indirect. Instead of classes that are directly associated with each other, they are associated indirectly through a third class. Consider the class diagram shown in Figure 2.13. The association shows that instances of the Cache class refer to instances of the Object class through an instance of the ObjectID class.

There is another use for the ellipsis in a class diagram. Some class diagrams need to show that a class has a large or open-ended set of subclasses, while showing only a few subclasses as examples of the sort of subclasses that the class has. Figure 2.14 shows how an ellipsis can be used to show just that.

The class diagram in Figure 2.14 shows a class named DataQuery that has subclasses named JDBCQuery, OracleQuery, SybaseQuery, and an indefinite number of other classes that are indicated by the ellipsis.

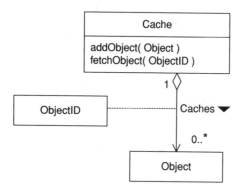

FIGURE 2.13 Association class.

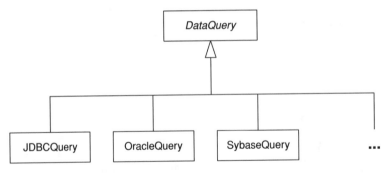

FIGURE 2.14 Open-ended subclasses.

The classes in a class diagram can be organized into *packages*. A package is drawn as a large rectangle with a small rectangle above it. The small rectangle contains the name of the package. The small and large rectangles are arranged with a shape similar to that of a manila folder. The class diagram in Figure 2.15 contains a package named `ServicePackage`.

A visibility indicator can precede the name of a class or interface that appears within a package. Public classes are accessible to classes outside of the package; private classes are not.

Sometimes there are aspects of a design that cannot be made sufficiently clear without a comment in a diagram. A comment in UML is drawn as a rectangle with its upper right corner turned down. The comment is attached by a dashed line to the diagram element that it relates to. The class diagram in Figure 2.16 contains a comment.

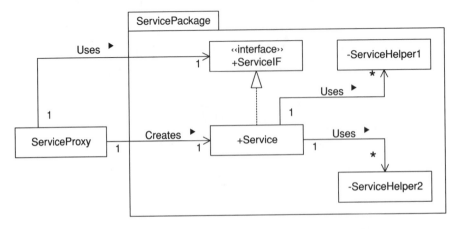

FIGURE 2.15 Package.

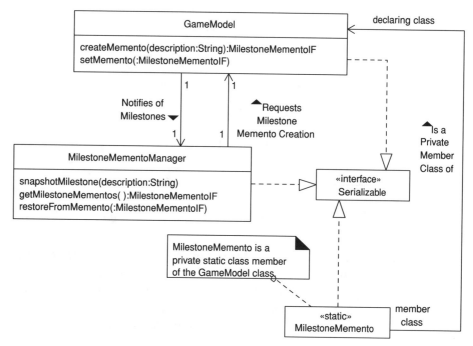

FIGURE 2.16 Private-static classes with a comment.

Figure 2.16 shows the static class `MilestoneMemento`, which is a private member of the `GameModel` class. There is no standard way in UML to represent a static, private-member class. The diagram uses a stereotype as an extension to UML to indicate that the `MilestoneMemento` class is static. It uses an association to indicate that the `MilestoneMemento` is a private member of the `GameModel` class. To make the relationship even more clear, there is a comment about it in the class diagram.

Class diagrams can include objects. Most of the objects in the diagrams found in this book are drawn as in Figure 2.17.

The object shown in Figure 2.17 is an instance of a class named `Area`. The underline in the object tells you that it's an object. A name may appear to the left of the colon (:). The only significance of the name is that you can use it to identify the individual object.

Some diagrams indicate an object as just an empty rectangle with nothing inside of the rectangle. Obviously, blank objects cannot be used to

> :Area

FIGURE 2.17 Object in a class diagram.

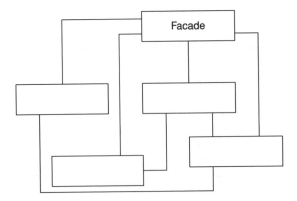

FIGURE 2.18 Blank objects.

identify any particular kind of object. However, they can be used in a diagram that shows a structure in which the objects of unspecified type are connected. Figure 2.18 shows such a structure.

The lines that connect two objects are not associations. They are called *links*. Links are connections between objects, whereas associations are relationships between classes. A link is an occurrence of an association, just as an object is an instance of a class. Links can have association names, navigation arrows, and most of the other embellishments that associations can have. However, since a link is a connection between two objects, links may not have multiplicity indicators or aggregation diamonds.

Some diagrams consist of just objects and links. Such diagrams are considered a kind of class diagram. However, there is a special name for diagrams that consist of only objects and links: *object diagram*. Figure 2.19 is an example of an object diagram.

Collaboration Diagram

Class and object diagrams show relationships between classes and objects. They also provide information about the interactions that occur between classes. They don't show the sequence in which the interactions occur or any concurrency that they may have.

Collaboration diagrams show objects, the links that connect them, and the interactions that occur over each link. They also show the sequence and concurrency requirements for each interaction. Figure 2.20 is a simple example of a collaboration diagram.

Any number of interactions can be associated with a link. Each interaction involves a method call. Next to each interaction or group of interac-

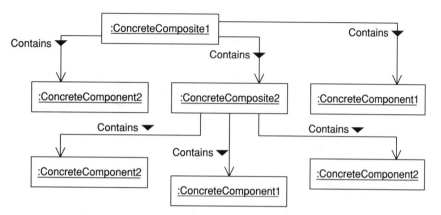

FIGURE 2.19 Object diagram.

tions is an arrow that points to the object whose method is called by the interaction. The entire set of objects and interactions shown in a collaboration diagram is collectively called a *collaboration*.

Each of the interactions shown in Figure 2.20 starts with a sequence number and a colon. Sequence numbers indicate the order in which

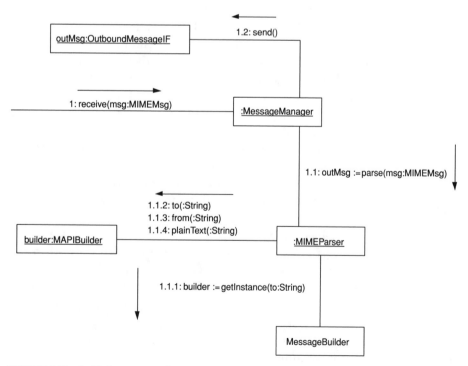

FIGURE 2.20 Collaboration diagram.

method calls occur. An interaction with the number 1 must come before an interaction with the number 2, and so on.

Multilevel sequence numbers consist of two or more numbers separated by a period. Notice that most of the sequence numbers in Figure 2.20 are multilevel sequence numbers. Multilevel sequence numbers correspond to multiple levels of method calls. The area of the multilevel sequence number to the left of its rightmost period is called its *prefix*. For example, the prefix of 1.3.4 is 1.3.

Interactions numbered with a multilevel sequence number occur during another interaction's method call. The other method call is determined by the interaction's prefix. So the method calls of the interactions numbered 1.1 and 1.2 are made during the method call of interaction 1. Similarly, interactions numbered 1.1.1, 1.1.2, 1.1.3, and so on, occur during the method call of interaction 1.1.

Among interactions numbered with the same prefix, their methods are called in the order determined by the number following their sequence number prefix. Therefore, the methods of interactions numbered 1.1.1, 1.1.2, 1.1.3, and so on, are called in that order.

As mentioned previously, links represent a connection between two objects. Because of that, links cannot have multiplicity indicators. This works well for links that represent an occurrence of an association between a definite number of objects. However, associations that have a star multiplicity indicator on either end involve an indefinite number of objects. For this type of association, there is no way to draw an indefinite number of links to an indefinite number of objects. UML provides a symbol that allows us to draw links that connect to an indefinite number of projects. That symbol is called a *multiobject*. It represents an indefinite number of objects. It looks like a rectangle behind a rectangle. The collaboration diagram in Figure 2.21 contains a multiobject. It shows an ObservableIF object calling a Multicaster object's notify method. The Multicaster object's implementation of the notify method calls the notify method of an indefinite number of ObserverIF objects linked to the Multicaster object.

Objects created as a result of a collaboration are marked with the property {new}. Temporary objects that exist only during a collaboration are marked with the property {transient}.* The collaboration diagram in Figure 2.22 shows a collaboration that creates an object.

---

* UML's use of the word *transient* is very different from the way that Java uses it. Java uses *transient* to mean that a variable is not part of an object's persistent state. UML uses it to mean that an object has a bounded lifetime.

FIGURE 2.21 Multiobject.

Some interactions occur concurrently, rather than sequentially. A letter at the end of a sequence number indicates concurrent interactions. For example, the methods of interactions numbered 2.2a and 2.2b are called concurrently and each call runs in a separate thread. Consider the collaboration diagram shown in Figure 2.23. Notice that the top-level interaction is numbered 1. During that interaction, first interaction 1.1 is invoked. Then interactions 1.2a and 1.2b are invoked at the same time. After that, interactions 1.3 and 1.4 are invoked, in that order. An asterisk after a sequence number indicates a repeated interaction, as shown in Figure 2.24.

The collaboration diagram in Figure 2.24 begins by calling the `TollBooth` object's `start` method. That method repeatedly calls the object's `collectNextToll` method. Each call to the `collectNextToll` method calls the `TollBasket` object's `collectToll` method and the `TollGate` object's `raiseGate` method.

One other thing to notice about this collaboration diagram is the «`self`» stereotype that appears next to the link for interaction 1.1. This stereotype serves to clarify the fact that the link is a self-reference.

Unlike the example shown in Figure 2.24, most repetitive interactions occur conditionally. UML allows a condition to be associated with a repetitive interaction by putting it after the asterisk inside of square brackets. Figure 2.25 shows an example of a conditional repetitive interaction where the `Iterator` object is passed to a `DialogMediator` object's `refresh`

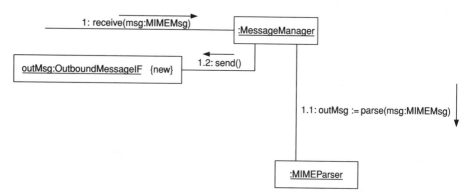

FIGURE 2.22 New object.

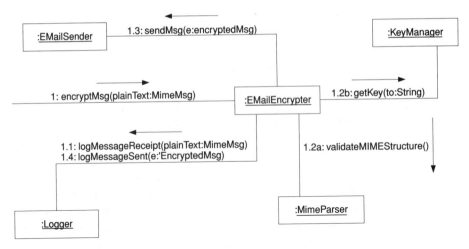

FIGURE 2.23 E-mail encrypter.

method. Its `refresh` method, in turn, calls a `Widget` object's `reset` method and then repeatedly calls its `addData` method, while the `Iterator` object's `hasNext` method returns true.

You can indicate that a non-repetitive interaction is conditional, by including a condition without an asterisk in the interaction.

It's important to note that the definition of UML does not define the meaning of conditions associated with repetitive interactions very precisely. In particular, the definition of UML says that what appears between the square brackets can "be expressed in pseudocode or an actual programming language." This book consistently uses Java for that purpose.

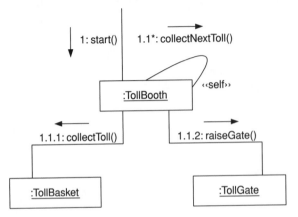

FIGURE 2.24 Tollbooth collaboration diagram.

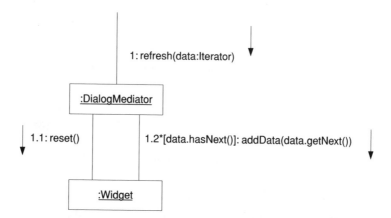

FIGURE 2.25 Refresh.

When dealing with multiple threads, something that often requires specification about methods is what happens when two threads try to call the same method at the same time. UML specifies this by placing one of the following constructs after a method:

```
{concurrency = sequential}
```

This means that only one thread at a time calls a method. No guarantee is made about the correctness of the method's behavior if the method is called with multiple threads at a time.

```
{concurrency = guarded}
```

This means that if multiple threads call a method at the same time, they all execute it concurrently and correctly.

```
{concurrency = concurrent}
```

This means that if multiple threads call a method at the same time, only one thread at a time is allowed to execute the method. While one thread executes the method, other threads are forced to wait until it's their turn. This is similar to the behavior of synchronized Java methods. Figure 2.26 shows an example of a synchronized method.

There are refinements to thread synchronization used in this book for which there is no standard representation in UML. This book uses some extensions to the `{concurrency = guarded}` construct to represent those refinements.

FIGURE 2.26 Synchronized method call.

In some cases, the object on which threads must synchronize is not the same object whose method is called by an interaction. Consider Figure 2.27. In this collaboration diagram, `{concurrency=guarded:out}` refers to the object labeled `out`. Before the method call can actually take place, the thread that controls the call must own the lock associated with the `out` object. That is identical to Java's semantics for a synchronized statement.

Sometimes there are preconditions beyond acquiring ownership of a lock that must be met before a thread may proceed with a method call. This book represents such preconditions with a vertical bar followed by the precondition. Figure 2.28 shows such preconditions following `guarded` and a vertical bar.

The collaboration diagram in Figure 2.28 shows two asynchronous interactions. One interaction calls a `PrintQueue` object's `addPrintJob` method to add a print job to the `PrintQueue` object. In the other interaction, a `PrintDriver` object calls the `PrintQueue` object's `getPrintJob` method to get a print job from the `PrintQueue` object. Both interactions

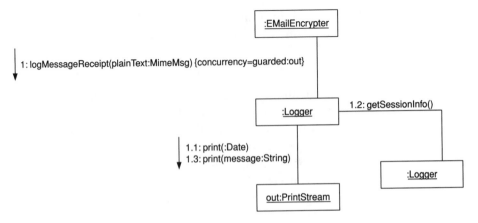

FIGURE 2.27 Synchronization using a third object.

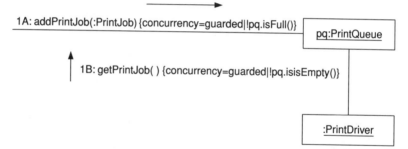

FIGURE 2.28 Print queue.

have synchronization preconditions. If the print queue is full, then the interaction that calls the `addPrintJob` method waits until the print queue is not full before proceeding to make the call to the `addPrintJob` method. If the print queue is empty, then the interaction that calls the `getPrintJob` method waits until the print queue is not empty before proceeding to make the call to the `getPrintJob` method.

These mechanisms determine when the methods of a collaboration are called. They don't say anything about when method calls return. The arrows that point at the objects whose methods are called provide information about when the methods can return.

All the arrows in Figure 2.28 have closed heads, which indicate that the calls are synchronous. The method calls do not return until the method has completed doing whatever it does.

An open arrowhead indicates an asynchronous method call. An asynchronous method call returns to its caller immediately, while the method does its work asynchronously in a separate thread. The collaboration diagram in Figure 2.29 shows an asynchronous method call.

UML defines arrowheads only for synchronous and asynchronous calls. As extensions to UML, UML allows other types of arrows to indicate different types of method calls. To indicate a balking call, this book uses a bent-back arrow, as shown in Figure 2.30.

When a balking call is made to an object's method and there is no other thread executing that object's method, the method returns when it is finished doing what it does. However, when a balking call is made and

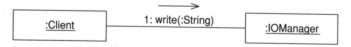

FIGURE 2.29 Asynchronous method call.

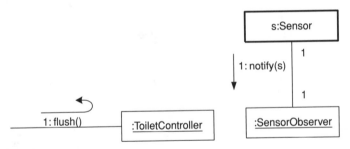

FIGURE 2.30 Balking call depicted with a bent-back arrow.

FIGURE 2.31 Active object Sensor.

there is another thread currently executing that object's method, the method returns immediately without performing anything.

You may have noticed that the object that makes the top-level call that initiates a collaboration is not shown in all of the collaboration diagrams. This means that the object that initiates the collaboration is not considered to be a part of the collaboration.

The objects in UML that you have seen up to this point are passive in nature. They don't do anything until one of their methods is called.

Some objects are active. They have a thread associated with them that allows them to initiate operations asynchronously and independently of whatever else is going on in a program. An *active object* is indicated as an object with a thick border. Figure 2.31 contains an example of an active object.

In the diagram an active Sensor object calls a SensorObserver object's method without another object first calling one of its methods.

Statechart Diagram

Statechart diagrams are used to model a class's behavior as a state machine. Figure 2.32 is an example of a simple state diagram.

A statechart diagram shows each state as a rounded rectangle. All of the states shown in Figure 2.32 are divided into two compartments. The upper compartment contains the name of the state. The lower compartment contains a list of events to which the object responds while in that state, without changing state. Each event in the list is followed by a slash and the action it performs in response to the event. UML predefines two such events:

1. The enter event occurs when an object enters a state.
2. The exit event occurs when an object leaves a state.

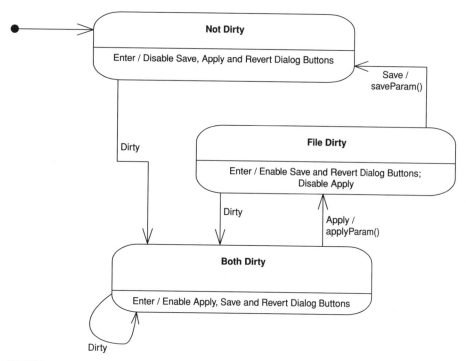

FIGURE 2.32 Statechart diagram.

If there are no events to which a state responds without changing state, then its rectangle is not divided into two compartments. Such a state is drawn as a simple, rounded rectangle that contains only the state's name.

Every state machine has an initial state that it is in before the first transition occurs. The initial state is drawn as a small, solid circle.

Transitions between states are shown in statechart diagrams as lines between states with an arrowhead showing the direction of the transition. Normally, a transition line is required to have a label that indicates the event that triggers the transition. The event can be followed with a slash and the action that occurs when the transition takes place.

If a statechart includes a final state, the final state is drawn as a small, solid circle inside of a larger circle.

The Software Life Cycle

This volume is devoted to patterns used during the object-oriented design phase of the software life cycle. This chapter first describes the software life cycle, then presents the object-oriented design portion of a case study.

There are a variety of activities that take place during the lifetime of a piece of software. Figure 3.1 shows some of the activities that lead up to the deployment of a piece of business software. Figure 3.1 is not intended to show all of the activities that take place during a software project. It merely shows some common activities that occur for the purpose of understanding the context in which the patterns discussed in this book are used. This volume and Volume 2 describe recurring patterns that occur during the portion of the software life cycle labeled in Figure 3.1 as "Build."

Figure 3.1 shows very clear boundaries between each activity. In practice, the boundaries are not always so clear. Sometimes it is difficult to determine whether a particular activity belongs in one box or another. The precise boundaries are not important. What is important is to understand the relationships between these activities.

Earlier activities, such as defining requirements and object-oriented analysis, established the course of activities that followed them, such as defining essential use cases or object-oriented design. However, in the

Business Planning: Business Case, Budget				

Detailed Planning	Define Requirements: Requirements Specification			
	Define High Level Essential Use Cases			
	Create Prototype			

Build	Object Oriented Analysis: Low Level Essential Use Cases, Conceptual Model, Sequence diagrams			Write Documentation and Help
	Design User Interface	Object Oriented Design: Class Diagrams, Collaboration Diagrams, State Diagrams	Logical Database Design	
	Usability Testing	Coding	Physical Database Design	
	Testing			

Deployment				

FIGURE 3.1 Activities that lead to software deployment.

course of those later activities, deficiencies in the products of earlier activities emerged. For example, in the course of defining a use case, it may become apparent that there is an ambiguous or conflicting requirement. Making the necessary changes to the requirements generally results in the need to modify existing use cases or to write new ones. You should expect such iterations. So long as the trend is for later iterations to produce fewer changes than earlier iterations, consider the iterations to be part of the normal development process.

Following are brief descriptions of some of the activities shown in Figure 3.1. The purpose of these descriptions is to provide enough background information on these activities for the user to understand how the patterns discussed in this work apply to a relevant activity. The case study that follows the descriptions provides deeper insights into these activities.

Business Planning   This typically starts with a proposal to build or modify a piece of software. The proposal evolves into a *business case*. A business case is a document that describes the pros and cons of the software project and also includes estimates of the resources that are required to complete the project. If a decision is made to proceed with the project, then a preliminary schedule and budget are prepared.

Define Requirements   The purpose of this activity is to produce a *requirements specification* that indicates what the software produced by the project will and won't do. This typically begins with goals and high-level requirements from the business case. Additional requirements are obtained from appropriate sources to produce an initial requirements specification. As the requirements specification is used in subsequent activities, necessary refinements to the requirements are discovered. The refinements are incorporated into the requirements specification. The products of subsequent activities are then modified to reflect the changes to the requirements specification.

Define Essential Use Cases   A *use case* describes the sequence of events that occurs in a specific circumstance between a system and other entities. The other entities are called *actors*. Developing use cases improves our understanding of the requirements, analysis, or design that the use case is based on. As we develop a better understanding of requirements, analysis, and design, we are able to refine them.

Essential use cases describe events in terms of the problem domain. Use cases that describe events in terms of the internal organization of software are called *real use cases*.

The type of use case most appropriate for refining requirements is the *high-level essential use case*. Such use cases are high level in the sense that they explore the implications of what they are based on, but do not try to add additional details.

Create Prototype   The purpose of this activity is to create a prototype of the proposed software. A prototype can be used to get reactions to a proposed project. Reactions to a prototype can be used to refine requirements and essential use cases.

Define High-Level System Architecture   The purpose of this activity is to determine the major components of the system that are obvious from the original proposal and their relationships.

Object-Oriented Analysis   The purpose of this activity is to understand what the software produced by the project will do and how it will interact with other entities in its environment. The goal of analysis is to create a conceptual model of the problem to be solved. The products of object-oriented analysis model the situation in which the software operates, from the perspective of an outside observer. The analysis does not concern itself with what goes on inside the software.

Object-Oriented Design   The purpose of this activity is to determine the internal organization of the software. The products of the design effort identify the classes that constitute the internal logic of the software. They also determine the internal structure of the classes and their interrelationships.

More decisions are made during object-oriented design than during any other activity. For that reason, this book focuses on those patterns that apply to object-oriented design more than any other activity.

Coding The purpose of this activity is to write the code that makes the software work.

Testing The purpose of this phase is to ensure that the software performs as expected.

Case Study

What follows is a case study that involves the design and development of an employee timekeeping system for a fictitious business called Henry's Food Market. To keep the size of this example reasonable, the artifacts of the development process are simplified and abbreviated. The details for deriving those artifacts are also abbreviated. The point of this case study is to set the stage for a situation in which applications of design patterns are demonstrated.

Business Case

Here is an abbreviated business case that lays out the motivation and schedule for building an employee timekeeping system.

Henry's Food Market operates five retail stores. To support these stores, it also operates a warehouse and a commercial bakery that produces the baked goods that the stores sell. Most of its employees are paid by the hour. Employee hours are tracked by a time-clock system. When employees start work, go on breaks, return from breaks, or leave work they are supposed to slide their employee badges through a timekeeping clock that records their hours.

Henry's Food Market wants to expand, increasing the number of its stores from 5 to 21 over the next 2 years at a rate of 2 stores every 3 months. One of the challenges that faces the company is that if it continues to use its existing timekeeping system, it will have to hire more people to handle the administrative side of timekeeping. Currently, each location requires a person working half-time as a timekeeper to administer its timekeeping system. The activities the timekeeper is required to perform are as follows:

- The timekeeper prints reports for supervisors that show the number of hours that each employee worked the previous day. This allows supervisors the ability to verify that their subordinates worked the stated number of hours. Some common errors that are uncovered by supervisors who review these reports are:

Employees don't clock out when they go on break or leave work.

Coworkers clock in employees who are late to work.

Employees clock in before the start of their shift.

- The timekeeper enters corrections into the timekeeping system.
- The timekeeper prepares weekly reports that show the number of hours every employee in a location worked and sends those reports to the payroll department.

The existing timekeeping system only provides employee hours in the form of a printed report. There is currently one person working full-time to enter employee hours into the payroll system and review the entered hours. That person costs the company $24,000 a year. If the company continues to use this system, it will have to hire an additional person to enter employee hours at an additional cost of $24,000 a year.

The cost of having a person work part-time as a timekeeper in each location is $9000 per person per year. The current cost of paying people to be timekeepers is $63,000 per year.

The total current cost of labor for timekeeping is $87,000 per year. In two years, when the company's expansion is complete, that labor cost will have increased to $237,000.

The proposed project is to build a replacement timekeeping system that will keep the labor cost of timekeeping at current or lower levels after the expansion. The timekeeping system will be expected to pay for itself in 18 months. Deployment for the system is expected within 6 months of the start of the project.

Define Requirements Specification

Minimally, a requirements specification should specify the required functions and attributes of what is produced by a project. *Required functions* are things that the system must do, such as record the time that an employee starts work. *Required attributes* are characteristics of the system that are not functions—for example, requiring that the use of the timekeeping terminals not require more than an eighth-grade education. Some other things that are normally found in a requirements document, but are not in the following example, are:

Assumptions   This is a list of things that are assumed to be true, such as the minimum educational requirement for employees or the fact that the company will not become unionized.

Risks   This is a list of things that can go wrong, leading to a delay or failure of the project. This list can include technical uncertainties, such as the availability of devices that are suitable for use as timekeeping terminals. It can also include nontechnical concerns such as anticipated changes to labor laws.

Dependencies   This is a list of resources that this project can depend on, such as the existence of a wide-area network.

It's helpful to number the requirements in a requirements specification. This allows decisions based on a requirement to be easily noted in use cases, design documents, and even code. If inconsistencies are found later on, it's easy to trace them to the relevant requirements. It's also common to number requirements hierarchically by functions. Here are some of the required functions for the timekeeping system.

R1   The system must document the hours that employees start work, go on break, return from break, and leave work.

R1.1   In order to work with the timekeeping terminal, employees are required to identify themselves by sliding their employee badges through a badge reader on the timekeeping terminal.

R1.2   After an employee is identified to a timekeeping terminal, the employee can press a button to indicate if he or she is starting a work shift, going on break, returning from break, or ending a work shift. The timekeeping system keeps a permanent record for each such event in a form that it can later incorporate into a report documenting the employee's hours.

R2   Supervisors must be able to review the hours of subordinates at a timekeeping terminal without any need to get hard copy.

R2.1   The timekeeping terminal presents options that allow supervisors to review and modify an employee's recorded hours.

R2.1.1   All revisions made to an employee's timekeeping record leave an audit trail that retains the original records and identifies the person who made each revision.

R2.2   To ensure the simplest possible user interface for nonsupervisors, nonsupervisors don't see any options related to supervisory functions when they use a timekeeping terminal.

R2.3   Supervisors can modify the timekeeping records only of their own subordinates.

R3 At the end of each pay period, the timekeeping system must automatically transmit employee hours to the payroll system.

As we develop some use cases, you can expect to discover additional required functions.

Develop High-Level Essential Use Cases

When you develop use cases, it's usually best to focus first on the most common cases and then develop use cases for the less common cases. Use cases for common situations are called *primary use cases*. Use cases for less common situations are called *secondary use cases*. Here is a use case for the most common use of the timekeeping system.

Use case:	Employee Uses Timekeeping Terminal, version 1
Actor:	Employee
Purpose:	Inform timekeeping system of an employee's comings and goings.
Synopsis:	An employee is about to start a work shift, go on break, return from break, or end a work shift. The employee identifies him- or herself to the timekeeping system and lets it know which of those four things he or she is about to do.
Type:	Primary and essential
Cross-references:	Requirements R1, R1.1, R1.2, R1.3, and R2.2

Course of Events

Employee	*System*
1. Employee slides his or her badge through a timekeeping terminal's badge reader.	2. The timekeeping terminal reads the employee ID from the badge and verifies that it's a legitimate employee ID. The timekeeping terminal then prompts the employee to tell it if he or she is starting a work shift, going on break, returning from break, or ending a work shift.
3. The employee indicates to the timekeeping terminal whether he or she is starting a work shift, going on break, returning from break, or ending a work shift.	4. The timekeeping terminal makes a permanent record of the employee's indication. It then acknowledges the employee with a display of the current time, indicating that it is ready for use by the next employee.

Now let's consider a larger use case that contains less detail.

Use case:	Employee Uses Multiple Timekeeping Terminals to Track Hours, version 1
Actor:	Employee
Purpose:	Inform timekeeping system of an employee's comings and goings during an entire shift.
Synopsis:	An employee who is not restricted to the use of a single timekeeping terminal notifies the timekeeping system when he or she starts a shift, goes on break, returns from break, and ends a shift.
Type:	Primary and essential
Cross-references:	Requirements R1 and R1.2

Course of Events

Employee	System
1. An employee uses a timekeeping terminal to notify the timekeeping system that he or she is starting a shift.	2. The system makes a record of the time that the employee began the shift.
3. An employee uses a timekeeping terminal to notify the timekeeping system that he or she is going on break.	4. The system makes a record of the time that the employee went on break.
5. An employee uses a timekeeping terminal to notify the timekeeping system that he or she has returned from break.	6. The system makes a record of the time that the employee returned from break.
7. An employee uses a timekeeping terminal to notify the timekeeping system that he or she is ending a shift.	8. The system makes a record of the time that the employee ended the shift.

When we analyze the less detailed use case, we find a potential problem. There is no requirement that all the timekeeping terminals keep the correct time. Employees are likely to notice if the times on different timekeeping terminals are not the same. They will want to start their shift on the terminal that shows the earlier time and end their shift on the terminal that shows the later time. To prevent employees from cheating the company in this way, we need to add another requirement:

R1.3 The times displayed and recorded by different timekeeping terminals must be within five seconds of each other.

As we develop more essential use cases, additional refinements to the requirements will be found. However, this is all that we present in this case study.

Object-Oriented Analysis

Object-oriented analysis is concerned with building a model of the problem that must be solved. It answers the question of what the software will do without concern for how it will do it.

The primary product of object-oriented analysis is a conceptual model of the problem that shows the proposed system and the real-world entities with which the system interacts. The conceptual model also includes the relationships and interactions between the problem domain entities and between the entities and the system.

Conceptual models are usually constructed in two phases:

1. Identify the entities that are involved in the problem. It's very important to identify all of the entities involved. When in doubt, it's best to include an entity in the model. If the entity is unnecessary for subsequent design activities, then that becomes apparent as the design develops. On the other hand, if an entity is missing from the analysis, the missing entity may not be detected later in the project.
2. Identify the relationships between the entities.

UML uses the same symbols to represent the entities and relationships of a conceptual model as it uses to represent classes and associations in a class model. Figure 3.2 is a diagram that shows just the entities that are apparent from the requirements and the use cases. The entities in Figure 3.2 are in no particular order. The diagram shown in Figure 3.3 adds some of the more obvious relationships.

When you examine Figure 3.3, notice two entities that are not involved in any of the indicated relationships: TimekeepingSystem and EmployeeID. This diagram is supposed to be a conceptual model of the problem to be solved. Because the TimekeepingSystem entity does not seem to have a relationship to anything else in the problem, we conclude that it's really part of the solution rather than the problem. For that reason, we drop it from the model.

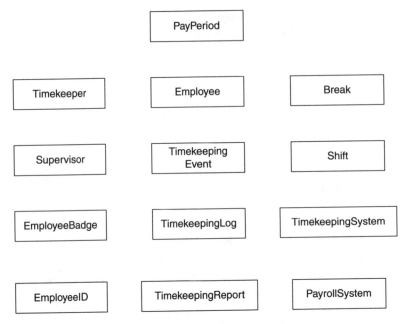

FIGURE 3.2 Conceptual model with entities only.

The EmployeeID entity is very closely related to the Employee entity. In fact, it's so closely related to the Employee entity that it seems more appropriate to represent it as an attribute. Figure 3.4 shows the conceptual model with attributes added.

The diagram depicted in Figure 3.4 is as far as we take the analysis of this problem.

Object-Oriented Design

Object-oriented design is concerned with the design of the internal logic of a program—in this case, we are concerned with the internal logic of the timekeeping system. It's not concerned with how the user interface presents that logic, nor is it concerned with how data is stored in a database. The ultimate goal of object-oriented design is to produce a detailed design of the classes that will provide that internal logic.

There are various strategies for using the results of analysis to produce a design. The strategy that we use here is to create a class diagram that models the structural relationships in the conceptual model. We then develop collaboration diagrams to model the behavioral relationships in the conceptual model. After that, we refine the class diagrams with what we learned from the collaboration diagrams. Finally, we refine the collaboration and

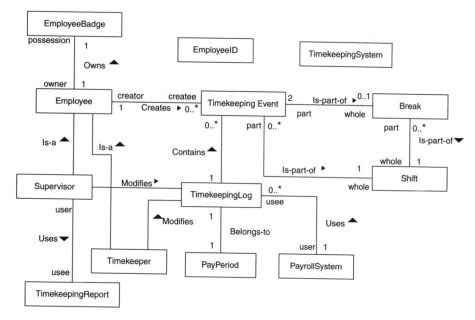

FIGURE 3.3 Conceptual model with associations.

class diagrams with requirements that are not covered by the conceptual model. Throughout that process, we use design patterns to guide us.

Let's construct our first class diagram by assuming that there is a class to represent each entity in the conceptual model, as shown in Figure 3.5. Rather than assume the representation of the entity attributes in the conceptual model, the class diagram shown in Figure 3.5 indicates *accessor methods* for the attributes. An accessor method is a method that provides access to a piece of information encapsulated by an object. Representing a conceptual entity's attributes as a class's private variables ensures that other classes can only access the attributes through the accessor methods. The way the class represents the attributes is hidden from other classes. This allows the representation to be changed without any impact on other classes.

Accessor methods that fetch the value of an attribute usually have a name that consists of the word "get" followed by the name of the attribute. In the conceptual model, the Employee entity has an attribute named employeeID. In Figure 3.5, that entity is represented by the Employee class. The Employee class has an accessor method named getEmployeeID. It returns the value of an Employee object's employee id attribute.

Accessor methods that set the value of an attribute usually have a name that consists of the word "set" followed by the name of the attribute.

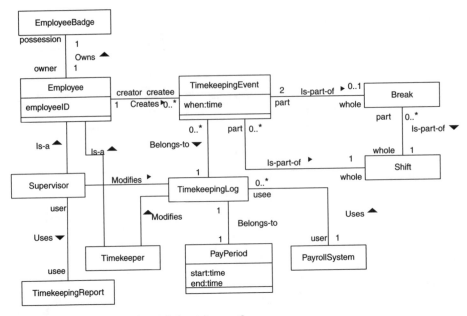

FIGURE 3.4 Conceptual model with attributes.

None of the classes in the class diagram have set methods because the conceptual model presents no reason to change any entity's attribute after the entity exists.

Next we need to consider the "Is-a" relationships in the conceptual model. The relationships marked "Is-a" in the conceptual model indicate that one kind of entity is also another kind of entity. For example, the model shows that a supervisor is also an employee. Though an obvious way to represent "Is-a" relationships in a class diagram is through inheritance, the Delegation pattern tells us that it's not always the best way to represent "Is-a" relationships. In particular, it tells us to use delegation instead of inheritance to depict "Is-a" relationships that represent roles that instances of a class may play at different times. Since a nonsupervisor employee may be promoted to supervisor, transferred from another job to the timekeeper job, or become a timekeeping supervisor, we use delegation to represent those roles (see Figure 3.6).

The "Is-part-of" relationships in the conceptual diagram are another structural relationship that we can consider designing into the class diagram at this point. The relationships in the model marked "Is-part-of" indicate an aggregation. For example, a shift can be thought of as an aggregation of timekeeping events, so the model indicates that a TimekeepingEvent entity

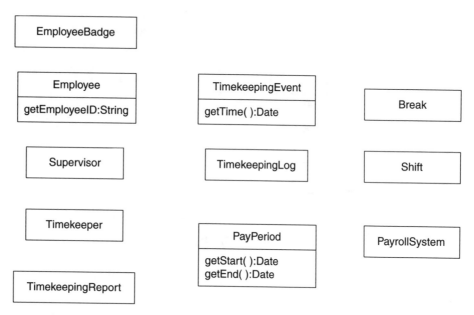

FIGURE 3.5 Class diagram, version 1.

has an "Is part-of" relationship with a `Shift` entity. Notice that there is some redundancy between two sets of "Is-part-of" relationships: The "Is-part-of" relationship between `Shift` and `TimekeepingEvent` appears to have some redundancy with the set of "Is-part-of" relationships between `Shift` and `Break` and between `Break` and `TimekeepingEvent`. For that reason we will postpone including those relationships in the design until we have clarified the relationships through the construction of collaboration diagrams.

We guide the construction of collaboration diagrams with use cases, so we assemble the following real use case to describe a typical employee's use of the timekeeping system for one day.

Use case:	Employee Uses Timekeeping Terminal to Track Hours, version 1
Actor:	Employee
Purpose:	Inform timekeeping system of an employee's comings and goings.
Synopsis:	An employee is about to start a work shift, go on break, return from break, or end a work shift. The employee identifies him- or herself to the timekeeping system and lets it know which of those four things he or she is about to do.

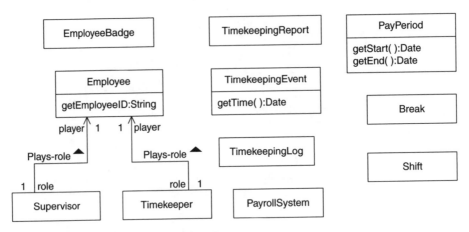

FIGURE 3.6 Class diagram, version 2.

Type: Primary and real

Cross-references: Requirements R1, R1.1, R1.2, R1.3, and R2.2

                               Essential use case "Employee Uses
                               Timekeeping Terminal"

Course of Events

Employee	*System*
1. Employee slides his or her badge through a timekeeping terminal's badge reader.	2. The timekeeping terminal replaces its display of the current time—indicating its availability for use—with a display that tells the employee that it's looking up the employee ID detected by the badge reader. After the timekeeping terminal finds the employee's information, it verifies that the employee is allowed to use this particular timekeeping terminal. The timekeeping terminal then prompts the employee to tell it if he or she is starting a work shift, going on break, returning from break, or ending a work shift.
3. The employee indicates to the timekeeping terminal whether he or she is starting a work shift, going on break, returning from break, or ending a work shift.	4. The timekeeping terminal makes a permanent record of the employee's choice. It acknowledges the completion of the timekeeping transaction by displaying the current time, indicating that it is ready for use by the next employee.

This use case involves classes that are not in the previous class diagram. The use case talks about a timekeeping terminal that interacts with a user, so we need to include a user interface class in our design. We may refine that into additional classes if deemed necessary later on.

The use case also mentions the creation of a permanent record of timekeeping events. To manage that and the employee information the timekeeping terminal looks up, we infer the existence of a database object. Again, we leave open the possibility of additional refinement later.

We want to minimize the number of dependencies between the user interface and the classes that implement the timekeeping terminal's internal logic. Retaining loose coupling between the user interface and the internal logic makes the software more maintainable. To achieve that, we use the Façade pattern. The Façade pattern tells us that we can maintain low coupling between a functionally related set of classes and their client classes by interposing an additional façade class between the set of classes and their clients. Most or all of the client's access to the set of classes is through the façade class. The façade class also encapsulates the common logic that is needed to use the set of classes.

The façade class that we add to the design is called `TimekeepingController`. It is responsible for controling the sequence of events that occurs when a timekeeping terminal interacts with a user.

Based on the preceding use case, we can construct the collaboration diagram shown in Figure 3.7. Here is a description of the interactions found in the start-shift collaboration diagram.

1. The `UserInterface` object begins the collaboration by passing an employee ID to the `TimekeepingController` object's `doTransaction` method.

   1.1 The `TimekeepingController` object passes the employee ID to the `Database` object's `LookupEmployee` method to get information about the employee associated with the employee ID. The `LookupEmployee` method returns an `Employee` object that encapsulates information about the employee.

   1.2 The `TimekeepingController` object calls the `UserInterface` object's `getEventType` method, which causes the user interface to prompt the employee for the type of event that should be recorded. The method returns a value that indicates the type of event to record.

   1.3 The `TimekeepingController` object passes the event type it got from the user interface to the `TimekeepingEvent` class's `createEvent` method. The `createEvent` method returns an object that encapsulates the event.

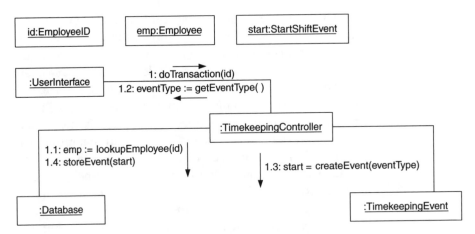

FIGURE 3.7 Start-shift collaboration diagram.

1.4 The `TimekeepingController` object passes the event object to the Database object's `storeEvent` method so it can be stored in the database.

Here is some of the rationale behind the construction of the collaboration diagram shown in Figure 3.7:

■ The `Database` class's `lookupEmployee` operation creates an object to encapsulate the employee information that it finds. The Creator pattern, described in Volume 2, says that if an object contains, aggregates, records instances of, or provides initializing data for instances of a class, then that object is a good choice of creator for instances of that class. Therefore, the objects that the `Database` class's `lookupEmployee` operation creates will be instances of the `Employee` class.

■ Since a start-of-shift event is a kind of timekeeping event, objects that represent a start-of-shift event are instances of a subclass of `TimekeepingEvent`. There will be other subclasses of the `TimekeepingEvent` class to represent other kinds of timekeeping events. We don't want the user interface to know about the subclasses of the `TimekeepingEvent` class because we want to minimize the dependencies between the user interface and the internal logic. To achieve that we use the Factory Method pattern.

The Factory Method pattern puts one class in charge of creating instances of other classes that have a common superclass or implement a common interface. Following that pattern, we put the `TimekeepingEvent` class in charge of creating instances of its subclasses.

Figure 3.8 shows another version of our class diagram that includes refinements from what we have learned since Figure 3.7. The `EmployeeBadge` class has been removed from the design, since the mechanism for capturing an employee's employee ID is part of the user interface and not part of the internal logic.

For the next refinement of the design, we take a closer look at the `Database` class. The intent of the `TimekeepingLog` entity in the conceptual model was to maintain a log of all timekeeping events. We created a class that corresponds to it in our initial design. Now we notice that the `Database` class has been given that responsibility. That means that we don't need the `TimekeepingLog` class in the design, so we must remove it.

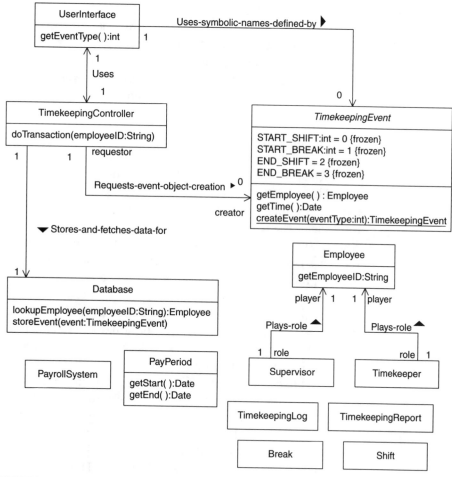

FIGURE 3.8 Class diagram, version 3.

An area of the design that we have not yet addressed is the generation of timekeeping reports. Supervisors use timekeeping reports to review the hours that their subordinates have worked. Specially formatted timekeeping reports are fed to the payroll system.

Timekeeping reports organize timekeeping events into shifts. A shift is a range of time during which an employee is at work. During a shift, an employee is supposed to work, except for periods within a shift called *breaks*. Breaks are periods when an employee stops working for such reasons as eating lunch, using the rest room, or smoking a cigarette.

For the purposes of computing an employee's pay, the time during a shift is broken down into three categories:

1. *Regular time* is time that an employee is paid at his or her usual hourly rate.
2. *Overtime* is time beyond the time that an employee is normally expected to work. An employee is paid for overtime at a multiple of his or her regular-time rate.
3. *Unpaid time* is time for which an employee is not paid. Some or all of an employee's break time may be unpaid time.

Timekeeping reports must break down the time an employee has worked into these three categories and indicate the amount of money an employee has earned before taxes and other deductions.

The rules that determine how to classify time as regular time, overtime, and unpaid time vary from state to state. The rules for computing the multiple of the regular rate that is paid for overtime also vary from state to state. Henry's Food Market currently operates in only one state. However, there are plans to expand into other states. Therefore, the design must account for different rules used to classify an employee's hours and compute the employee's pay.

To allow different sets of rules to be selected for timekeeping computations, we need to devise a way to organize a set of rules as a set of objects. We can represent a set of rules as finite state machines that take timekeeping events as input and then respond to the input by performing timekeeping computations. The statechart diagram in Figure 3.9 shows a sample state machine, omitting states and transitions for error handling, that models the timekeeping rules for the state of Georgia.

To implement the state machine shown in Figure 3.9, we can use the State pattern. The State pattern tells us to implement the states of a state class as subclasses of a common superclass. The class diagram in Figure

3.10 shows how the State pattern is used to implement the state machine shown in Figure 3.9.

Here is the way that the classes in Figure 3.10 are used. A program that retrieves an employee's timekeeping events from the database creates a GATimekeepingState object. It uses an instance of each of its subclasses to represent each of the state machine's states. The GATimekeepingState object's start method returns the state machine's initial state and makes that state the current state.

After a program creates an instance of GATimekeepingState, it calls its start method to retrieve the initial state. Then the program starts to fetch an employee's timekeeping events from the database. It passes each timekeeping event object it locates to the processEvent method of the current state object. The processEvent method causes the state machine to transition to another state based on the type of timekeeping event that

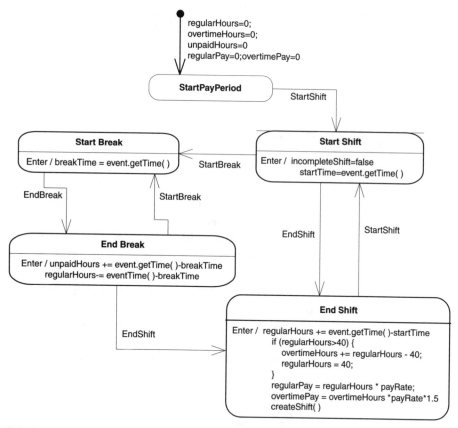

FIGURE 3.9 Sample state-based timekeeping computation.

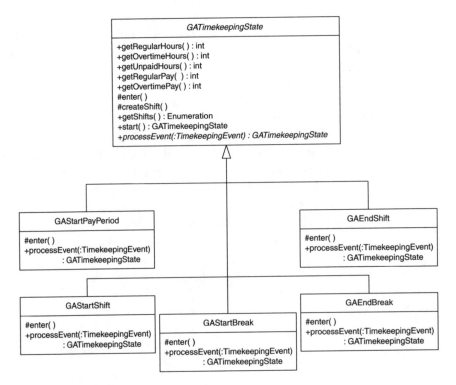

FIGURE 3.10 Timekeeping state classes.

is passed to it. The `processEvent` method returns the new current state. When the `processEvent` method causes the state machine to enter a state, it calls that state object's `enter` method.

As the state machine shifts from state to state, it computes the employee's hours and gross pay. It also organizes the timekeeping events into shifts. When the program is finished passing an employee's timekeeping events to the state machine, it can call appropriate methods of the `GATimekeepingState` object to get the employee's hours, gross pay, or an `Enumeration` of the shifts that the employee worked.

This is as far as we take this case study. This should provide you with some insight into how to use design patterns.

Design Pattern Catalog

4

Fundamental Design Patterns

The patterns in this chapter are the most fundamental and important design patterns to know. You will find these patterns used extensively in other design patterns.

Delegation (When Not to Use Inheritance) [Grand98]

SYNOPSIS

Delegation is a way to extend and reuse the functionality of a class by writing an additional class with added functionality that uses instances of the original class to provide the original functionality.

CONTEXT

Inheritance is a common way to extend and reuse the functionality of a class. Delegation is a more general way for extending a class's behavior that involves a class calling another class's methods rather than inheriting them. Inheritance is inappropriate for many situations that delegations are appropriate for.

For example, inheritance is useful for capturing "is-a-kind-of" relationships because these types of relationships are very static in nature. However, "is-a-role-played-by" relationships are awkward to model by inheritance. Instances of a class can play multiple roles. Let's look at an example of an airline reservation system. This airline reservation system includes such roles as passenger, ticket selling agent, and flight crew. It's possible to represent this as a class called `Person` that has subclasses corresponding to these roles, as shown in Figure 4.1.

The problem with the diagram depicted in Figure 4.1 is that the same person can fill more than one of these roles. A person who is normally part of a flight crew can also be a passenger. Some airlines occasionally float the flight crew to the ticket counter. This means that the same person can fill any combination of these roles. To model this situation, you need 7 subclasses for `Person`, as shown in Figure 4.2. The number of subclasses needed increases exponentially with the number of roles. Therefore, you need 63 subclasses to model 6 roles.

A more serious problem is that the same person can play different combinations of roles at different times. Inheritance is a static relationship that does not change over time. Using inheritance necessitates using multiple objects to represent the same person in order to capture changes in role.

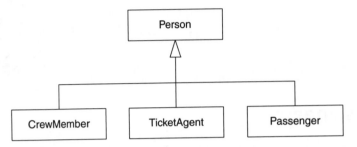

FIGURE 4.1 Modeling roles with inheritance.

On the other hand, it's possible to represent persons in different roles using delegation without having any of those problems, as shown in Figure 4.3.

FORCES

If you find that an object needs to be a different subclass of a class at different times, then it should not be a subclass of that class in the first place. If an object is created as an instance of a class, it will always be an instance of that class. On the other hand, an object can delegate behavior to different objects at different times.

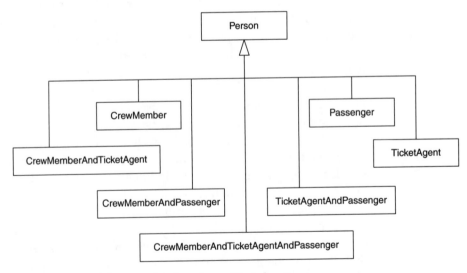

FIGURE 4.2 Modeling multiple roles with inheritance.

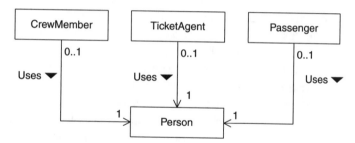

FIGURE 4.3 Modeling roles with delegation.

If you find that a class attempts to hide a method or variable inherited from a superclass from other classes, then that class should not inherit from that subclass. There is no way to effectively hide methods or variables that are inherited from a superclass. On the other hand, it is possible for an object to use the methods and variables of another object while ensuring that it is the only object that has access to the other object.

Declaring a class that is related to a program's problem domain as a subclass of a utility class is usually not a good idea for two reasons:

1. When you declare that a class is a subclass of a class such as `Vector` or `Hashtable`, you run the risk that these classes that you do not control will change in an incompatible way in the future. Though it's a low risk, there is usually no corresponding benefit to offset it.
2. When people write a problem-domain-specific class as a subclass of a utility class, the intent is usually to use the functionality of the utility class to implement problem-domain-specific functionality. The problem is that it weakens the encapsulation of the problem domain class's implementation.

   Client classes that use the problem domain class can be written in a way that assumes the problem domain class is a subclass of the utility class. If the implementation of the problem domain changes in a way that results in its having a different superclass, those client classes that rely on its original superclass will break.

   An even more serious problem is that client classes can call the public methods of the utility superclass, which defeats its encapsulation.

Some inappropriate uses of inheritance are so common that they can be classified as AntiPatterns. In particular, subclassing utility classes and using inheritance to model roles are common design flaws.

Many or possibly most reuse situations and extensions of a class are not appropriately done through inheritance.

By determining its superclass, a class's declaration determines the behavior that a class inherits from its superclass. Inheritance is not useful when the behavior that a class builds on is determined at runtime.

SOLUTION

Delegation is a way to reuse and extend class behavior. It works by writing a new class that incorporates the functionality of the original class by using an instance of the original class and calling its methods, as shown in Figure 4.4. The diagram in Figure 4.4 shows that a class that is in a Delegator role uses a class in the Delegate role.

Delegation is more general purpose than inheritance. Any extension to a class that can be accomplished by inheritance can also be accomplished by delegation.

CONSEQUENCES

Delegation can be used without the problems that accompany inheritance. Another advantage of delegation is that it is easy to compose behavior at runtime.

The main disadvantage of delegation is that it is less structured than inheritance. Relationships between classes built using delegation are less obvious than those built with inheritance. Here are some strategies for improving the clarity of delegation-based relationships:

■ Use consistent naming schemes to refer to objects in a particular role. For example, if multiple classes delegate the creation of widget objects, the role of the delegate object becomes more obvious if all of

FIGURE 4.4 Delegation used to reuse and extend class behavior.

the classes that delegate that operation refer to delegate objects through a variable called `widgetFactory`.
- You can always clarify the purpose of a delegation by writing comments.
- Follow the Don't Talk to Strangers pattern (described in Volume 2). It states that if a class without a delegation only has an indirect association with another class, then the delegation should be indirect. Do not directly delegate behavior to an indirectly associated class that provides the behavior. Instead, delegate it to a directly associated class and have that class delegate the behavior to the class that provides the behavior. This simplifies the overall design by minimizing the number of associations between objects.
- Use well-known design and coding patterns. A person reading code that uses delegation will be more likely to understand the role that the objects play if the roles are part of a well-known pattern or a pattern that recurs frequently in your program.

Note that it's possible and advantageous to use all of these strategies at the same time.

IMPLEMENTATION

The implementation of delegation is very straightforward. It simply involves the acquisition of a reference to an instance of the class to which you want to delegate and call its methods.

JAVA API USAGE

The Java API is full of examples of delegation. It's the basis for Java's delegation event model. In that model, event source objects send events to event listener objects. Event source objects don't generally decide what to do with an event. Instead they delegate the responsibility for processing the event to listener objects.

CODE EXAMPLE

For an example of delegation, we look at another part of an airline reservation system. Suppose the reservation system is responsible for keeping

FIGURE 4.5 Classes for check luggage example.

track of checked pieces of luggage. We can expect this part of the system to include classes to represent a flight segment,* a luggage compartment, and pieces of luggage, as shown in Figure 4.5.

In Figure 4.5, the `FlightSegment` class has a method called `checkLuggage` that checks a piece of luggage onto a flight. The flight class delegates that operation to an instance of the `LuggageCompartment` class.

Another common use for delegation is to implement a collection. Consider the class diagram in Figure 4.6. A class such as `LuggageCompartment` that maintains a collection of other objects normally delegates that collection to another object such as an instance of `java.util.Vector`. Because implementing a collection with delegation is so common, the separate collection class is usually omitted from design drawings.

Here are code fragments that implement the design shown in Figures 4.5 and 4.6. First, let's look at the `FlightSegment` class that delegates the `checkLuggage` operation to the `LuggageCompartment` class:

```
class FlightSegment {
...
   LuggageCompartment luggage;
...
   void checkLuggage(Luggage piece) throws LuggageException {
       luggage.checkLuggage(piece);
   } // checkLuggage(Luggage)
} // class FlightSegment
```

Here is the `LuggageCompartment` class that delegates the collection of pieces of luggage to the `Vector` class:

```
class LuggageCompartment {
...
   // The pieces of luggage in this LuggageCompartment
   private Vector pieces = new Vector();
...
   void checkLuggage(Luggage piece) throws LuggageException {
...
       pieces.addElement(piece);
   } // checkLuggage(Luggage)
} // class LuggageCompartment
```

*A flight segment is a portion of a trip that you take on an airline without changing planes.

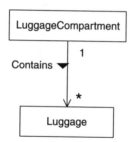

FIGURE 4.6 Luggage compartment example.

RELATED PATTERNS

Almost every other pattern uses delegation. Some of the patterns that rely most clearly on delegation are the Decorator pattern and the Proxy pattern.

Interface [Grand98]

SYNOPSIS

Keep a class that uses data and services provided by instances of other classes independent of those classes by having it access those instances through an interface.

CONTEXT

Suppose that you are writing an application to manage the purchase of goods for a business. Among the entities your program needs information about are vendors, freight companies, receiving locations, and billing locations. One thing these entities have in common is that they all have street addresses. These street addresses appear in different parts of the user interface. You want to have a class that can display and edit street addresses. This will ensure that you can reuse it wherever there is an address in the user interface. Let's call that class AddressPanel.

You want AddressPanel objects to be able to retrieve and set address information in a separate data object. That raises the question of what instances of the AddressPanel class can assume about the class of the data objects that will be with them. Clearly, you should use different classes to represent vendors, freight companies, and the like. If you program in a language like C++ that supports multiple inheritance, you can arrange for the data objects that instances of AddressPanel use to inherit from an address class in addition to the other classes they inherit from. If you program in a language like Java that uses a single inheritance object model, then you must explore other solutions.

You can solve the problem by creating an address interface. Then instances of the AddressPanel class simply require data objects that implement the address interface. They can then call the accessor methods declared by the interface and set the object's address information. Using the indirection that the interface provides, instances of the AddressPanel are able to call the methods of the data object without knowing what class it belongs to. Figure 4.7 is a class diagram that shows these relationships.

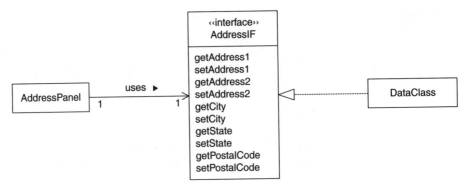

FIGURE 4.7 Indirection through address interface.

FORCES

- If the instances of a class must use another object and that object is assumed to belong to a particular class, then the reusability of the class is compromised.
- Suppose that instances of a class use other objects and all that they require of those objects is that they implement certain methods. You can limit the class's dependency to just this requirement by defining an interface that has just those methods and designing the class to use the interface.

SOLUTION

To avoid the coupling of classes because one uses the other, make the usage indirect through an interface. Figure 4.8 shows this organization. Here are the roles that these classes and the interface play.

Client   The Client class uses other classes that implement the IndirectionIF interface.

IndirectionIF   The IndirectionIF interface provides the indirection that keeps the Client class independent of the class that is in the Service role.

FIGURE 4.8 Class decoupling relationship.

Service Classes in this role provide a service to classes in the `Client` role.

CONSEQUENCES

Applying the Interface pattern keeps a class that needs a service from another class from being coupled to any specific class.

Like any other indirection, the Interface pattern can make a program more difficult to understand.

IMPLEMENTATION

Implementation of the Interface pattern is straightforward: Define an interface to provide a service, write client classes to access the service through the interface, and write classes that provide the service to implement the interface.

JAVA API USAGE

The Java API defines the interface `java.io.FilenameFilter`. That interface declares a method that you can use to decide if a named file is included in a collection. The Java API also defines the `java.awt` `.FileDialog` class that can use a `FilenameFilter` object to filter the files that it displays. You can pass the `list` method of the `java.io.File` class a `FilenameFilter` object to filter the files that it puts in the array that it returns.

CODE EXAMPLE

The example for the Interface pattern is the `AddressPanel` class and `AddressIF` interface discussed under the Context heading. Here is code for the `AddressPanel` class:

```
class AddressPanel extends Panel {
    private AddressIF data; // Data object
```

```
...
   /**
    * Save the contents of the TextFields into the data object.
    */
   public void save() {
       if (data != null) {
           data.setAddress1(address1Field.getText());
...
           data.setPostalCode(postalCodeField.getText());
       } // if data
   } // save()
} // class AddressPanel
```

Notice that the Interface pattern only manifests itself in the fact that the AddressPanel class declares its data instance variable as an interface type.

The heart of the Interface pattern is the interface that provides the indirection between the client class and the service class. Here is the code for the AddressIF interface that provides that indirection for the AddressPanel class:

```
public interface AddressIF {
    public String getAddress1();
    public void setAddress1(String address1);
...
    public String getPostalCode() ;
    public void setPostalCode(String PostalCode);
} // interface AddressIF
```

The interface simply declares the methods required for the needed service.

Finally, here is code for the service class. The only impact that the Interface pattern has on the class is that it implements the AddressIF interface.

```
class ReceivingLocation extends Facility implements AddressIF{
    private String address1;
    private String postalCode;
...
    public String getAddress1() { return address1; }
    public void setAddress1(String address1) {
    this.address1 = address1;
}
...
    public String getPostalCode() { return postalCode; }
    public void setPostalCode(String postalCode) {
        this.postalCode = postalCode;
```

```
      } // setPostalCode(String)
} // class ReceivingLocation
```

RELATED PATTERNS

Delegation   The Delegation and Interface patterns are often used
together.

Many other patterns use the Interface pattern.

Immutable [Grand98]

The Immutable pattern is fundamental in a different sense from the other patterns presented in this chapter. The Immutable pattern is considered fundamental because the more appropriate places you use it, the more robust and maintainable your programs will be.

SYNOPSIS

The Immutable pattern increases the robustness of objects that share references to the same object and reduces the overhead of concurrent access to an object. It accomplishes this by forbidding any of an object's state information to change after the object is constructed. The Immutable pattern also avoids the need to synchronize multiple threads of execution that share an object.

CONTEXT

The Immutable pattern is useful in a great variety of contexts. What these contexts have in common is that they use instances of a class that are shared by multiple objects and whose states are fetched more often than changed.

In situations where multiple objects share access to the same object, a problem can arise if changes to the shared object are not properly coordinated between the objects that share it. That can require careful programming that is easy to get wrong. If the changes to and fetches of the shared object's state are done asynchronously, then, in addition to the greater likelihood of bugs, correctly functioning code will have the overhead of synchronizing the accesses to the shared object's state.

The Immutable pattern avoids these problems. It organizes a class so that the state information of its instances never changes after they are constructed.

Suppose that you are writing a game program that involves the placement and occasional movement of objects on a playing field. In the course of designing the classes for that program, you decide that you want to use immutable objects to represent the position of objects on the playing field.

The organization of a class for modeling a position that way might look like Figure 4.9.

In Figure 4.9, a class called Position has *x* and *y* values associated with its instances. The class has a constructor that specifies the *x* and *y* values. It also has methods to fetch the *x* and *y* values associated with its instances. Last, it has a method that creates a new Position object that is given an *x* and *y* offset from an existing position. It does not have any methods to modify its own *x* or *y* value.

FORCES

- Your program uses instances of a class that are passive in nature. The instances don't ever need to change their own state. The instances of that class are used by multiple other objects.
- Correctly coordinating changes to the state information of an object used by multiple other objects is difficult and bug prone, even if the changes are sequential and not concurrent. When the state of such an object changes, all the objects that use it may need to be informed. Also, when multiple objects use an object, they may attempt to change its state in inconsistent ways.
- If access to a shared object's state information involves multiple threads and modifications of its state information, then the threads that access the state information must be synchronized in order to ensure consistency.
- The overhead of synchronizing the threads may add an unacceptable overhead to accessing the shared object's state information.

SOLUTION

To avoid having to manage the propagation and synchronization of changes to the state information of objects used by multiple other objects,

```
┌─────────────────────────────────┐
│            Position             │
├─────────────────────────────────┤
│ ‹‹constructor››                 │
│ Position(x:int, y:int)          │
│ ‹‹misc››                        │
│ getX( ):int                     │
│ getY( ):int                     │
│ Offset(x:int, y:int):Position   │
└─────────────────────────────────┘
```

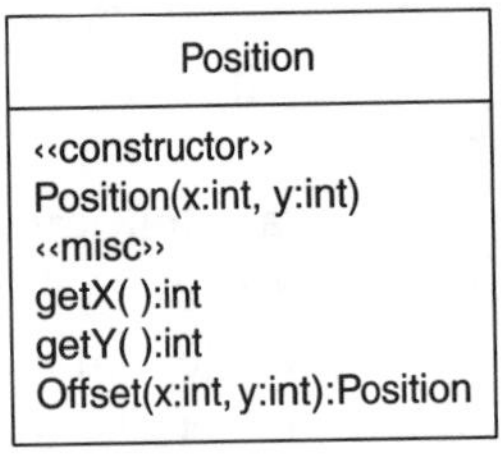

FIGURE 4.9 Immutable position.

make the shared objects immutable, disallowing any changes to their state after they are constructed. You can accomplish that by not including any methods, other than constructors, in their class that modify state information. You can organize such a class like that shown in Figure 4.10.

Notice that the class has accessor methods to retrieve state information but not to set it.

CONSEQUENCES

Since the state of immutable objects never changes, there is no need to write code to manage such changes. Also, there is no need to synchronize threads that access immutable objects.

Operations that would otherwise have changed the state of an object must create a new object. Mutable objects do not incur this overhead.

IMPLEMENTATION

There are two concerns to be aware of when you implement the Immutable pattern:

1. No method, other than a constructor, should modify the values of a class's instance variables.
2. Any method that computes new state information must store that information in a new instance of the same class, rather than modify the existing object's state.

One possible, unexpected detail for implementing the Immutable pattern is that it usually does not involve the declaration of variables with the `final` modifier. The values of final instance variables are normally provided from within their class. However, the values of an immutable object's

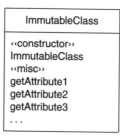

FIGURE 4.10 Immutable class.

instance variables normally are provided by another class that instantiates the object.

A common variation on the Immutable pattern is called the Read Only Object. The Immutable pattern cannot be used if there is even one other class that needs to modify instances of a class after they are created. To get most of the robustness that the Immutable pattern provides, you can define a read-only interface that most other classes can use to access the class's instances. The class diagram in Figure 4.11 shows the organization for Read Only Object.

In the Read Only Object diagram, the Foo class has accessor methods to retrieve and set the values of its attributes. The ReadOnlyFooIF interface has the same get methods as the Foo class, which implements the interface. The interface does not include any of the Foo class's set methods. Some clients of the Foo class, such as the MutatorClient class, use the Foo class directly and call its set methods. Other classes, such as the Client class, access the Foo class indirectly through the ReadOnlyFooIF interface. Classes that access the Foo class through the ReadOnlyFooIF interface are not able to access its set methods.

JAVA API USAGE

Instances of the String class are immutable. The sequence of characters that a String object represents is determined when it is constructed. The String class does not provide any methods to change the sequence of characters represented by a String object. Methods of the String class,

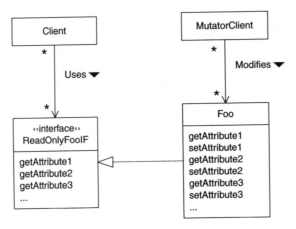

FIGURE 4.11 Read Only Object organization.

such as `toLowerCase` and `substring`, that compute a new sequence of characters return the new sequence of characters in a new `String` object.

CODE EXAMPLE

Here is what the declaration for the `Position` class described under the Context heading looks like:

```
class Position {
    private int x;
    private int y;

    public Position(int x, int y) {
        this.x = x;
        this.y = y;
    } // Position(int, int)

    public int getX() { return x; }

    public int getY() { return y; }

    public Position offset(int xOffset, int yOffset) {
        return new Position(x+xOffset, y+yOffset);
    } // offset(int, int)
} // class Position
```

RELATED PATTERNS

Single Threaded Execution   The Single Threaded Execution pattern is the pattern most frequently used to coordinate access by multiple threads to a shared object. The Immutable pattern can be used to avoid the need for the Single Threaded Execution pattern or any other kind of access coordination.

Marker Interface [Grand98]

The Marker Interface pattern occurs rarely outside of utility classes. However, it's included in this chapter because it takes advantage of the fundamental nature of class declarations.

SYNOPSIS

The Marker Interface pattern uses interfaces that declare no methods or variables to indicate semantic attributes of a class. It works particularly well with utility classes that must determine something about objects without assuming they are an instance of any particular class.

CONTEXT

Java's `Object` class defines a method called `equals` that takes an argument that can be a reference to any object. Since Java's `Object` class is the ultimate superclass of all other classes in Java, all other classes inherit the `equals` method from the `Object` class. The implementation of `equals` provided by the `Object` class returns true if the object passed to it is the same object as the object it's associated with. Classes that want their instances considered equal if they contain the same values override the `equals` method appropriately.

Container objects, such as `java.util.Vector`, call an object's `equals` method when performing a search of their contents to find an object that is equal to a given object. Such searches might call an object's `equals` method for each object in the container objects. This is wasteful in those cases where the object searched for belongs to a class that does not override the `equals` method. It's faster to use the == operator to determine if two objects are the same object instead of calling the `Object` class's implementation of the `equals` method. If the container class is able to determine that the object searched for belongs to a class that does not override the `equals` method, then it can use the == operator instead of calling `equals`. The problem with this approach is that there is no way to determine if an arbitrary object's class overrides the `equals` method.

It is possible to provide container classes with a hint to let them know that it's correct to use the `==` operator for an equality test on instances of a class. You can define an interface called `EqualByIdentity` that declares no methods or variables. You can then write container classes to assume that if a class implements `EqualByIdentity`, then the equality comparison is done with the `==` operator.

An interface that does not declare methods or variables and is used to indicate attributes of classes that implement them is said to be a *marker interface*.

FORCES

- Utility classes may need to know something about the intended use of an object's class without relying on an object being an instance of a particular class.
- Classes can implement any number of interfaces.
- It's possible to determine if an object's class implements a known interface without relying on the object being an instance of any particular class.

SOLUTION

When a utility class needs to determine if another class's instances are included in a classification without the utility class knowing of other classes, it can determine if other classes implement a marker interface. As stated previously, a marker interface is an interface that does not declare any methods or variables. You declare that a class implements a marker interface to indicate that it belongs to the classification associated with the marker interface.

These relationships are shown in Figure 4.12.

Figure 4.13 shows a diagram that contains a marker interface called `MarkerIF`. There is a class called `Marked` that implements `MarkerIF` and a class called `Unmarked` that doesn't. There is also a utility class called `Utility` that is aware of the `MarkerIF` interface. Instances of `UtilityClass` receive calls to their `operation1` method. The parameter passed to that method can be an object that implements or does not implement `MarkerIF`.

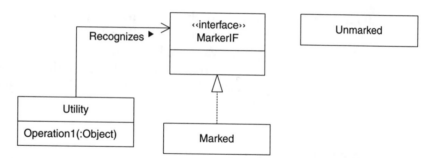

FIGURE 4.12 Marker interface class diagram.

CONSEQUENCES

Instances of utility classes are able to make inferences about objects passed to their methods without depending on the objects to be instances of any particular class.

The relationship between the utility class and the marker interface is transparent to all other classes except for those classes that implement the interface.

IMPLEMENTATION

The essence of the Marker Interface pattern is that an object that either does or does not implement a marker interface is passed to a method of a utility class. The formal parameter that corresponds to that object is typically declared as Object. It is sometimes appropriate to declare that formal parameter to be a more specialized class.

It is also possible to use an interface that declares methods in the Marker Interface method. In such cases, the interface used as a marker interface usually extends an interface that declares methods.

Declaring that a class implements a marker interface implies that the class is included in the classification implied by the interface. It also

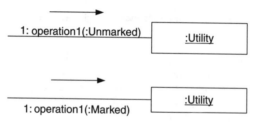

FIGURE 4.13 Marker interface collaboration.

implies that all subclasses of that class are included in the classification. If there is any possibility that someone will declare a subclass that does not fit the classification, then you should take measures to prevent that from happening. Such measures might include declaring the class final to prevent it from being subclassed, or its equals method to be final to prevent it from being overridden.

JAVA API USAGE

A class indicates that its instances may be serialized by implementing the Serializable interface. Instances of the ObjectOutputstream class write objects as a stream of bytes that an instance of the ObjectInputStream class can read and turn back into an object. The conversion of an object to a stream of bytes is called *serialization*. There are a number of reasons why instances of some classes should not be serialized. Because of that, the ObjectOutputstream class refuses to serialize objects unless their class implements the Serializable interface to indicate that its serialization is allowed.

CODE EXAMPLE

For an example of an application of the Marker Interface pattern, see the following class that implements a linked list data structure. At the bottom of the listing, you will see methods called find, findEq, and findEquals. The purpose of all three methods is to find a LinkedList node that refers to a specified object. The find method is the only one of the three that is public. The findEq method performs the necessary equality tests using the == operator. The findEquals method performs the necessary equality tests using the equals method of the object being searched for. The find method decides which of the other two methods to call by determining if the object to search for implements the marker interface EqualByIdentity.

```
public class LinkedList implements Cloneable, java.io.Serializable {
...
    /**
     * Find an object in a linked list that is equal to the given
     * object. Equality is normally determined by calling the given
     * object's equals method. However, if the given object
     * implements the EqualByIdentity interface, then equality will be
     * determined by the == operator.
     */
```

```
public LinkedList find(Object target) {
    if (target == null || target instanceof EqualByIdentity)
      return findEq(target);
    else
      return findEquals(target);
} // find(Object)

/**
 * Find an object in a linked list that is equal to the given
 * object. Equality is determined by the == operator.
 */
private synchronized LinkedList findEq(Object target) {
...
} // find(Object)

/**
 * Find an object in a linked list that is equal to the given
 * object. Equality is determined by calling the given
 * object's equals method.
 */
private synchronized LinkedList findEquals(Object target) {
...
} // find(Object)
} // class LinkedList
```

RELATED PATTERNS

Snapshot   The Marker Interface pattern is used by the Snapshot pattern to allow serialization of objects.

Proxy

SYNOPSIS

Proxy is a very general pattern that occurs in many other patterns, but never by itself in its pure form. The Proxy pattern forces method calls to an object to occur indirectly through a proxy object that acts as a surrogate for the other object, delegating method calls to that object. Classes for proxy objects are declared in a way that usually eliminates client objects' awareness that they are dealing with a proxy.

CONTEXT

A proxy object is an object that receives method calls on behalf of another object. Client objects call the proxy object's methods. The proxy object's methods do not directly provide the service that its clients expect. Instead, the proxy object's methods call the methods of the object that provides the actual service. Figure 4.14 shows a diagram of that structure.

Though a Proxy object's methods don't directly provide the service that its clients expect, the Proxy object provides some management of those services. Proxy objects generally share a common interface or superclass with the service-providing object. That makes it possible for client objects to be unaware that they are calling the methods of a proxy object rather than the methods of the actual service-providing object. Transparent management of another object's services is the basic reason for using a proxy.

There are many different types of service management that a proxy can be used to provide. Some of the more important ones are documented elsewhere in this book as patterns in their own right. Here are some of the more common uses for proxies:

- A proxy makes a method that can take a long time to complete appear to return immediately.

FIGURE 4.14 Method calls through a Proxy.

- A proxy creates the illusion that an object that exists on a different machine is an ordinary local object. This kind of proxy is called a *remote proxy*. It is used by Remote Method Invocation (RMI).
- A proxy controls access to a service-providing object. This kind of proxy is called an *access proxy*.
- A proxy creates the illusion that a service object exists before it actually does. This can be useful if a service object is expensive to create and its services are not needed. This use of proxies is documented as the Virtual Proxy pattern.

FORCES

- It is not possible for a service-providing object to provide a service at a time or place that is convenient.
- Gaining visibility to an object is nontrivial and you want to hide that complexity.
- Access to a service-providing object must be controlled without adding complexity to the service-providing object or coupling the service to the access control policy.
- The management of a service should be provided in a way that is as transparent as possible to the clients of that service.

SOLUTION

Transparent management of a service-providing object can be accomplished by forcing all access to the service-providing object through a proxy object. In order for the management to be transparent, the proxy object and the service-providing object must either be instances of a common superclass or implement a common interface, as shown in Figure 4.15.

By referring to the superclass or interface that is common to both the proxy and service providing classes, client classes avoid having to care which is the actual class that they refer to at run time.

Figure 4.15 does not show any details for implementing any particular service management policy. However, the Proxy pattern is not very useful unless it implements some particular service management policy. The Proxy pattern is so commonly used with some service management policies that the combinations are described elsewhere as patterns in their own right.

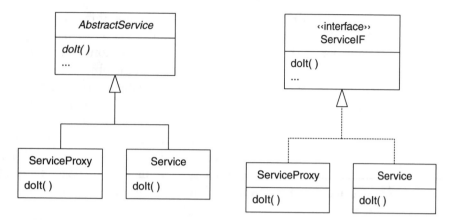

FIGURE 4.15 Proxy class diagram.

CONSEQUENCES

The service provided by a service-providing object is managed in a manner transparent to that object and its clients.

Unless the use of proxies introduces new failure modes, there is normally no need for the code of client classes to reflect the use of proxies.

IMPLEMENTATION

Without any specific management policy, the implementation of the Proxy pattern simply involves creating a class that shares a common superclass or interface with a service-providing class and delegates operations to instances of the service-providing class.

CODE EXAMPLE

The Proxy pattern is not useful in its pure form. It must be combined with a service management behavior to accomplish anything useful. The example for the Proxy pattern uses proxies to defer an expensive operation until it is actually needed. If the operation is not needed, the operation is never performed.

The example is a subclass of `java.util.Hashtable` that is functionally equivalent to `Hashtable`. The difference is the way that it handles the clone operation. A `Hashtable` object's `clone` method returns a new

Hashtable object that contains all the same things as the original Hashtable object. Cloning a Hashtable is an expensive operation.

One of the more common reasons for cloning an object like a Hashtable is to avoid holding a lock on the object for a long time when all that is desired is to fetch multiple key-value pairs. In a multithreaded program, to ensure that a Hashtable is in a consistent state when you are fetching key-value pairs from it, you can use a synchronized method to obtain exclusive access to the Hashtable. While that is going on, other threads will wait to gain access to the same Hashtable, which may be unacceptable. In some other cases it may not be possible to retain exclusive access. An example of that is the Enumeration object returned by the Hashtable class's elements object.

Cloning a Hashtable prior to fetching values out of it is a defensive measure. Cloning the Hashtable avoids the need to obtain a synchronization lock on a Hashtable beyond the time that it takes for the clone operation to complete. When you have a freshly cloned copy of a Hashtable, you can be sure that no other thread has access to the copy. Since no other thread has access to the copy, you will be able to fetch key-value pairs from the copy without any interference with other threads.

If, after you clone a Hashtable, there is no subsequent modification to the original Hashtable, then the time and memory spent in creating the clone was wasted. The point of this example is to avoid that waste. It does this by delaying the cloning of a Hashtable until a modification to it actually occurs.

The main class in the example is LargeHashtable. Instances of LargeHashtable are a copy-on-write proxy for a Hashtable object. When a proxy's clone method is called, it returns a copy of the proxy but does not copy the Hashtable object. At this point, both the original and the copy of the proxy refer to the same Hashtable object. When either of the proxies is asked to modify the Hashtable, they recognize that they are using a shared Hashtable and clone the Hashtable before they make the modification.

The way the proxies know that they are working with a shared Hashtable object is that the Hashtable object that the proxies work with is an instance of a private subclass of Hashtable called ReferenceCountedHashTable. A ReferenceCountedHashTable object keeps a count of how many proxies refer to it.

```
public class LargeHashtable extends Hashtable {
    // The ReferenceCountedHashTable that this is a proxy for.
    private ReferenceCountedHashTable theHashTable;
```

```
...
    public LargeHashtable() {
        theHashTable = new ReferenceCountedHashTable();
    } // constructor()

    /**
     * Return the number of key-value pairs in this hashtable.
     */
    public int size() {
        return theHashTable.size();
    } // size()
...
    /**
     * Return the value associated with the specified key in this
     * Hashtable.
     */
    public synchronized Object get(Object key) {
        return theHashTable.get(key);
    } // get(key)

    /**
     * Add the given key-value pair to this Hashtable.
     */
    public synchronized Object put(Object key, Object value) {
        copyOnWrite();
        return theHashTable.put(key, value);
    } // put(key, value)
...
    /**
     * Return a copy of this proxy that accesses the same Hashtable as this
     * proxy. The first attempt for either to modify the
     * contents of the Hashtable results in that proxy accessing a
     * modified clone of the original Hashtable.
     */
    public synchronized Object clone() {
        Object copy = super.clone();
        theHashTable.addProxy();
        return copy;
    } // clone()

    /**
     * This method is called before modifying the underlying
     * Hashtable. If it
     * is being shared, then this method clones it.
     */
    private void copyOnWrite() {
        if (theHashTable.getProxyCount() > 1) {
            // Synchronize on the original Hashtable to allow
            // consistent recovery on error.
            synchronized (theHashTable) {
```

```
                    theHashTable.removeProxy();
                    try {
                        theHashTable
                          = (ReferenceCountedHashTable)
                          theHashTable.clone();
                    } catch (Throwable e) {
                        theHashTable.addProxy();
                    } // try
                } // synchronized
            } // if proxyCount
        } // copyOnWrite()
...
        private class ReferenceCountedHashTable extends Hashtable {
            private int proxyCount = 1;
...
            public ReferenceCountedHashTable() {
                super();
            } // constructor()
            /**
             * Return a copy of this object with proxyCount set to 1.
             */
            public synchronized Object clone() {
                ReferenceCountedHashTable copy;
                copy = (ReferenceCountedHashTable)super.clone();
                copy.proxyCount = 1;
                return copy;
            } // clone()

            /**
             * Return the number of proxies using this object.
             */
            synchronized int getProxyCount() {
                return proxyCount;
            } // getProxyCount()

            /**
             * Increment the number of proxies using this object by one.
             */
            synchronized void addProxy() {
                proxyCount++;
            } // addProxy()

            /**
             * Decrement the number of proxies using this object by one.
             */
            synchronized void removeProxy() {
                proxyCount--;
            } // removeProxy()
        } // class ReferenceCountedHashTable
    } // class LargeHashtable
```

RELATED PATTERNS

Access Proxy   The Access Proxy pattern uses a proxy to enforce a security policy on access to a service-providing object. Access Proxy is not documented in this work.

Broker   The Proxy pattern is sometimes used with the Broker pattern to provide a transparent way of forwarding service requests to a service object selected by the Broker/Proxy object. The Broker pattern is not documented in this work.

Facade   The facade pattern uses a single object as a front end to a set of interrelated objects.

Remote Proxy   The Remote Proxy pattern uses a proxy to hide the fact that a service object is located on a different machine from the client objects that want to use it. The Remote Proxy pattern is not documented in this work.

Virtual Proxy   This pattern uses a proxy to create the illusion that a service-providing object exists before it has actually been created. It is useful if the object is expensive to create and its services may not be needed. The copy-on-write proxy discussed under the "Code Example" heading for the Proxy pattern is a kind of virtual proxy.

Decorator   The Decorator pattern is structurally similar to the Proxy pattern in that it forces access to a service-providing object to be done indirectly through another object. The difference is a matter of intent. Instead of trying to manage the service, the indirection object in some way enhances the service.

5

Creational Patterns

Creational patterns provide guidance as to how to create objects when their creation requires making decisions. These decisions will typically involve dynamically deciding which class to instantiate or which objects an object will delegate responsibility to. The value of creational patterns is to tell us how to structure and encapsulate these decisions.

Often, there is more than one creational pattern that you can apply to a situation. Sometimes you can combine multiple patterns advantageously.

In other cases, you must choose between competing patterns. For these reasons, it is important to be acquainted with all five of the patterns described in this chapter.

   If you only have time to learn one pattern in this chapter, the most commonly used one is Factory Method.

Factory Method [GoF95]

SYNOPSIS

You write a class for reuse with arbitrary data types. You organize this class so that it can instantiate other classes without being dependent on any of the classes it instantiates. The reusable class is able to remain independent of the classes it instantiates by delegating the choice of which class to instantiate to another object and referring to the newly created object through a common interface.

CONTEXT

Consider the problem of writing a framework for desktop applications. Such applications are typically organized in a document- or file-centered manner. Their operation usually begins with a command to create or edit a word-processing document, spreadsheet, time line, or whatever document or file the application is intended to work with. In the case of a word processor, the program may be required to work with many different types of files.

A framework to support this type of application includes high-level support for common operations, such as creating, opening, or saving documents. Such support generally includes a consistent set of methods to call when the user issues a command. For the purpose of this discussion, we call the class that provides the methods the `Application` class.

Because the logic to implement most of these commands varies with the type of document, the `Application` class usually delegates most of the commands to some sort of document object. The logic in document objects for implementing these commands varies with the type of document. However, there are operations, such as displaying the title string for a document, that are common to all document objects. This suggests an organization that includes an application-independent abstract `Document` class and application subclasses for specific types of documents. Figure 5.1 shows a class diagram that illustrates that organization.

What neither the application framework diagram nor the preceding discussion show is how an `Application` object can create instances of application-specific document classes without being application specific itself. One way to accomplish this is for the programmer using the frame-

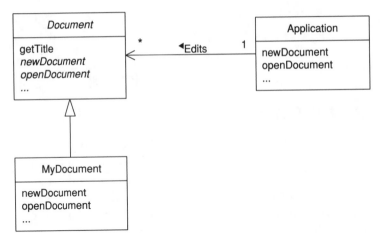

FIGURE 5.1 Application framework.

work to provide a class that encapsulates the logic for selecting and instantiating application-specific subclasses of the Document class. For the Application class to call the programmer-provided class without having any dependencies on it, the framework must provide an interface that the programmer-provided class would have to implement. The interface would declare a method that the programmer-provided class would implement to select and instantiate a class. Figure 5.2 shows a class diagram that includes that organization.

Using the organization shown in Figure 5.2, an Application object calls the createDocument method of an object that implements the DocumentFactoryIF interface. It passes a string to the createDocument method that tells that method which subclass of the Document class to instantiate. The Application class does not need to know the actual class of the object whose method it calls or which subclass of the Document class it instantiates.

FORCES

- It should be possible to organize a class so it can create objects that inherit from a given class or implement a given interface. To be reusable, the class must create objects without knowing what subclasses of the given class are available or what classes that implement the given interface are available. That use-specific knowledge should come from a separate use-specific class.

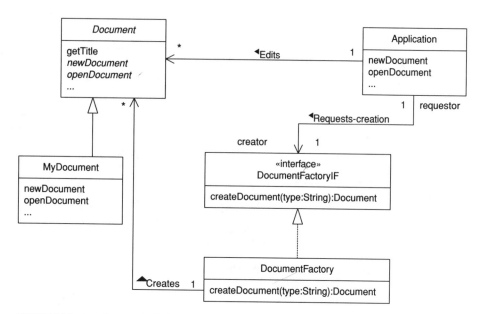

FIGURE 5.2 Application framework with document factory.

- The set of classes a class may be expected to instantiate may be dynamic as new classes become available.

SOLUTION

The Factory Method pattern provides an application-independent object with an application-specific object to which it can delegate the creation of other application-specific objects. Figure 5.3 shows a class diagram with the interfaces and classes that typically make up the Factory Method pattern.

Figure 5.3 also shows the roles that classes and interfaces play in the Factory Method pattern. These roles are:

Product   A class in this role is the abstract superclass of objects produced by the Factory Method pattern. An actual class in this role is usually not called `Product`, but has a name like `Document` or `Image`.

Concrete Product   This is any concrete class instantiated by the objects that participate in the Factory Method pattern. If these classes share no common logic, then the product role can be played by an interface instead of an abstract class. An actual class in this role is usually not

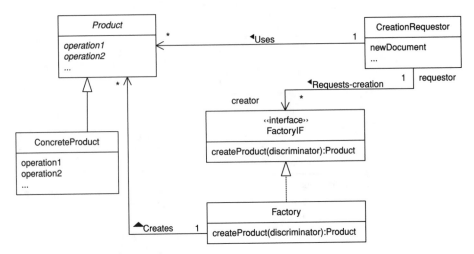

FIGURE 5.3 Factory method pattern.

called `ConcreteProduct`, but has a name like `RTFDocument` or `JPEGImage`.

Creation Requestor   The creation requestor is an application-independent class that needs to create application-specific classes. It does so indirectly through an instance of a factory class.

Factory IF   This is an application-independent interface. Objects that create `Product` objects on behalf of `CreationRequestor` objects must implement this interface. Interfaces of this sort declare a method that is called by a `CreationRequestor` object to create concrete product objects. The method typically has a name like `createDocument` or `createImage`. The method takes whatever arguments are needed to deduce the class to instantiate. Interfaces that fill this role typically have a name like `DocumentFactoryIF` or `ImageFactoryIF`.

Factory Class   This is an application-specific class that implements the appropriate factory interface and has a method to create `ConcreteProduct` objects. Classes that fill this role typically have a name like `DocumentFactory` or `ImageFactory`.

CONSEQUENCES

The primary consequences of using the Factory Method pattern are:

■ The creation requester class is independent of the class of concrete product objects actually created.

- The set of product classes that can be instantiated may change dynamically.

IMPLEMENTATION

In situations where all the concrete product classes are known in advance, the indirection of a product interface may not be necessary. In these situations, the only benefit realized by using the Factory Method pattern is that the creation requestor class is kept independent of the actual concrete product classes instantiated. The way this works is that the creation requestor class refers directly to a factory object. That factory object has a `createProduct` method implemented with the necessary logic to instantiate the correct concrete product class.

If each class that implements a product interface creates only one kind of concrete product, then the `createProduct` method defined by the interface may not need any parameters. However, if factory objects are required to create multiple kinds of product objects then their `createProduct` method needs to take the necessary parameters to allow the method to deduce which product class to instantiate. Parametric `createProduct` methods often look something like this:

```
Image createImage (String ext) {
    if (ext.equals("gif")
      return new GIFImage();
    if (ext.equals("jpeg"))
      return new JPEGImage();
    ...
} // createImage(String)
```

This code sequence of `if` statements works well for `createProduct` methods that have a fixed set of product classes to instantiate. To write a `createProduct` method that handles a variable or large number of product classes, you can use the Hashed Adapter Objects pattern (a coding pattern described in Volume 2). Alternatively, you can use the various objects that indicate which class to instantiate as keys in a hash table, with `java.lang.reflect.Constructor` objects for values. Using this technique, you look up an argument value in the hash table and the use the Constructor object that is its value in the hash table to instantiate the desired object.

Another point that the code segment illustrates is that factory methods are a reasonable place to find switch statements or chains of `if` statements. In many situations, the presence of `switch` statements or chains of `if` statements in code indicates that a method should be implemented as a polymorphic method. Factory methods cannot be implemented using polymorphism, because polymorphism works only after an object has been created.

For many implementations of the Factory Method pattern, the valid arguments to the factory object's `createProduct` method are a set of predetermined values. It is often convenient for the factory class to define symbolic names for each of those predetermined values. Classes that ask the factory class to create objects can use the constants that define the symbolic names to specify the type of object to be created.

JAVA API USAGE

The Java API uses the Factory Method pattern in a few different places to allow the integration of the applet environment with its host program. For example, each URL object has a `URLConnection` object associated with it. You can use `URLConnection` objects to read the raw bytes of a URL. `URLConnection` objects also have a method called `getContent` that returns the content of the URL packaged in an appropriate sort of object. For example, if the URL contains a `gif` file, then the `URLConnection` object's `getContent` method returns an Image object.

The way it works is that `URLConnection` objects play the role of creation requester in the Factory Method pattern. They delegate the work of the `getContent` method to a `ContentHandler` object. `ContentHandler` is an abstract class that serves as a product class that knows about handling a specific type of content. The way that a `URLConnection` object gets a `ContentHandler` object is through a `ContentHandlerFactory` object. The `ContentHandlerFactory` class is an abstract class that participates in the Factory Method pattern as a factory interface. The `URLConnection` class also has a method called `setContentHandlerFactory`. Programs that host applets call that method to provide a factory object used for all `URLConnection` objects.

CODE EXAMPLE

For our example, let's suppose that we are developing an extension to the `Socket` class to encrypt the stream of bytes written to a socket and decrypt the bytes read from the socket. We call this class `EncryptedSocket`.

We want the `EncryptedSocket` class to support multiple encryption algorithms. Because of U.S. legal restrictions on the import and export of encryption software, we want to keep the `EncryptedSocket` class independent of the encryption classes used.

The requirement that `EncryptedSocket` objects be able to work with multiple encryption algorithms without knowing in advance what classes encapsulate those algorithms suggests the use of the Factory Method pattern. Figure 5.4 shows a class diagram to illustrate this.

Here is a description of the classes and the interface used in Figure 5.4:

`EncryptedSocket` This subclass of `java.net.Socket` fills the role of creation requestor.

`EncryptionFactoryIF` This interface fills the role of factory interface.

`EncryptionFactory` This class fills the role of factory class.

`Encryption` This class fills the role of product.

`RSAEncryption` This class is in the role of concrete product.

`DESEncryption` This class is in the role of concrete product.

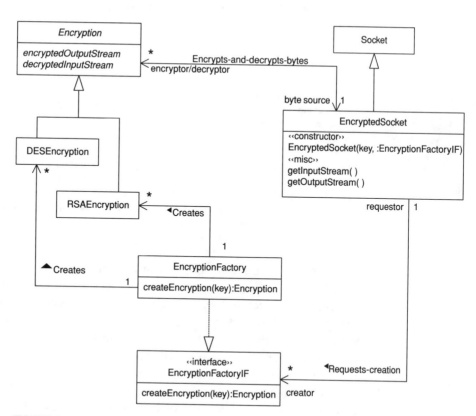

FIGURE 5.4 Factory method example.

Let's look at the code that implements these classes. Following is the code for the `EncryptedSocket` class. The `EncryptedSocket` class extends `Socket` to encrypt and decrypt the stream of bytes that goes over the net.

```
public class EncryptedSocket extends Socket {
    private static Encryption crypt;
    private Key key;
    /**
     * Constructor
     * @param key The key to use for encryption and decryption. This
     *             object will determine the encryption technique to use
     *             by calling the key object's getAlgorithm() method.
     * @param factory The Factory object for creatig Encryption objects.
     * @exception NoSuchAlgorithmException if the key specifies an
     *             encryption technique that is not available.
     */
    public EncryptedSocket(Key key, EncryptionFactoryIF factory)
                    throws NoSuchAlgorithmException {
        this.key = key;
        crypt = factory.createEncryption(key);
    } // Constructor(Key, EncryptionFactoryIF)


    /**
     * Return an input stream that decrypts the inbound stream of bytes.
     */
    public InputStream getInputStream() throws IOException {
        return crypt.decryptInputStream(super.getInputStream());
    } // getInputStream()


    /**
     * Return an output stream that encrypts the outbound stream of bytes.
     */
    public OutputStream getOutputStream() throws IOException {
        return crypt.encryptOutputStream(super.getOutputStream());
    } // getOutputStream()
} // class EncryptedSocket
```

An `EncryptedSocket` object works by first getting an Encryption object from the `EncryptionFactoryIF` object that is passed to its constructor. It then accomplishes the encryption and decryption using the Filter pattern. It extends the `getInputStream` and `getOutputStream` methods so that the `inputStream` objects and `outputStream` objects that they would otherwise return are filtered through objects created by the Encryption object.

Following is code for the `EncryptionFactoryIF` interface. All factory classes used to create instances of subclasses of `Encryption` must implement the `EncryptionFactoryIF` interface.

```
public interface EncryptionFactoryIF {
    /**
     * Return an instance of the appropriate subclass of Encryption as
     * determined from information provided by the given Key object.
     */
    public Encryption createEncryption(Key key)
                        throws NoSuchAlgorithmException;
} // interface EncryptionFactoryIF
```

Here is the code for the EncryptionFactory class. Its
createEncryption method creates an instance of an appropriate subclass
of Encryption. Its createEncryption method selects a subclass of
Encryption based on information it gets from the key object that is
passed to the method.

```
public class EncryptionFactory implements EncryptionFactoryIF {
    public Encryption createEncryption(Key key)
                        throws NoSuchAlgorithmException{
        String algorithm = key.getAlgorithm();
        if ("DES".equals(algorithm))
          return new DESEncryption(key);
        if ("RSA".equals(algorithm))
          return new RSAEncryption(key);
        throw new NoSuchAlgorithmException(algorithm);
    } // createEncryption(Key)
} // class EncryptionFactory
```

Finally, here is the code for the Encryption class. The Encryption
class is the abstract superclass of classes that perform specific types of
encryption or decryption.

```
abstract public class Encryption {
    private Key key;
    /**
     * Constructor
     * @param key The key to use to perform the encryption.
     */
    public Encryption(Key key) {
        this.key = key;
    } // Constructor(Key)
...
    /**
     * This method returns an OutputStream writes encrypted bytes to the
     * given OutputStream.
     */
    abstract OutputStream encryptOutputStream(OutputStream out);
```

```
/**
 * This method returns an InputStream that decrypts bytes from the
 * given InputStream.
 */
abstract InputStream decryptInputStream(InputStream in);
} // class Encrypt
```

RELATED PATTERNS

Abstract Factory   The Factory Method pattern is useful for constructing individual objects for a specific purpose without the construction requestor knowing the specific classes being instantiated. If you need to create a matched set of such objects, then the Abstract Factory pattern is a more appropriate pattern to use.

Template Method   The full Factory Method pattern is often used with the Template Method pattern.

Prototype   The Prototype pattern provides an alternate way for an object to work with other objects without knowing the details of their construction.

Hashed Adapter Objects   This coding pattern (described in volume 2) is a good way to implement a factory class when there are many different classes to instantiate or the set of classes to instantiate changes dynamically.

Abstract Factory [GoF95]

Abstract Factory is also known as Kit or Toolkit.

SYNOPSIS

Given a set of related abstract classes, the Abstract Factory pattern provides a way to create instances of those abstract classes from a matched set of concrete subclasses. The Abstract Factory pattern can be very useful for allowing a program to work with a variety of complex external entities, such as different windowing systems with similar functionality.

CONTEXT

Suppose you have the task of building a user-interface framework that works on top of multiple windowing systems, such as MS-Windows, Motif, or MacOS. You can make it work on each platform with the platform's native look and feel. You can do that by creating an abstract class for each type of widget (text field, push button, list box, etc.) and then writing a concrete subclass of each of those classes for each supported platform. To make this robust, you will need to ensure that the widget objects created are all for the desired platform. This is where the abstract factory comes into play.

In this situation, an abstract factory class defines methods to create an instance of each abstract class that represents a user-interface widget. Concrete factories are concrete subclasses of an abstract factory that implement its methods to create instances of concrete widget classes for the same platform.

In a more general context, an abstract factory class and its concrete subclasses organize sets of concrete classes that work with different but related products. For a broader perspective, consider another situation.

Suppose you are writing a program that performs remote diagnostics on computers for a computer manufacturer called Stellar Microsystems. Over time, Stellar has produced computer models having substantially different architectures. Its oldest computers used CPU chips from Enginola that had a traditional complex instruction set. Since then, it has released three generations of computers based on its own RISC architectures, called ember, superember, and ultraember. The core components used in these models perform similar functions, but involve different sets of components.

For the program you are writing to know what tests to run and how to interpret the results, it will need to instantiate objects that correspond to each one of the core components in the computer being diagnosed. The class of each object will correspond to the type of component to be tested. This means that you will have a set of classes for each computer architecture. There will be a class in each set corresponding to the same type of computer component. Because this situation fits the Abstract Factory so well, you can use that pattern to organize the creation of objects that correspond to core computer components.

Figure 5.5 shows a class diagram that illustrates classes for only two types of components in only two architectures.

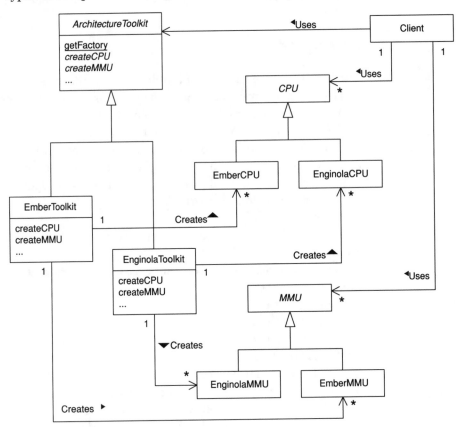

FIGURE 5.5 Abstract factory example.

An instance of the `Client` class manages the remote diagnostic process. When it determines the architecture of the machine it has to diagnose, it calls the `ArchitectureToolkit` class' `getFactory` method. This static method returns an instance of a class, such as `EmberToolkit` or `EnginolaToolkit`, that corresponds to the architecture that the `Client` object passed to the `getFactory` method. The `Client` object can then use that toolkit object to create objects that model CPUs, MMUs, and other components of the required architecture.

FORCES

- A system that works with multiple products should function in a way that is independent of the specific product that it is working with.
- It should be possible to configure a system to work with one or multiple members of a family of products.
- Instances of classes intended to interface with a product should be used together and only with that product. This constraint must be enforced.
- The rest of a system should work with a product without being aware of the specific classes used to interface with the product.
- A system should be extensible so that it can work with additional products by adding additional sets of classes and changing, at most, only a few lines of code.

SOLUTION

Figure 5.6 shows a class diagram that illustrates the roles that classes play in the Abstract Factory pattern.

Here are descriptions of the roles classes play in the Abstract Factory pattern:

Client   Classes in the `Client` role use various widget classes to request or receive services from the product that the client is working with. Client classes only know about the abstract widget classes. They should have no knowledge of any concrete widget classes.

AbstractFactory   `AbstractFactory` classes define abstract methods for creating instances of concrete widget classes. They have a static method, shown in Figure 5.6 as `getFactory`. Another common name for this method is `getToolkit`. A `Client` object calls that method to get an

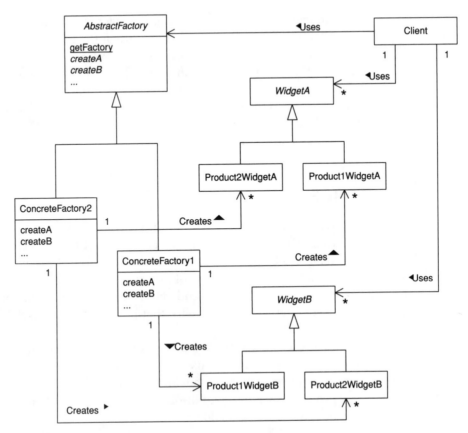

FIGURE 5.6 Abstract factory.

instance of a concrete factory appropriate for creating widgets that
work with a particular product.

ConcreteFactory1, ConcreteFactory2   Classes in this role implement
the methods defined by their abstract factory superclasses to create
instances of concrete widget classes. Client classes that call these methods should not have any direct knowledge of these concrete factory
classes, but instead should access singleton instances of these classes as
instances of their abstract factory superclass.

WidgetA, WidgetB   Classes in this role are abstract classes that correspond to a feature of a product that their concrete subclasses will work
with. You can generically refer to classes in this role as *abstract widgets*.

Product1WidgetA, Product2WidgetA   Classes in this role are concrete
classes that correspond to a feature of a product that they work with.
You can generically refer to classes in this role as *concrete widgets*.

CONSEQUENCES

- Concrete widget classes are independent of the classes that use them and initiate their creation, because the abstract factory class encapsulates the process of creating widget objects.
- Adding (as opposed to writing) classes to work with additional products is simple. The class of a concrete factory object usually needs to be referenced in only one place. It is also easy to change the concrete factory used to work with a particular product.
- By forcing client classes to go through concrete factory objects to create concrete widget objects, the Abstract Factory pattern ensures that client objects use a consistent set of objects to interface with the features of a product.
- The main drawback to the Abstract Factory pattern is that it can be a lot of work to write a set of classes to interface with a new product. It can also take a lot of work to extend the set of features that the existing set of classes is able to exercise in the products that they work with.

  Adding support for a new product involves writing a complete set of concrete widget classes to support that product. You must write a concrete widget class for each abstract widget class. If there is a large number of abstract widget classes, then it will be a lot of work to support an additional product.

  Adding access to an additional feature of the interfacing products can also take a lot of work if there are many supported products. It involves writing a new abstract widget class corresponding to the new feature and a new concrete widget class corresponding to each product.

- Client objects may have a need to organize widget classes into a hierarchy that serves the needs of client objects. The basic Abstract Factory pattern does not lend itself to this, because it requires organizing concrete widget classes into a class hierarchy that is independent of client objects. That difficulty can be overcome by mixing the Bridge pattern with the Abstract Factory pattern: Create a hierarchy of product-independent widget classes that suits the needs of the client classes. Have each product-independent widget class delegate product-specific logic to a product-specific instance of an abstract widget class. Java's `java.awt` package contains a number of classes that are implemented using this variation. Classes like `Button` and `TextField` contain logic that is independent of the windowing system being used. These classes provide a native look and feel by delegating windowing system operations to concrete widget classes that implement interfaces defined in the `java.awt.peer` package.

IMPLEMENTATION

If you implement the abstract factory class as an abstract class, as recommended, then its `getFactory` method will have to be static. The reason for this is to be able to call the `getFactory` method without having to create an instance of the abstract factory class.

A deeper implementation issue for the Abstract Factory pattern is the mechanism the abstract factory class's `getFactory` method uses to select the class of the concrete factory it supplies to client objects. The simplest situation is when client objects need to work with only one product during the run of a program. In that case, the abstract factory class will typically have a static variable set to the concrete factory class that will be used for the duration of the program run. The abstract factory class's `getFactory` method can then just return an instance of that class.

If the abstract factory object will use information provided by the requesting client to select among multiple concrete factory objects, you can hard code the selection logic and choice of concrete factory objects in the abstract factory class. This strategy has the advantage of simplicity. It has the drawback of requiring a source code modification to add a new concrete factory class.

A different strategy is to use the Hashed Adapter pattern described in Volume 2. To use this pattern, separate the selection logic for concrete factories from the data it uses to make the selection. You do this by putting references to concrete factory classes, along with the information used to select them, into a data structure. The data structure allows an abstract factory to select a concrete factory object by performing a look on the data structure. The advantage of using the data structure is that it is possible to devise schemes for building the data structure that allow an abstract factory to work with new concrete factory classes without any source code modification.

JAVA API USAGE

The Abstract Factory pattern is used in the Java API to implement the `java.awt.Toolkit` class. The `java.awt.Toolkit` class is an abstract factory class used to create objects that work with the native windowing system. The concrete factory class it uses is determined by the initialization code and the singleton concrete factory object is returned by its `getDefaultToolkit` method.

CODE EXAMPLE

Here is some of the Java code that implements the design for remote computer diagnostics presented under the "Context" heading. The abstract widget classes have the obvious structure:

```
public abstract class CPU {
    . . .
} // class CPU
```

The concrete widget classes are simply concrete subclasses of the abstract widget classes:

```
class EmberCPU extends CPU {
    . . .
} // class EmberCPU
```

Code for a concrete factory class that creates instances of classes to test ember architecture computers follows:

```
class EmberToolkit extends ArchitectureToolkit {
    public CPU createCPU() {
        return new EmberCPU();
    } // createCPU()
    public MMU createMMU() {
        return new EmberMMU();
    } // createMMU()
    . . .
} // class EmberFactory
```

Here is the code for the abstract factory class:

```
public abstract class ArchitectureToolkit {
    private static final EmberToolkit emberToolkit
      = new EmberToolkit();
    private static EnginolaToolkit enginolaToolkit
      = new EnginolaToolkit();
...

    /**
     * Returns a concrete factory object that is an instance of the
     * concrete factory class appropriate for the given architecture.
```

```
    */
    static final ArchitectureToolkit getFactory(int architecture) {
        switch (architecture) {
          case ENGINOLA:
              return enginolaToolkit;

          case EMBER:
              return emberToolkit;
          ...
        } // switch
        String errMsg = Integer.toString(architecture);
        throw new IllegalArgumentException(errMsg);
    } // getFactory()

    public abstract CPU createCPU() ;
    public abstract MMU createMMU() ;
...
} // AbstractFactory
```

Client classes typically create concrete widget objects using code that looks something like this:

```
public class Client {
    public void doIt () {
        AbstractFactory af;
        af = AbstractFactory.getFactory(AbstractFactory.EMBER);
        CPU cpu = af.createCPU();
        ...
    } //doIt
} // class Client
```

RELATED PATTERNS

Factory Method   In the preceding example, the abstract factory class uses the Factory Method pattern to decide which concrete factory object to give to a client class.

Singleton   Concrete Factory classes are usually implemented as Singleton classes.

Builder [GoF95]

SYNOPSIS

The Builder pattern allows a client object to construct a complex object by specifying only its type and content. The client is shielded from the details of the object's construction.

CONTEXT

Consider the problem of writing an e-mail gateway program. The program receives e-mail messages that are in MIME format.* It forwards them in a different format for a different kind of e-mail system. This situation is a good fit for the Builder pattern. It is very straightforward to organize this program with an object that parses MIME messages. For each message to parse, the message is paired with a builder object that the parser uses to build a message in the new format. As the parser recognizes each header field and message body part, it calls the corresponding method of the builder object that it is working with.

Figure 5.7 shows a class diagram that illustrates that structure.

In Figure 5.7, the MessageManager class is responsible for collecting MIME-formatted e-mail messages and initiating their transmission. The e-mail messages that it directly manages are instances of the MIMEMsg class.

Instances of the MIMEMsg class represent MIME-formatted e-mail messages. When a MessageManager object wants to transmit one of its messages in a format other than MIME, it must build a message in the desired format. The content of the new message must be the same as the MIME message or as close to it as the format will allow.

The MIMEParser class is a subclass of the MessageParser class (a class invented for but not included in this example) that can parse MIME-formatted e-mail messages and pass their contents to a builder object.

MessageBuilder is an abstract builder class. It defines methods that correspond to the various header fields and body types that MIME sup-

---

* MIME is an acronym for Multipurpose Internet Mail Extensions. It is the standard that most e-mail messages on the internet conform to. You can find a description of MIME at http://www.mindspring.com/~mgrand/mime.html.

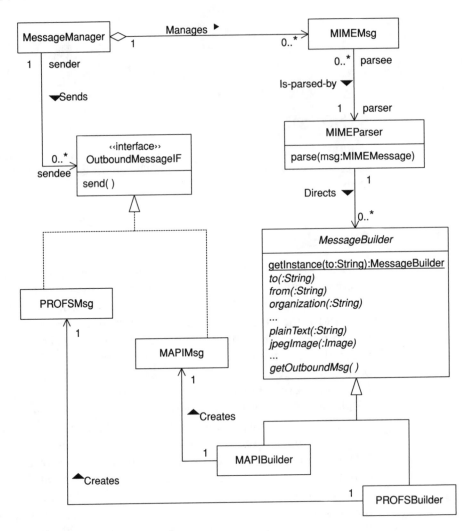

FIGURE 5.7 Builder example.

ports. It declares abstract methods that correspond to required header fields and the most common body types. It declares those methods abstract because all concrete subclasses of `MessageBuilder` should define those methods. However, some of the optional header fields, such as `organization`, and fancier body types, such as `Image/Jpeg`, may not be supported in all message formats, so the `MessageBuilder` class provides do-nothing implementations of those methods.

The `MessageBuilder` class also defines a static method called `getInstance`. A `MIMEParser` object passes the `getInstance` method the destination address of the message it is parsing. From the message's destination address, the `getInstance` method determines the message format needed for the new message. It returns an instance of the subclass of `MessageBuilder` appropriate for the format of the new message to the `MIMEParser` object.

The `MAPIBuilder` and `PROFSBuilder` classes are concrete builder classes for building **MAPI** and **PROFS** messages, respectively.

The builder classes create product objects that implement the `OutboundMsgIF` interface. That interface defines a method called `send` that is intended to send the e-mail message wherever it is supposed to go.

Figure 5.8 shows a collaboration diagram that illustrates how these classes work together.

Here is what's happening in Figure 5.8:

1 A `MessageManager` object receives a MIME compliant e-mail message.

  1.1 The `MessageManager` object calls the `MIMEParser` class's `parse` method. It will return an `OutboundMessageIF` object that encapsulates the new message that is in the needed format.

    1.1.1 The `MIMEParser` object calls the `MessageBuilder` class's `getInstance` method, passing it the destination e-mail

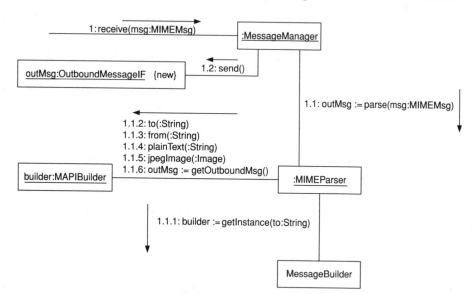

FIGURE 5.8 Builder example collaboration.

address. By analyzing the address, the method selects a concrete subclass of the `MessageBuilder` class and creates an instance of it.

1.1.2 The `MIMEParser` object passes the destination e-mail address to the `MessageBuilder` object's `to` method.

1.1.3 The `MIMEParser` object passes the originating e-mail address to the `MessageBuilder` object's `from` method.

1.1.4 The `MIMEParser` object passes the e-mail message's simple content to the `MessageBuilder` object's `plainText` method.

1.1.5 The `MIMEParser` object passes the e-mail message's attached jpeg image to the `MessageBuilder` object's `jpegImage` method.

1.1.6 The `MIMEParser` object calls the `MessageBuilder` object's `getOutboundMsg` method to complete and fetch the new message.

1.2 The `MessageManager` object calls the `OutboundMsg` object's `send` method. That sends the message off, and completes the processing of that message.

FORCES

- A program is required to produce multiple external representations of the same data.
- The class(es) responsible for providing content should be independent of any external data representation and the classes that build them. If content-providing classes have no dependencies on external data representations, then modifications to external data representation classes will not require any maintenance to content-providing classes.
- The classes responsible for building external data representations are independent of the class(es) that provides the content. Their instances can work with any content-providing object without knowing anything about the content-providing object.

SOLUTION

Figure 5.9 shows a class diagram that illustrates the participants in the Builder pattern.

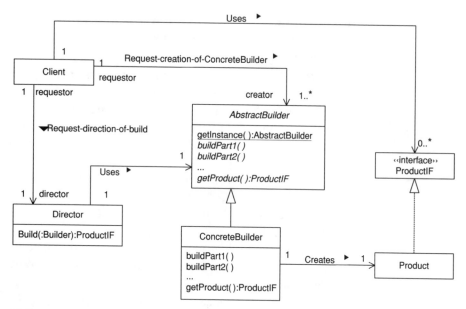

FIGURE 5.9 Builder pattern.

Here are the roles that these classes and the interface play in the Builder pattern:

Product   A class in this role defines a type of data representation. All Product classes should implement the ProductIF interface so that other classes can refer to Product objects through the interface without having to know an object's class.

ProductIF   The Builder pattern is used to build a variety of different kinds of Product objects for use by Client objects. To avoid the need for Client objects to know the actual class of Product objects built for them, all Product classes implement the ProductIF interface. Client objects refer to Product objects built for them through the ProductIF interface, so they don't need to know the actual class of the objects built for them.

Client   An instance of a client class initiates the actions of the Builder pattern. It calls the AbstractBuilder class's getInstance method. It passes information to getInstance that tells it what sort of product it wants to have built. The getInstance method determines the subclass of AbstractBuilder to instantiate and returns it to the Client object. The Client object then passes the object it got from getInstance to a Director object's build method, which builds the desired object.

Concrete Builder A class in this role is a concrete subclass of the `AbstractBuilder` class that is used to build a specific kind of data representation of a `Director` object.

AbstractBuilder A class in this role is the abstract superclass of `ConcreteBuilder` classes. An `AbstractBuilder` class defines a static method, typically called `getInstance`, which takes an argument that specifies a data representation. The `getInstance` method returns an instance of a concrete builder class that produces the specified data representation.

An `AbstractBuilder` class also defines methods, shown in the class diagram as `buildPart1`, `buildPart2`... that a `Director` object calls to tell the object returned by the `getInstance` method what content to put in the created object.

Finally, the builder class defines a method, typically called `getProduct`, which returns the product object created by a concrete builder object.

Director A `Director` object calls the methods of a concrete builder object to provide the concrete builder with the content for the product object that it builds.

Figure 5.10 shows how these classes work together.

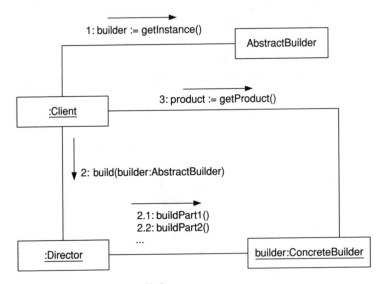

FIGURE 5.10 Builder collaboration.

CONSEQUENCES

Content determination and the construction of a specific data representation are independent of each other. The data representation of the product can change without any impact on the objects that provide the content. Builder objects can work with different content-providing objects without requiring any changes.

Builder provides finer control over construction than other patterns, such as Factory Method, by giving the director object step-by-step control over creation of the product object. Other patterns simply create the entire object in one step.

IMPLEMENTATION

The essential design and implementation issue for the Builder pattern is the set of methods defined by the builder class to provide content to concrete builder objects. These methods can be a major concern because there can be a large number of them. The methods should be general enough to allow all reasonable data representations to be constructed. On the other hand, an excessively general set of methods can be more difficult to implement and to use. The consideration of generality versus difficulty of implementation raises these issues in the implementation phase:

- Each of the content-providing methods declared by the builder class can be abstract or provided with a default do-nothing implementation. Abstract method declarations force concrete builder classes to provide an implementation for that method. Forcing concrete builder classes to provide implementations for methods is good in those cases where the method provides essential information about content. It prevents implementers of those classes from forgetting to implement those methods.

    However, methods that provide optional content or supplementary information about the structure of the content may be unnecessary or even inappropriate for some data representations. Providing a default do-nothing implementation for such methods saves effort in the implementation of concrete builder classes that do not need those methods.

- Organizing concrete builder classes so that calls to content-providing methods simply add data to the product object is often good enough.

In some cases, there will be no simple way to tell the builder where in the finished product a particular piece of the product will go. In those situations, it may be simplest to have the content-providing method return an object that encapsulates such a piece of the product to the director. The director object can then pass the object to another content-providing method in a way that implies the position of the piece of the product within the whole product.

CODE EXAMPLE

Let's look at some sample code for the classes in this example that collaborate in the Builder pattern. Instances of the MIMEParser class fill the role of director objects. Here is the source for the MIMEParser class:

```java
class MIMEParser extends MessageParser {
    private MIMEMessage msg;        // The message being parsed
    private MessageBuilder builder; // The builder object
    ...
    /**
     * parse a MIME message, calling the builder methods that
     * correspond to the message's header fields and body parts.
     */
    OutboundMessageIF parse() {
        builder = MessageBuilder.getInstance(getDestination());
        MessagePart hdr = nextHeader();
        while (hdr != null) {
            if (hdr.getName().equals("to"))
              builder.to((String)hdr.getValue());
            else if (hdr.getName().equals("from"))
              builder.from((String)hdr.getValue());

            ...
            hdr = nextHeader();
        } // while hdr
        MessagePart bdy = nextBodyPart();
        while (bdy != null) {
            if (bdy.getName().equalsIgnoreCase ("text/plain"))
              builder.plainText((String)bdy.getValue());
            else if (bdy.getName().equalsIgnoreCase ("image/jpeg"))
              builder.jpegImage((Image)bdy.getValue());

            ...
            bdy = nextBodyPart();
        } // while bdy
        return builder.getOutboundMsg();
    } // parse(Message)
    ...
```

```
        private class MessagePart {
            private String name;
            private Object value;

            MessagePart(String name, Object value) {
                this.name = name;
                this.value = value;
            } // Constructor(String, String)

            String getName() { return name; }

            Object getValue() { return value; }
        } // class MessagePart
    } // class MIMEParser
```

The chains of `if` statements that occur in the `parse` method of the preceding class would be rather long if the method were fully fleshed out. MIME supports over 25 different kinds of header fields alone. A less awkward way to organize a chain of tests of object equality that result in a method call is to use the Hashed Adapter Objects coding pattern described in Volume 2.

Here is code for the `MessageBuilder` class, which fills the role of abstract builder class:

```
abstract class MessageBuilder {
    /**
     * Return an object of the subclass appropriate for the e-mail
     * message format implied by the given destination address.
     * @param dest The e-mail address the message is to be sent to
     */
    static MessageBuilder getInstance(String dest) {
        MessageBuilder builder = null;
        ...
        return builder;
    } // getInstance(String)

    /**
     * pass the value of the "to" header field to this method.
     */
    abstract void to(String value);

    /**
     * pass the value of the "from" header field to this method.
     */
    abstract void from(String value);

    /**
     * pass the value of the "organization" header field to this
     * method.
```

```
     */
    void organization(String value) { }

    /**
     * pass the content of a plain text body part to this method.
     */
    abstract void plainText(String content);

...

    /**
     * complete and return the outbound e-mail message.
     */
    abstract OutboundMessageIF getOutboundMsg() ;
} // class MessageBuilder
```

Finally, here is the code for the OutboundMsgIF interface:

```
public interface OutboundMsgIF {
    public void send() ;
} // interface OutboundMsgIF
```

RELATED PATTERNS

Interface   The Builder pattern uses the Interface pattern to hide the class of a ProductIF object.

Composite   The object built using the Builder pattern is typically a Composite.

Factory Method   The Builder pattern uses the Factory Method pattern to decide which concrete builder class to instantiate.

Layered Initialization   The Builder pattern uses the Layered Initialization pattern to create ConcreteBuilder objects.

Marker Interface   The ProductIF interface uses the Marker Interface pattern.

Null Object   The Null Object pattern may be used by the Builder pattern to provide do-nothing implementations of methods.

Visitor   The Visitor pattern allows the client object to be more closely coupled to the construction of the new complex object. Instead of describing the content of the objects to be built through a series of method calls, the information is presented in bulk as a complex data structure.

Prototype [GoF95]

SYNOPSIS

The Prototype pattern allows an object to create customized objects without knowing their exact class or the details of how to create them. It works by giving prototypical objects to an object that initiates the creation of objects. The creation-initiating object then creates objects by asking the prototypical objects to make copies of themselves.

CONTEXT

Suppose that you are writing a CAD program that allows its users to draw diagrams from a palette of symbols. The program has a core set of built-in symbols. However, people with different and specialized interests use the program. The core set of symbols is not adequate for people with specialized interests. Those people want additional symbols that are specific to their interests. Most users of this program are in that category. Therefore, it must be possible to provide additional sets of symbols that users can add to the program to meet their needs.

This pattern addresses the problem of how to provide these palettes of additional symbols. You can easily organize things so all symbols, both core and additional, are descended from a common ancestor class. This gives the rest of your diagram-drawing program a consistent way of manipulating symbol objects. It does leave open the question of how the program will create these objects. Creating objects such as these is often more complicated than simply instantiating a class. It may also involve setting values for data attributes of objects or combining objects to form a composite object.

The solution that the Prototype pattern suggests is to provide the drawing program with previously created objects to use as prototypes to create similar objects. The most important requirement for objects to be used as prototypes is that they have a method, typically called clone, that returns a new object that is a copy of the original object. The class diagram in Figure 5.11 is shows this organization.

The drawing program maintains a collection of prototypical Symbol objects. It uses the Symbol objects by cloning them. SymbolBuilder objects create Symbol objects and register them with the drawing program.

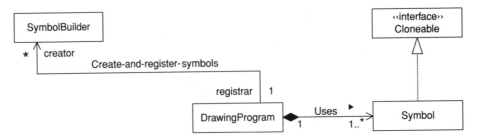

FIGURE 5.11 Symbol prototype class diagram.

All Java classes inherit a method from the `Object` class called `clone`. An object's `clone` method returns a copy of the object. It only does so for instances of classes that give permission to be cloned. A class gives permission for its instance to be cloned if, and only if, it implements the `Cloneable` interface. Because the `Symbol` class implements the `Cloneable` interface, the drawing program is able to clone the `Symbol` objects that it manages and is able to incorporate those objects into drawings.

FORCES

- A system must be able to create objects without knowing their exact class, how they are created, or what data they represent.
- Classes to be instantiated are not known by the system until runtime, when they are acquired on the fly by techniques like dynamic linkage.
- The following approaches that allow for the creation of a large variety of objects are undesirable:

    The classes that initiate the creation of objects directly create the objects. This makes them aware of and dependent on a large number of other classes.

    The classes that initiate the creation of objects create the objects indirectly through a factory method class. A factory method that is able to create a large variety of objects may be very large and difficult to maintain.

    The classes that initiate the creation of objects create the objects indirectly through an abstract factory class. In order for an abstract factory to be able to create a large variety of objects, it must have a large variety of concrete factory classes in a hierarchy that parallels the classes to be instantiated.

The different objects that a system must create may be instances of the same class that contain different state information or data content.

SOLUTION

Figure 5.12 shows the classes and interfaces that participate in the Prototype pattern.

Here are descriptions of the roles these classes and interfaces play in the Prototype pattern:

Client   The `Client` class represents the rest of the program for the purposes of the Prototype pattern. The `Client` class needs to create objects that it knows little about. The `Client` class will have a method that can be called to add a prototypical object to a `Client` object's collection. In Figure 5.12, that method is indicated with the name `registerPrototype`. However, a name that reflects the sort of object being prototyped, such as `registerSymbol`, is more appropriate in an actual implementation.

Prototype   Classes in this role implement the `PrototypeIF` interface and are instantiated for the purpose of being cloned by the client.

PrototypeBuilder   This corresponds to any class that is instantiated to supply prototypical objects to the `Client` object. Such classes should have a name that denotes the type of prototypical object that they build, such as `SymbolBuilder`.

A `PrototypeBuilder` object creates `Prototype` objects. It passes each newly created `Prototype` object to a `Client` object's `registerPrototype` method.

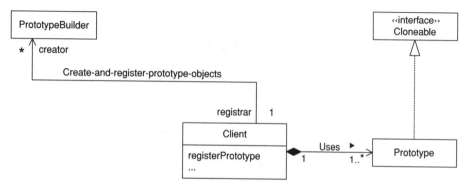

FIGURE 5.12 Prototype pattern.

CONSEQUENCES

- A program can dynamically add and remove prototypical objects at runtime. This is a distinct advantage offered by none of the other creational patterns in this book.
- A `PrototypeBuilder` object can simply supply a fixed set of prototypical objects. A `PrototypeBuilder` object provides the additional flexibility of allowing new kinds of prototypical objects to be created by object composition and changes to the values of object attributes.
- The client object may also be able to create new kinds of prototypical objects. In the drawing program example we looked at previously, the client object could very reasonably allow the user to identify a subdrawing and then turn the subdrawing into a new symbol.
- The client class is independent of the exact class of the prototypical objects that it uses. Also, the client class does not need to know the details of how to build the prototypical objects.
- The `PrototypeBuilder` objects encapsulate the details of constructing prototypical objects.
- By insisting that prototypical objects implement an interface such as `PrototypeIF`, the Prototype pattern ensures that the prototypical objects provide a consistent set of methods for the client object to use.
- A drawback of the Prototype pattern is the additional time spent writing `PrototypeBuilder` classes.
- Programs that use the Prototype pattern rely on dynamic linkage or similar mechanisms. Installation of programs that rely on dynamic linkage or similar mechanisms can be more complicated.
- There is no need to organize prototypical objects into any sort of class hierarchy.

IMPLEMENTATION

An essential implementation issue is how the `PrototypeBuilder` objects add objects to a client object's palette of prototypical objects. The simplest strategy is for the client class to provide a method for that purpose that `PrototypeBuilder` objects can call. A possible drawback is that the `PrototypeBuilder` objects will need to know the class of the client object. If this is a problem, the `PrototypeBuilder` objects can be shielded from knowing the exact class of the client objects by providing an interface or abstract class for the client class to implement or inherit.

How to implement the clone operation for the prototypical objects is another important implementation issue. There are two basic strategies for implementing the clone operation:

1. *Shallow copying* means that the variables of the cloned object contain the same values as the variables of the original object and that all object references are to the same objects. In other words, shallow copying copies only the object being cloned, not the objects that it refers to.

2. *Deep copying* means that the variables of the cloned object contain the same values as the variables of the original object, except that those variables that refer to objects refer to copies of the objects referred to by the original object. In other words, deep copying copies the object being cloned and the objects that it refers to. Implementing deep copying can be tricky. You will need to decide if you want to make deep or shallow copies of the indirectly copied objects. You will also need to be careful about handling any circular references.

Shallow copying is easier to implement because all classes inherit a `clone` method for the `Object` class that does just that. However, unless an object's class implements the `Cloneable` interface, the `clone` method will refuse to work. If all of the prototypical objects your program uses will be cloning themselves by shallow copying, you can save some time by declaring the `PrototypeIF` interface to extend the `Cloneable` interface. That way, all classes that implement the `PrototypeIF` interface also implement the `Cloneable` interface.

Some objects, such as threads and sockets, cannot be simply copied or shared. Whichever copying strategy you use, if it involves references to such objects then you will need to construct equivalent objects for the use of the copied objects.

Unless the `Client` object's palette of prototypical objects consists of a fixed number of objects having fixed purposes, it is inconvenient to use individual variables to refer to each prototypical object. It is easier to use a collection object that can contain a dynamically growing or shrinking palette of prototypical objects. A collection object that plays this role in the Prototype pattern is called a *prototype manager*. Prototype managers can be fancier than just a simple collection. They may allow objects to be retrieved by their attribute values or other keys.

If your program will have multiple client objects, then you have another issue to consider. Will the client objects have their own palette of prototypical objects, or will they all share the same palette? The answer will depend on the needs of your application.

JAVA API USAGE

The Prototype pattern is the very essence of JavaBeans. JavaBeans are instances of classes that conform to certain naming conventions. The naming conventions allow a bean creation program to know how to customize them. After a bean object has been customized for use in an application, the object is saved to a file to be loaded by the application while it is running. Saving an object to a file to be loaded later by other applications is a time-delayed way of cloning objects.

CODE EXAMPLE

Suppose that you are writing an interactive role-playing game. That is, a game that allows the user to interact with computer-simulated characters. One of the expectations for this game is that the people who play it will grow tired of interacting with the same characters and will want to interact with new characters. Because of that expectation, you are also developing an add-on to the game that consists of a few pregenerated characters and a program to generate additional characters.

The characters in the game are instances of a relatively small number of classes, such as Hero, Fool, Villain, and Monster. What makes instances of the same class different from each other is the different attributes values that are set for them, such as the images that are used to represent them on the screen, height, weight, intelligence, and dexterity.

Figure 5.13 shows a class diagram that illustrates some of the classes involved in the game.

Here is the code for the Character class, an abstract class that serves the role of `PrototypeIF`:

```
public abstract class Character implements Cloneable {
...
    /**
     * Override clone to make it public.
     */
    public Object clone() {
        try {
            return super.clone();
        } catch (CloneNotSupportedException e) {
```

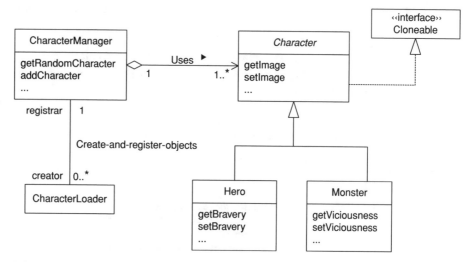

FIGURE 5.13 Prototype example.

```
            // should never happen because this class implements
            // Cloneable.
            throw new InternalError();
        } // try
    } // clone()

    public String getName() { return name; }

    public void setName(String name) { this.name = name; }

    public Image getImage() { return image; }

    public void setImage(Image image) { this.image = image; }
...
} // class Character
```

As you can see, most of this is just simple accessor methods. The one less than obvious method is the clone method. All objects inherit a clone method from the Object class. Because that clone method is not public, the character class must override it with a public declaration, just to make it accessible to other classes.

Here is the source code for the Hero class that serves as Prototype classes:

```
public class Hero extends Character {
    private int bravery;
...
    public int getBravery() { return bravery; }
```

```
        public void setBravery(int bravery) { this.bravery = bravery; }
} // class Hero
```

The Monster class is similar to the Hero class.

Here is the code for the `CharacterManager` class that serves in the role of client class:

```
public class CharacterManager {
    private Vector characters = new Vector();
...
    /**
     * Return a copy of random character from the collection.
     */
    Character getRandomCharacter() {
        int i = (int) (characters.size()*Math.random());
        return (Character)
        ((Character)characters.elementAt(i)).clone();
    } // getRandomCharacter()

    /**
     * Add a prototypical object to the collection.
     */
    void addCharacter(Character character) {
        characters.addElement(character);
    } // addCharacter(Character)
...
} // class CharacterManager
```

Here is the code for the `CharacterLoader` class that fills the role of `PrototypeBuilder`:

```
/**
 * This class loads character objects and adds them to the
 * CharacterManager.
 */
class CharacterLoader {
    private CharacterManager mgr;
    /**
     * Constructor
     * @param cm The CharacterManager that this object will work with.
     */
    CharacterLoader(CharacterManager cm) {
        mgr = cm;
    } // Constructor(CharacterManager)

    /**
     * Load character objects from the specified file.
     * Since failure only affects the rest of the program to the
     * extent that new character objects are not loaded, we need
```

```
        * not throw any exceptions.
        */
    int loadCharacters(String fname) {
        int objectCount = 0; // The number of objects loaded
        // If construction of the InputStream fails, just return
        try {
            InputStream in;
            in = new FileInputStream(fname);
            in = new BufferedInputStream(in);
            ObjectInputStream oIn = new ObjectInputStream(in);
            while(true) {
                Object c = oIn.readObject();
                if (c instanceof Character) {
                    mgr.addCharacter((Character)c);
                } // if
            } // while
        } catch (Exception e) {
        } // try
        return objectCount;
    } // loadCharacters(String)
} // class CharacterLoader
```

RELATED PATTERNS

Composite   The Prototype pattern is often used with the Composite pattern.

Abstract Factory   The Abstract Factory pattern can be a good alternative to the Prototype pattern where the dynamic changes that the Prototype pattern allows to the prototypical object palette are not needed.

   `PrototypeBuilder` classes may use the Abstract Factory pattern to create a set of prototypical objects.

Façade   The client class commonly acts as a façade that separates the other classes that participate in the Prototype pattern from the rest of the program.

Factory Method   The Factory Method pattern can be an alternative to the Prototype pattern when the palette of prototypical objects never contains more than one object.

Decorator   The Prototype pattern is often used with the Decorator pattern.

Singleton [GoF95]

SYNOPSIS

The Singleton pattern ensures that only one instance of a class is created. All objects that use an instance of that class use the same instance.

CONTEXT

Some classes should have exactly one instance. These classes usually involve the central management of a resource. The resource may be external, as is the case with an object that manages the reuse of database connections. The resource may be internal, such as an object that keeps an error count and other statistics for a compiler.

Suppose that you need to write a class that an applet can use to ensure that no more than one audio clip is played at a time. If an applet contains two pieces of code that independently play audio clips, then it is possible for both to play at the same time. When two audio clips play at the same time, the results depend on the platform. The results may range from confusing, with users hearing both audio clips together, to terrible, with the platform's sound-producing mechanism unable to cope with playing two different audio clips at once.

To avoid the undesirable situation of playing two audio clips at the same time, the class that you write should stop playing an audio clip before starting to play the next audio clip. A way to design a class to implement this policy while keeping that class simple is to ensure that there is only one instance of that class shared by all objects that use that class. If all requests to play audio clips go through the same object, then it is simple for that object to stop an audio clip before starting the next audio clip. Figure 5.14 shows a class diagram with such a class.

The constructor for the AudioClipManager class is private. That prevents another class from directly creating an instance of the AudioClipManager class. Instead, to get an instance of the AudioClipManager class, other classes must call its getInstance method. The getInstance method is a static method that always returns the same instance of the AudioClipManager class. The instance it returns is the instance referred to by its private static variable instance.

The rest of the `AudioClipManager` class's methods are responsible for audio clip play control. The `AudioClipManager` class has a private instance variable named `prevClip`, which is initially null and later refers to the last audio clip played. Before playing a new audio clip, the instance of the `AudioClipManager` class stops the audio clip referred to by the `prevClip`. This ensures that the previously requested audio clip stops before the next audio clip starts.

FORCES

- There must be exactly one instance of a class.
- The one instance of a class must be accessible to all clients of that class.

SOLUTION

The Singleton pattern is relatively simple, since it only involves one class (see Figure 5.15).

A singleton class has a static variable that refers to the one instance of the class that you want to use. This instance is created when the class is loaded into memory. You should implement the class in a way that prevents other classes from creating any additional instances of a singleton class. This means you should ensure that all of the class's constructors are private.

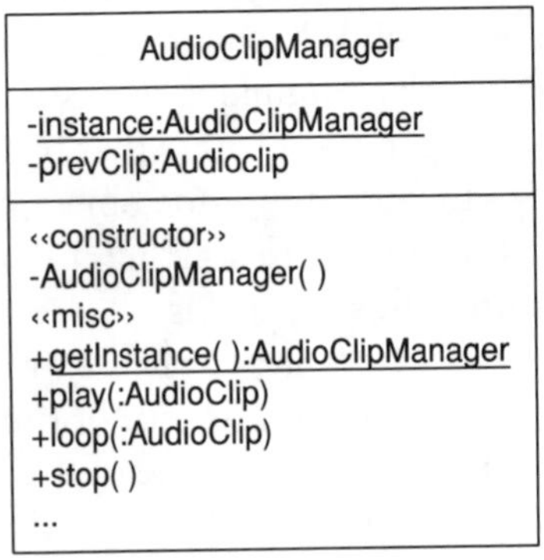

FIGURE 5.14 Audio clip manager.

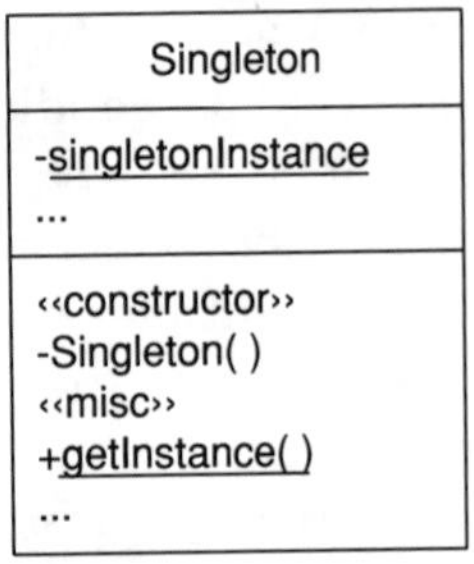

FIGURE 5.15 Singleton class.

To access the one instance of a singleton class, the class provides a static method, typically called `getInstance` or `getClassname`, which returns a reference to the one instance of the class.

CONSEQUENCES

- Exactly one instance of a singleton class exists.
- Other classes that want a reference to the one instance of the singleton class must get that instance by calling the class's `getInstance` static method, rather than by constructing the instance themselves.
- Subclassing a singleton class is awkward and results in imperfectly encapsulated classes. To subclass a singleton class, you must give it a constructor that is not private. Also, if you want to define a subclass of a singleton class that is also supposed to be a singleton, you will want the subclass to override the singleton class's `getInstance` method. This will not be possible, since methods such as `getInstance` must be static. Java does not allow static methods to be overridden.

IMPLEMENTATION

To enforce the nature of a singleton class, you must code the class in a way that prevents other classes from directly creating instances of the class. The way to accomplish this is to declare all of the class's constructors private. Be careful to declare at least one private constructor. If a class does not declare any constructors, then a default public constructor is automatically generated for it.

A common variation on the Singleton pattern occurs in situations where the instance of a Singleton may not be needed. In situations like this, you can postpone creation of the instance until the first call to `getInstance`.

Another variation on the Singleton pattern stems from the fact that it has a class's instantiation policy encapsulated in the class itself. Because the instantiation policy is encapsulated in the class's `getInstance` method, it is possible to vary the creation policy. One possible policy is to have `getInstance` alternately return one of two instances or to periodically create a new instance for `getInstance` to return.

There is a rather subtle bug than can occur in implementations of the Singleton pattern. It can cause a singleton class to create and initialize more than one instance of itself. The problem occurs in programs that refer to a singleton class only through other classes that are dynamically loaded, as described in the Dynamic Linkage pattern.

Some programs are organized so that they dynamically load a set of classes, use them for a while, and then stop using them. When a program stops using classes, the classes that it is finished with may be garbage collected. This is normally a good thing. If a program keeps no references to classes after it is finished with them and garbage collection of classes is enabled, the unused classes will eventually be garbage collected.

This behavior can be a problem for singleton classes. If a singleton class is garbage collected, it will be loaded again if there is another dynamic reference to it. After the class has been loaded a second time, the first request for its instance will return a new instance. This can produce unexpected results.

Suppose that you have a singleton class whose purpose is to maintain performance statistics. Consider what will happen if it is garbage collected and reloaded. The first time its getInstance method is called after it is loaded a second time, it will return a new object. Its instance variables will have their initial values, and previously collected statistics will be lost.

If a class is loaded by a ClassLoader object, then it will not be garbage collected until the ClassLoader object is eligible to be garbage collected. If that is not a practical way for you to manage the lifetime of a singleton object, there is a more general way. This is to ensure there is a reference, direct or indirect, from a live thread to the object not to be garbage collected. The class listed here can be used to do just that:

```
public class ObjectPreserver implements Runnable {
    // This keeps this class and everything it references from
    // being garbage collected
    private static ObjectPreserver lifeLine
      = new ObjectPreserver();
    // Since this class won't be garbage collected, neither will
    // this HashSet or the object that it references.
    private static HashSet protectedSet = new HashSet();

    private ObjectPreserver() {
        new Thread(this).start();
    } // constructor()

    public void run() {
        try {
            wait();
```

```
        } catch (InterruptedException e) {
        } // try
    } // run()

    /**
     * Garbage collection of objects passed to this method will be
     * prevented until they are passed to the unpreserveObject method.
     */
    public static void preserveObject(Object o) {
        protectedSet.add(o);
    } // preserveObject()

    /**
     * Objects passed to this method lose the protection that the
     * preserveObject method gave them from garbage collection.
     */
    public static void unpreserveObject(Object o) {
        protectedSet.remove(o);
    } // unpreserveObject(Object)
} // class ObjectPreserver
```

If the class object that encapsulates a class or one of a class's instances is passed to the `preserveObject` method of the `ObjectPreserver` class shown in the preceding listing, then that class will not be garbage collected.

JAVA API USAGE

The Java API class `java.lang.Runtime` is a singleton class. It has exactly one instance. It has no public constructors. To get a reference to its one instance, other classes must call its static method `getRuntime`.

CODE EXAMPLE

Following is a Java class you can use to avoid playing two audio clips at the same time. The class is a singleton class. You can access its instance by calling its static `getInstance` method. When you play audio clips through that object, it stops the last audio clip it was playing before it starts the newly requested one. If you play all audio clips through the `AudioClipManager` object, there will never be more than one audio clip playing at the same time.

```
public class AudioClipManager implements AudioClip{
    private static AudioClipManager instance = new AudioClipManager();
    private AudioClip prevClip; // previously requested audio clip
```

```
/**
 * This private constructor is defined so the compiler won't
 * generate a default public constructor.
 */
private AudioClipManager() { }
/**
 * Return a reference to the only instance of this class.
 */
public static AudioClipManager getInstance() {
    return instance;
} // getInstance()
```

. . .

```
/**
 * Stop the previously requested audio clip and play the given
 * audio clip.
 * @param clip the new audio clip to play.
 /
public void play(AudioClip clip) {
    if (prevClip != null)
      prevClip.stop();
    prevClip = clip;
    clip.play();
} // play(AudioClip)
```

. . .

```
/**
 * Stop the previously requested audio clip and play the given
 * audio clip in a loop.
 * @param clip the new audio clip to play.
 */
public void loop(AudioClip clip) {
    if (prevClip != null)
      prevClip.stop();
    prevClip = clip;
    clip.loop();
} // play(AudioClip)

/**
 * Stops playing this audio clip.
 */
public void stop() {
    if (prevClip != null)
      prevClip.stop();
} // stop()
} // class AudioClipManager
```

RELATED PATTERNS

You can use the Singleton pattern with many other patterns. In particular, it is often used with the Abstract Factory, Builder, and Prototype patterns.

The Singleton pattern has some similarity to the Cache Management pattern. A Singleton is functionally similar to a Cache that contains only one object.

If multiple threads will be receiving the instance of a singleton class, you can use the Double Checked Locking coding pattern (described in Volume 2) to ensure that only one instance is created. This avoids the overhead of unnecessary thread synchronization after the instance is created.

Object Pool [Grand98]

SYNOPSIS

Manages the reuse of objects when a type of object is expensive to create or only a limited number of objects can be created.

CONTEXT

Suppose that you have been given the assignment of writing a library to provide access to a proprietary database. Clients send queries to the database through a network connection. The database server receives queries through the network connection and returns the queries through the same connection.

In order for a program to query the database, it must have a connection to the database. The most convenient way to manage connections for the programmers who will use the library is to have each part of a program that needs a connection create its own connection. However, creating database connections that are not really needed is bad for a few reasons:

- It can take a few seconds to create each database connection.
- The more connections there are to a database, the longer it takes to create new connections.
- Each database connection uses a network connection. Some platforms limit the number of network connections that they allow.

Your design for the library must reconcile these conflicting forces—the convenience of programmers versus the high expense of creating database connection objects and a possible limit on the number of database connections that can exist at one time. One way to reconcile these forces is to have the library manage database connections on behalf of the application that uses the library.

The strategy that the library uses to manage database connections is based on the premise that a program's database connections are interchangeable. So long as a database connection is in a state that allows it to convey a query to the database, it does not matter which of a program's database connections is used. Using that observation, the database access library is designed to have a two-layer implementation of database connections.

A class called `Connection` implements the upper layer. Programs that use the database access library directly create and use `Connection` objects. `Connection` objects identify a database, but have no direct database connection. A `Connection` object is paired with a `ConnectionImpl` object only while it is used to send a query to a database and fetch the result. `ConnectionImpl` objects encapsulate an actual database connection. The database access library creates and manages `ConnectionImpl` objects. It manages `ConnectionImpl` objects by maintaining a pool of them that are not currently paired up with a `Connection` object. The library creates a `ConnectionImpl` object only when it needs to pair one up with a `Connection` object and the pool of `ConnectionImpl` objects is empty. The class diagram in Figure 5.16 shows the classes that are involved in managing the pool of `ConnectionImpl` objects.

A `Connection` object calls the `ConnectionPool` object's `AcquireImpl` method when it needs a `ConnectionImpl` object, passing it the name of the database it needs to be connected with. If there are any `ConnectionImpl` objects in the `ConnectionPool` object's collection that are connected to the needed database, it returns one of those objects. If there are no such `ConnectionImpl` objects in the `ConnectionPool` object's collection, it tries to create one and return it. If it is unable to create a `ConnectionImpl` object, it waits until an existing `ConnectionImpl` object

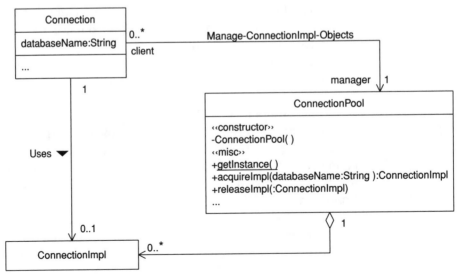

FIGURE 5.16 ConnectionImpl pool management.

is returned to the pool by a call to the `releaseImpl` method, and then it returns that object.

The `ConnectionPool` class is a singleton. There should be only one instance of the `ConnectionPool` class. The class's constructor is private. Other classes access the one instance of the `ConnectionPool` class by calling its `getInstance` method, which is static.

In addition to the other reasons why a `ConnectionPool` object's `AcquireImpl` method may be unable to create a `ConnectionImpl` object, you need to impose a maximum on the number of `ConnectionImpl` objects it may create that connect to the same database. The reason for this is to guarantee that a database will support a minimum number of clients. Since there is a maximum number of connections that each database can support, limiting the number of connections each client can have to a database allows you to guarantee support for a minimum number of client programs.

FORCES

- A program may not create more than a limited number of instances for a particular class.
- If creating instances of a particular class is sufficiently more expensive, then creating new instances for that class should be avoided.
- A program can avoid creating some objects by reusing objects when it has finished with them rather than discarding them as garbage.

SOLUTION

If instances of a class are reused, avoid creating new instances of the class. Figure 5.17 shows a class diagram that demonstrates the roles that classes play in the Object Pool pattern.

Here are descriptions of the roles that classes in the Object Pool pattern play in Figure 5.17:

Reusable   Instances of classes in this role collaborate with other objects for a limited amount of time, then they are no longer needed for that collaboration.

Client   Instances of classes in this role use `Reusable` objects.

ReusablePool   Instances of classes in this role manage `Reusable` objects for use by `Client` objects. Usually, it is desirable to keep all `Reusable`

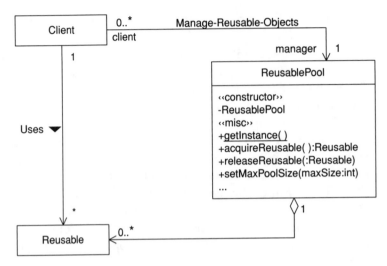

FIGURE 5.17 Object pool pattern.

objects that are not currently in use in the same object pool so that they can be managed by one coherent policy. To achieve this, the ReusablePool class is designed to be a singleton class. Its constructor(s) are private, which forces other classes to call its getInstance method to get the one instance of the ReusablePool class.

A Client object will call a ReusablePool object's acquireReusable method when it needs a Reusable object. A ReusablePool object maintains a collection of Reusable objects. It uses the collection of Reusable objects to contain a pool of Reusable objects that are not currently in use. If there are any Reusable objects in the pool when the acquireReusable method is called, it removes a Reusable object from the pool and returns it. If the pool is empty, then the acquireReusable method creates a Reusable object if it can. If the acquireReusable method cannot create a new Reusable object, then it waits until a Reusable object is returned to the collection.

Client objects pass a Reusable object to a ReusablePool object's releaseReusable method when they are finished with the object. The releaseReusable method returns a Reusable object to the pool of Reusable objects that are not in use.

In many applications of the Object Pool pattern, there are reasons for limiting the total number of Reusable objects that may be created. In such cases, the ReusablePool object that creates Reusable objects is responsible for not creating more than a specified maximum number of

Reusable objects. If ReusablePool objects are responsible for limiting the number of objects they will create, then the ReusablePool class will have a method for specifying the maximum number of objects to be created. That method is indicated in Figure 5.17 as setMaxPoolSize.

CONSEQUENCES

Using the Object Pool pattern helps to avoid the need for object creation. It works best when the demand for objects does not vary greatly over time. When there are large variations in the demand for objects, performance problems may result.

Suppose that most of the time the demand for a kind of object managed by the Object Pool pattern is less than 10, but occasionally the demand briefly jumps to 1000. If the demand for more than 10 of those objects is very rare, then you can have a situation where there are over 990 objects in the pool that are not used for a long period of time. In fact, they may never be used again. If the memory used by those unused objects is needed for other purposes, performance may suffer.

Limiting the number of objects that may be in the object pool without limiting the total number of objects that can be created alleviates this problem. If the limit on the number of objects that are in the object pool is 10, then when a Reusable object is no longer in use it is discarded instead of being added to the object pool.

When the demand for objects exceeds the limit of the size of the object pool, the penalty is that additional objects need to be created. When the demand for objects exceeds a limit on the number of objects that may be created, the penalty is that requests for objects must wait for an object to become unused.

Keeping the logic to manage the creation and reuse of a class's instances in a separate class from the class whose instances are being managed results in a more cohesive design. It eliminates interactions between the implementation of a creation and reuse policy and the implementation of the managed class's functionality.

IMPLEMENTATION

When there is a limit on the number of objects that may be created or just a limit on the size of the object pool, using a simple array is usually the best way to implement the object pool. When there is no limit on the size of the object pool, using a `Vector` is an appropriate way to implement the object pool.

In many cases, the object that manages an object pool is supposed to limit the number of instances of a class that can be created. It is easy for an object to limit the number of objects it creates. However, to robustly enforce a limit on the total number of objects created, the object responsible for managing the object pool must be the only object able to create those objects.

You can ensure that a class is instantiated only by the class that manages the object pool. You can do that by making the managed class's constructor(s) private and implementing the pool management class as a static member class of the managed class. If you do not have control over the structure of the class whose instances are to be managed, you may be able to add that structure to the class through inheritance.

CODE EXAMPLE

Following is code that implements that design presented under the "Context" heading. The first listing shows part of the `Connection` class. The `Connection` class uses `ConnectionImpl` objects, which are managed in pools by the `ConnectionImpl.ConnectionPool` class.

```
public class Connection {
    private final static ConnectionImpl.ConnectionPool
      connectionPool = ConnectionImpl.ConnectionPool.getInstance();
    private String databaseName;
...
    /**
     * Send a request to the database and return the result.
     */
    Object sendRequest(Request request) {
        Object result;
        ConnectionImpl impl;
        impl = connectionPool.acquireImpl(databaseName);
        result = impl.sendRequest(request);
        connectionPool.releaseImpl(impl);
        return result;
    } // sendRequest(Request)
} // class Connection
```

The other listing presented here is of the `ConnectionImpl` class.

```
class ConnectionImpl {
    // Name of the database this object is connected to.
    private String dbName;
```

```
// Private Constructor
private ConnectionImpl(String dbName) {
    this.dbName = dbName;
    ...
} // constructor()
...

/**
 * return the name of the database that this object is
 * connected to.
 */
String getDatabaseName() {
    return dbName;
} // getDatabaseName()

/**
 * Send a request to the database and return the result.
 */
Object sendRequest(Request request) {
    Object result = null;
    ...
    return result;
} // sendRequest(Request)
```

The rest of the `ConnectionImpl` class is the part that is most interesting with respect to the Object Pool pattern. It is the `ConnectionImpl.CommectionPool` class, which manages a pool of `ConnectionImpl` objects. It is implemented as a static member of the `ConnectionImpl` class. Because it is a member of the `ConnectionImpl` class, it is allowed to access the `ConnectionImpl` class's constructor.

```
static class ConnectionPool {
    // The one instance of this class
    private static ConnectionPool thePool
      = new ConnectionPool();

    // This hash table associates database names with the
    // corresponding Vector that contains a pool of connections for
    // that database.
    private Hashtable poolDictionary = new Hashtable();

    // This constructor is private to prevent other classes
    // from creating instances of this class.
    private ConnectionPool() {}

    /**
     * Return the one instance of this class.
     */
    public static ConnectionPool getInstance() {
```

```
        return thePool;
} // getInstance()


/**
 * Return a ConnectionImpl from the appropriate pool or
 * if the pool is empty.
 * @param dbName The name of the database that a
 * ConnectionImpl is to be supplied for.
 */
public
synchronized ConnectionImpl acquireImpl(String dbName) {
    Vector pool = (Vector)poolDictionary.get(dbName);
    if (pool != null) {
        int size = pool.size();
        if (size > 0)
          return (ConnectionImpl)pool.remove(size-1);
    } // if null
    // No ConnectionImpl in pool, so create one.
    return new ConnectionImpl(dbName);
} // acquireImpl(String)
/**
 * Add a ConnectionImpl to the appropriate pool.
 */
public synchronized void releaseImpl(ConnectionImpl impl) {
    String databaseName = impl.getDatabaseName();
    Vector pool = (Vector)poolDictionary.get(databaseName);
    if (pool == null) {
        pool = new Vector();
        poolDictionary.put(databaseName, pool);
    } // if null
    pool.addElement(impl);
} // releaseImpl(ConnectionImpl)
} // class ConnectionPool
} // class ConnectionImpl
```

RELATED PATTERNS

Cache Management   The Cache Management pattern manages the reuse
of specific instances of a class. The Pool pattern manages and creates
instances of a class that can be used interchangeably.

Factory Method   The Factory Method pattern can be used to encapsulate
the creation logic for objects. However, it does not manage them after
their creation.

Singleton   Objects that manage object pools are usually singletons.

Partitioning Patterns

In the analysis stage, you examine a problem to identify the actors, concepts, requirements, and their relationships that constitute the problem. The patterns in this chapter provide guidance on how to partition complex actors and concepts into multiple classes.

Layered Initialization [Grand98]

SYNOPSIS

When you need multiple implementations of an abstraction, you usually define a class to encapsulate common logic and subclasses to encapsulate different specialized logic. This does not work when common logic is used to decide which specialized subclass to create. The Layered Initialization pattern solves this problem by encapsulating the common and specialized logic to create an object in unrelated classes.

CONTEXT

Suppose that you implement a business-rule server for an enterprise. The business-rule server is a central repository that encapsulates business rules for all the applications that a business uses.

A business-rule server may be asked questions such as, "What format should we use to display location numbers?" The answer to a question like this is normally embedded directly in one of the server's rules. More complicated questions may require the business-rule manager to consult some databases. Consider the question, "How far into the future can we guarantee a price quote for this item?" To answer this question, there are likely rules that break it down into subquestions such as:

> Do we have a price guarantee from our supplier, and if so, when does the guarantee expire? We don't have a price guarantee from our supplier. Based on the amount of times the item's price has changed in the past and our sales projections, how long will the amount of inventory we have for that item shield us from price changes?

Questions such as these require the business-rule manager to query information from databases. Clearly, the set of rules will be complex. Because of this, you will want to keep information about how to get different kinds of data from a database separate from business rules that request the information. This way any changes to the organization of the database that the business-rule manager works with will not require changes to the business rules themselves.

Having determined those requirements, during analysis you need to identify a set of entities that include an inference engine to interpret the business rules and a data query to fetch information requested by the inference engine. Designing classes to implement the data query entity poses an interesting challenge.

You will want to have a `DataQuery` class you can instantiate by passing its constructor a request for information. It will be up to the constructor to determine which databases to query to get the requested information.

The techniques for getting data from a database vary with the type of database, so you will want to have a class that corresponds to each type of supported database. There may be a class for accessing relational databases through JDBC, additional classes for natively accessing relational database engines such as Oracle and Sybase, and perhaps another class for accessing object-oriented databases.

JDBC does not provide access to object-oriented databases. Some queries to relational databases can be done much more efficiently through a database-engine-specific API rather than through JDBC.

The obvious way to organize this is with a `DataQuery` class that has subclasses like those shown in Figure 6.1. The problem with using this type of organization is that you must decide which kind of `DataQuery` object to create before you pass the request for information to its constructor. Since you want to hide the details of data queries from the business-rule inference engine, requiring it to decide which subclass of `DataQuery` to use is not a good thing.

To keep the business-rule inference engine independent of which of database is used, you can have a separate object to encapsulate the logic used to analyze the data request and determine the database that should be used. You will also want to have a factory method object that determines which class to use to access that database (see Figure 6.2).

The design shown in Figure 6.2 is an example of the Layered Initialization pattern. A data request is passed into the constructor for a `DataQuery` object. The constructor analyzes the data request to determine which database to consult to retrieve the necessary information. Using an object that implements the `DataQueryFactoryIF` interface, it creates instances of the appropriate classes that implement `DataQueryImplIF`. Those `DataQueryImplIF` objects retrieve the data. The `DataQueryFactoryIF` is passed to the `DataQuery` object at an earlier time through its `setFactory` method.

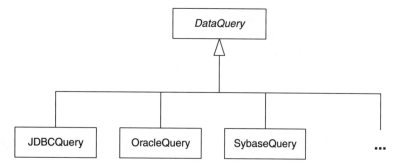

FIGURE 6.1 DataQuery class.

You can use the Layered Initialization pattern in any situation where preprocessing must be done on selection data before deciding which specialized class to instantiate.

FORCES

- A specialized class must be chosen to process complex data.
- The logic to choose a specialized class should be encapsulated so that it is transparent to the classes that provide data for an instance of the specialized class to process.
- The constructors of the specialized classes and their superclasses are invoked after it has been decided which specialized class to instantiate. This means that those constructors cannot participate in the decision of which class to instantiate.
- To maintain low coupling, only one of the objects that participates in the Layered Initialization pattern should be visible to the object that provides the complex data.
- Putting the decision of which class to instantiate into a separate class reduces the effort required to maintain the other classes. If a database migrates to a different type of engine or a new class becomes available that provides better access to it, then the corresponding change in the program is limited to the class that decides what class to instantiate.

SOLUTION

Objects that participate in the Layered Initialization pattern cooperate to provide a service to objects outside the pattern.

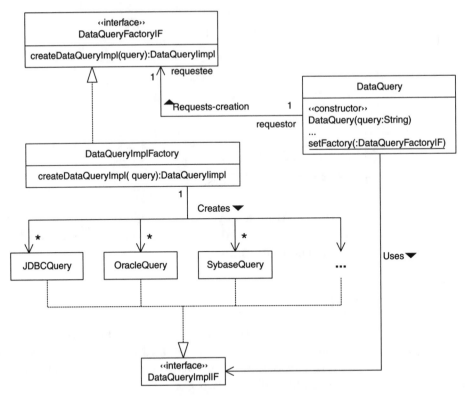

FIGURE 6.2 DataQuery factory method object.

The essence of the Layered Initialization pattern is that initialization of the objects participating in the pattern happens in layers. The layers are necessary because the normal sequence of events that occurs when an object is created does not fit the constraints of a problem. The normal sequence of events is shown in the following three steps:

1. Decide on the type of specialized logic that a situation requires and select the class that will be instantiated to provide that logic.
2. The constructors of the object's superclasses initialize instance variables to support common logic.
3. A constructor of the object's class initializes the object's instance variables to support the object's specialized logic.

Sometimes, it is necessary to initialize the common logic before selecting the specialized class to instantiate. This implies performing step 2 before step 1. Inheritance does not allow this sort of variation. However, this can be accomplished through delegation by having a class that contains common logic delegate the specialized logic to other classes.

First, objects that perform logic common to all cases are initialized. That initialization concludes by determining the class to instantiate that will supply the appropriate specialized logic. That class's constructor performs the next layer of initialization logic. After that initialization is done, it may create objects that belong to a more specialized layer, if there is one.

After the objects that participate in the Layered Initialization pattern have completed their initialization, there will be one top-level object whose methods are called by objects outside the pattern. If a method in that object requires any specialized logic, it calls the appropriate method in an object one layer down.

Figure 6.3 shows a class diagram with the roles in which classes and interfaces participate in the Layered Initialization pattern. This diagram shows only two layers. However, with recursive composition, each of the `service1`, `service2`, . . . classes can be the top-level class in another application of the Layered Initialization pattern.

Here are descriptions of the participants shown in Figure 6.3:

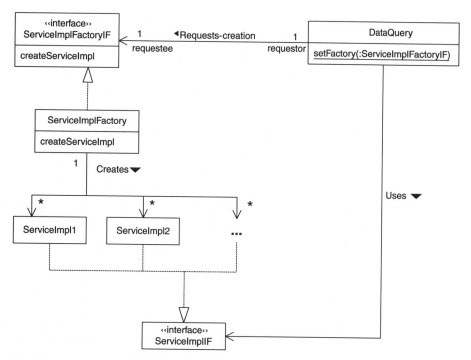

FIGURE 6.3 Layered initialization class diagram.

Service   All classes that participate in the Layered Initialization pattern cooperate to provide the same service. Instances of the `Service` class contribute to this in two ways:

1. Instances of the `Service` class are the only objects that participate in this pattern that are visible to objects outside this pattern.
2. The `Service` class encapsulates logic that is common to all of the specialized cases. It delegates specialized operations and specialized portions of common operations to classes that implement the `ServiceImplIF` interface.

After a service object is sufficiently initialized to have gathered the information needed to create a specialized object that implements the `ServiceImplIF` interface, it passes that information to a `ServiceImplFactory` object that is responsible for the creation of those objects.

If the `Service` class is intended to be reusable, then it will probably have a static method, indicated in the class diagram as `setFactory`, that sets the `ServiceImplFactory` object that all instances of the `Service` class will use. If that sort of reusability is not needed, then neither the `setFactory` method nor the `ServiceImplFactoryIF` interface is needed, and the service class can directly refer to a `ServiceImplFactory` class.

ServiceImplIF   The service object accesses `service1`, `service2`, . . . objects of the lower layer through this interface.

ServiceImplFactoryIF   The service object uses this interface to access a `ServiceImplFactory` object.

ServiceImplFactory   This corresponds to any class that creates `ServiceImpl` objects and implements the `ServiceFactoryIF` interface.

ServiceImpl1, ServiceImpl2, . . .   These classes implement the `ServiceImplIF` interface and provide the specialized logic needed by service class methods.

CONSEQUENCES

- The complexity of initializing an object using data that requires analysis before the initialization can proceed is hidden from client objects.

■ The clients of the service class have no dependencies on the objects that participate in the Layered Initialization pattern, except the service object.

IMPLEMENTATION

One idea in the Layered Initialization pattern is that out of all the objects that participate in this pattern, only the service object has clients that are outside of the pattern. A way to enforce this is to put the classes and interfaces that participate in an application of the Layered Initialization pattern into a separate package, making only the service class and the `ServiceImplFactoryIF` interface public.

Normally the `Service` class's `setFactory` method is called during a program's initialization. Once a factory object has been provided to the `Service` class, it is not normally necessary to provide it with another factory object. If you know that changing the factory object is unnecessary, then it is a reasonable assertion that calling the `Service` class's `setFactory` method a second time is an error. If this is the case, you can make the service class more robust by putting code in the `setFactory` method that signals an error if a factory object has previously been set.

JAVA API USAGE

The `java.net.URL` class uses the Layered Initialization pattern. When you create a `URL` object, you can pass a string that specifies a URL to the object's constructor. These strings can look like:

```
http://www.mindspring.com/~mgrand
```

or

```
mailto:mgrand@mindspring.com
```

The portion of the string located before the first colon is the protocol to use for the URL. The syntax of what follows the colon depends on the protocol specified before the colon. Because the `URL` object must parse the entire string before its initialization is complete, it uses the Layered Initialization pattern.

The `URL` class participates in the Layered Initialization pattern as the service class. It uses an abstract class called `URLStreamHandler`. The

URLStreamHandler class participates in the Layered Initialization pattern as a ServiceFactoryImplIF interface. To parse the portion of the URL string after the colon, the URL class creates an instance of the appropriate subclass of the URLStreamHandler class. It can pick the subclass of URLStreamHandler to instantiate using a default mechanism. Alternatively, if an object that implements the URLStreamHandlerFactory interface is passed to the URL class's setURLStreamHandlerFactory static method, then all instances of the URL use that object to indirectly create instances of the appropriate subclass of URLStreamHandler.

CODE EXAMPLE

The example for the Layered Initialization pattern is some skeletal code that implements the data query design shown under the "Context" heading for this pattern. Here is the code for the DataQuery class that takes a data query in its constructor so that its instances can produce a result:

```
public class DataQuery {
    // Factory object for creating DataQueryImplIF objects.
    private DataQueryFactoryIF factory;

    public void setFactory(DataQueryFactoryIF factory) {
        if (this.factory != null)
          throw new Error("Data query factory already defined");
        this.factory = factory;
    } // setFactory(DataQueryFactoryIF)

    /**
     * Constructor
     */
    public DataQuery(String query) {
        ...
        while ( ... ) {
            String dbName = null;
            ...
            // Construct a database specific query object
            DataQueryImplIF dq;
            dq = (DataQueryImplIF)
            factory.createDataQueryImpl (dbName);
            ...
        } // while
        ...
    } // Constructor (String)
    ...
} // class DataQuery
```

Here is the declaration of the `DataQueryFactoryIF` interface that all factory objects that create database-specific query objects must implement:

```
public interface DataQueryFactoryIF {
    public DataQueryFactoryIF createDataQueryImpl (String dbName);
} // DataQueryFactoryIF
```

Here is a sample class that implements the `DataQueryFactoryIF` interface:

```
class MyDataQueryFactory implements DataQueryFactoryIF {
    private static Hashtable classes = new Hashtable ();
    // populate the classes hashtable
    static {
    classes.put("INVENTORY", dataQuery.OracleQuery.class);
    classes.put("SALES",     dataQuery.SybaseQuery.class);
    classes.put("PERSONNEL", dataQuery.OracleQuery.class);
    ...
    } // static

    /**
     * Create a DataQueryImplIF object that retrieves data from the
     * specified database.
     * @param dbName the name of the database that will be queried
     * /
    public DataQueryFactoryIF createDataQueryImpl (String dbName) {
        Class clazz = (Class)classes.get(dbName);
        try {
            return (DataQueryFactoryIF)clazz.newInstance();
        } catch (Exception e) {
            return null;
        } // try
    } // createDataQueryImpl (String)
} // class MyDataQueryFactory
```

RELATED PATTERNS

Builder   The Builder pattern uses the Layered Initialization pattern to create a specialized object for representing data in a specific form.

Delegation (When not to use Inheritance)   The service class delegates specialized operations to objects that implement the `ServiceImpl` interface.

Façade   The Layered Initialization pattern uses the Façade pattern by hiding all of the other objects that participate in the pattern from clients of service objects.

Factory Method In situations where the choice of which kind of object to create does not involve any significant preprocessing of data, the Factory Method pattern may be a more appropriate choice. The Layered Initialization pattern may use the Factory Method pattern after it has decided what kind of specialized logic is needed.

Layered Architecture The Layered Initialization pattern recognizes a division of responsibilities into layers during design. The Layered Architecture pattern recognizes a division of responsibilities into layers during analysis.

Composite When more than two layers are needed for initialization, you can combine the Layered Initialization pattern with the Composite pattern to perform initialization in as many layers as needed.

Filter [BMRSS96]

SYNOPSIS

The Filter pattern allows objects that perform different transformations and computations on streams of data and that have compatible interfaces to dynamically connect in order to perform arbitrary operations on streams of data.

CONTEXT

There are many programs whose purpose is to perform computations or analysis on a stream of data. A program that performs simple transformations on the contents of a data stream is the UNIX `uniq` program. The `uniq` program organizes its input into lines. The `uniq` program normally copies all of the lines that it reads to its output. However, when it finds consecutive lines that contain identical characters, it copies only the first such line to its output. UNIX also comes with a program called `wc` that does a simple analysis of a data stream. It produces a count of the number of characters, words, and lines in the data stream. Compilers perform a complex series of transformations and analysis on their source code input to produce their binary output.

Since many programs perform transformations and analysis on data streams, it would clearly be beneficial to define classes that perform the more common transformations and analyses. Such classes will get a lot of reuse.

Classes that perform simple transformations and analysis on data streams tend to be very generic in nature. When writing such classes, it is not possible to anticipate all the possible ways they will be used. Some applications will want to apply some transformations and analyses to only selected parts of a data stream. Clearly, these classes should be written in a way that allows great flexibility in how their instances can be connected together. One way to accomplish that flexibility is to define a common superclass for all of these classes so an instance of one can use an instance of another without caring which class the object is an instance of (see Figure 6.4).

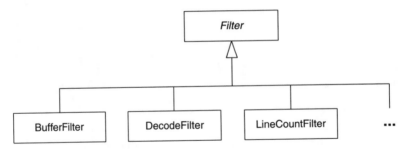

FIGURE 6.4 File filters.

FORCES

- Classes that implement common data transformations and analyses are used in a great variety of programs.
- It should be possible to dynamically combine data analysis and transformation objects by connecting them together.
- The use of transformation/analysis objects should be transparent to other objects.

SOLUTION

Through a combination of abstract classes and delegation, a solution is realized. The Filter pattern organizes the classes that participate in it as data sources, data sinks, and data filters. The data filter classes perform the transformation and analysis operations. There are two basic forms of the Filter pattern: data flows as a result of a data sink object calling a method in a data source object and data flows when a data source object passes data to a method of a data sink object.

Figure 6.5 shows a class diagram for the form of Filter in which data sink objects retrieve data by calling methods in data sources.

Here are descriptions of how the classes in Figure 6.5 participate in the Filter pattern:

AbstractSource   This abstract class declares a method, indicated in the diagram as getData, that returns data when it is called.

ConcreteSource   This corresponds to any concrete subclass of AbstractSource that is primarily responsible for providing data rather than transforming or analyzing data.

AbstractSourceFilter   This abstract class is the superclass of classes that transform and analyze data. It has a constructor that takes an argument

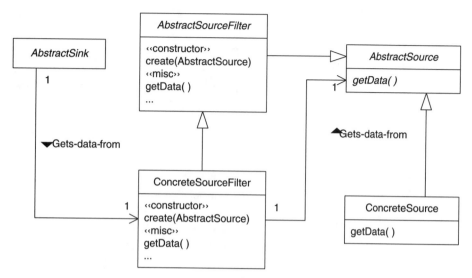

FIGURE 6.5 Source filter.

that is the instance of the AbstractSource class. Instances of an AbstractSourceFilter class delegate the fetching of data to the AbstractSource object passed to their constructor. Because instances of this class are also instances of the abstract source class, instances of the abstract sink class can treat instances of the AbstractSourceFilter class the same as instances of a concrete source class.

The AbstractSourceFilter class defines a getData method that simply calls the getData method of the abstract source object that was passed to its object's constructor.

ConcreteSourceFilter   This corresponds to any concrete subclass of AbstractSourceFilter. Subclasses of AbstractSourceFilter should extend the behavior of the getData method that they inherit from AbstractSourceFilter to perform the appropriate transformation or analysis operations.

AbstractSink   Instances of abstract sink classes call the getData method of an AbstractSouce object. Unlike ConcreteSourceFilter objects, instances of abstract sink classes use the data without passing it on to another AbstractSourceFilter object.

Figure 6.6 shows a class diagram for the form of Filter in which data source objects pass data to methods of data sink objects.

Here are the descriptions for the classes in Figure 6.6:

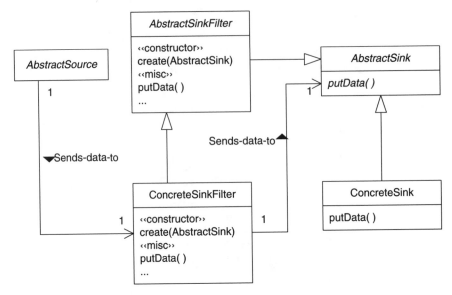

FIGURE 6.6 Sink filter.

AbstractSink   This abstract class declares a method, indicated in the diagram as `putData`, that takes data through one of its parameters.

ConcreteSink   This corresponds to any concrete subclass of `AbstractSink` that is primarily responsible for receiving data rather than transforming or analyzing data.

AbstractSinkFilter   This abstract class is the superclass of classes that transform and analyze data. It has a constructor that takes an argument that is the instance of the `AbstractSink` class. Instances of an `AbstractSinkFilter` class delegate putting of data to the `AbstractSink` object passed to their constructor. Because instances of this class are also instances of the abstract sink class, instances of the abstract source class can treat instances of the `AbstractSinkFilter` class the same as instances of a concrete sink class.

> The `AbstractSinkFilter` class defines a `putData` method that simply calls the `putData` method of the `AbstractSink` object that was passed to its object's constructor.

ConcreteSinkFilter   This corresponds to any concrete subclass of `AbstractSinkFilter`. Subclasses of `AbstractSinkFilter` should extend the behavior of the `putData` method that they inherit from `AbstractSinkFilter` to perform the appropriate transformation or analysis operations.

AbstractSource Instances of `AbstractSource` call the `putData` method of an `AbstractSink` object. Unlike `ConcreteSinkFilter` objects, instances of `AbstractSource` provide the data without getting it from another `AbstractSinkFilter` object.

CONSEQUENCES

- The portion of a program that follows the Filter pattern is structured as a set of sources, sinks, and filters.
- Filter objects that don't maintain internal state can be dynamically replaced while a program is running. This property of stateless filters allows dynamic change of behavior and adaptation to different requirements at runtime.
- It is quite reasonable for a program to incorporate both forms of the Filter pattern. However, it is unusual for the same class to participate in both forms.

IMPLEMENTATION

Filter classes should be implemented in a way that does not assume anything about the programs that they will be used in or which other filter classes they will be used with. Because of this, it follows that filter objects should not have side effects and should communicate with each other only through the data that they exchange.

Making filter classes independent of the programs that they are used in increases their reusability. However, in some cases there can be performance penalties if a filter object is not allowed to use context-specific information. The best design is sometimes a compromise between these considerations. For example, you could define one or more interfaces that declare methods for providing context-specific information to a filter object. If a program detects that a filter object implements one of those interfaces, it can use the interface to provide additional information to the filter.

JAVA API USAGE

The `java.io` package includes the `FilterReader` class that participates in the Filter pattern as an abstract source filter class. The corresponding abstract source class is Reader. Concrete subclasses of the FilterReader class include BufferedReader, FileReader and LineNumberReader.

The java.io package includes the FilterWriter class, which participates in the Filter pattern as an abstract sink filter class. The corresponding abstract sink class is Writer. Concrete subclasses of the FilterWriter class include BufferedWriter, FileWriter and PrintWriter.

Here is a common arrangement of FilterReader objects for a program that reads lines of text as commands and needs to track line numbers for producing error messages:

```
LineNumberReader in;
void init(String fName) {
    FileReader fin;
        try {
            fin = new FileReader (fName);
            in = new LineNumberReader(new BufferedReader (fin));
        } catch (FileNotFoundException e) {
            System.out.println("Unable to open "+fName);
            ...
        }
    ...
```

CODE EXAMPLE

For an example of classes that implement the Filter pattern, here are classes that read and filter a stream of bytes. First is a class that participates in the Filter pattern as an abstract source:

```
public abstract class InStream {
    /**
     * Read bytes from a stream of bytes and put them in an array.
     */
    public abstract int read(byte[] array) throws IOException;
} // class InStream
```

Second is a concrete subclass of InStream that participates in the Filter pattern as a concrete source:

```
/**
 * This class reads a stream of bytes from a file.
 */
public class FileInStream extends InStream {
    private RandomAccessFile file;

    /**
     * Constructor
```

```
    * @param fName The name of the file to read
    */
   public FileInStream(String fName) throws IOException {
       file = new RandomAccessFile (fName, "r");
   } // Constructor (String)
   /**
    * Read bytes from a file and fill an array with those bytes.
    */
   public int read(byte[] array) throws IOException {
       return file.read(array);
   } // read(byte[])
} // class FileInStream
```

The following class participates in the Filter pattern as an abstract source filter:

```
public class FilterInStream extends InStream {
   private InStream inStream;
   /**
    * Constructor
    * @param inStream The InStream that this object should delegate
    *                 read operations to.
    */
   public FilterInStream(InStream inStream) throws IOException {
       this.inStream = inStream;
   } // Constructor(InStream)

   /**
    * Read bytes from a stream of bytes and fill an array with those
    * bytes.
    */
   public int read(byte[] array) throws IOException {
       return inStream.read(array);
   } // read(byte[])
} // class FilterInStream
```

Next are some classes that participate in the Filter pattern as a concrete source filter. The first of these performs the simple analysis of counting the number of bytes it has read:

```
public class ByteCountInStream extends FilterInStream {
   private long byteCount = 0;

   /**
    * Constructor
    * @param inStream The InStream that this object should
    * delegate read operations to.
    */
   public byteCountInStream(InStream inStream)
       throws IOException {
```

```
        super(inStream);
    } // Constructor(InStream)


    /**
     * Read bytes from a stream of bytes into an array.
     */
    public int read(byte[] array) throws IOException {
        int count;
        count = super.read(array);
        if (count >0)
          byteCount += count;
        return count;
    } // read(byte[])


    /**
     * return the number of bytes this object has read.
     */
    public long getByteCount() {
        return byteCount;
    } // getByteCount()
} // class ByteCountInStream
```

Finally, here is a filter class that performs character code translations on a stream of bytes:

```
/**
 * This class treats bytes in a byte stream as eight bit character
 * codes and translates them to other character codes using a
 * translation table.
 */
public class TranslateInStream extends FilterInStream {
    private byte[] translationTable;
    private final static int TRANS_TBL_LENGTH = 256;


    /**
     * Constructor
     * @param inStream The InStream that this object should
     * delegate read operations to.
     * @param table An array of bytes used to determine translation
     *        values for character codes. The value to replace
     *        character code n with is at index n of the translation
     *        table. If the array is longer than TRANS_TBL_LENGTH
     *        elements, the additional elements are ignored. If the
     *        array is shorter than TRANS_TBL_LENGTH elements, then
     *        no translation is done on character codes greater
     *        than or equal to the length of the array.
     */
    public TranslateInStream(InStream inStream,
                             byte[] table) throws IOException {
        super(inStream);
```

```
        // Create translation table by copying translation data.
        translationTable = new byte[TRANS__TBL_LENGTH];
        System.arraycopy(table, 0, translationTable, 0,
                        Math.min(TRANS_TBL_LENGTH, table.length));
        for (int i = table.length; i < TRANS_TBL_LENGTH; i++) {
            translationTable[i] = (byte)i;
        } // for
    } // Constructor(InStream)

    public int read(byte[] array) throws IOException {
        int count;
        count = super.read(array);
        for (int i = 0; i < count; i++) {
            array[i] = translationTable[array[i]];
        } // for
        return count;
    } // read(byte[])
} // class ByteCountInStream
```

RELATED PATTERNS

Composite   The Composite pattern can be an alternative to the Filter
pattern when the objects involved do not have a consistent interface and
they can be composed statically.

Layered Architecture   The Layered Architecture pattern (described in
Volume 2) is similar to the Filter pattern. The most important difference
is that the objects involved in the Layered Architecture pattern correspond to different levels of abstraction.

Pipe   The Pipe pattern is sometimes an alternative to the Filter pattern
and is sometimes used with the Filter pattern.

This book does not contain a chapter for the Pipe pattern. Like the
Filter pattern, the Pipe pattern allows an object that is a data source to
send a stream of data to an object that is a data sink. Instead of the
movement of data being initiated by the source or the sink object, they
operate asynchronously of each other. The data source object puts data
in a buffer when it wants to. The data sink gets data from the buffer
when it wants to. If the buffer is empty when the data sink tries to get
data from it, the data sink waits until there is data in the buffer.

Decorator   The Filter pattern is a special case of the Decorator pattern,
in which a data source or data sink object is wrapped to add logic to the
handling of a data stream.

Composite [GoF95]

The Composite pattern is also known as the Recursive Composition pattern.

The following description of the Composite pattern describes it in terms of recursively building a composite object from other objects. It appears in this chapter because the Recursive Composition pattern is often used to recursively decompose a complex object during the design process.

SYNOPSIS

The Composite pattern allows you to build complex objects by recursively composing similar objects in a treelike manner. The Composite pattern also allows the objects in the tree to be manipulated in a consistent manner, by requiring all of the objects in the tree to have a common superclass or interface.

CONTEXT

Suppose that you are writing a document formatting program. It formats characters into lines of text, which are organized into columns, which are organized into pages. However, a document may contain other elements. Columns and pages can contain frames, which can contain columns. Columns, frames, and lines of text can contain images. Figure 6.7 shows a class diagram that demonstrates those relationships.

As you can see, there is a fair amount of complexity here. Page and Frame objects must know how to handle and combine two kinds of elements. Column objects must know how to handle and combine three kinds of elements. The Composite pattern removes that complexity by allowing these objects to know how to handle only one kind of element. It accomplishes this by insisting that document element classes all have a common superclass. Figure 6.8 shows how you can simplify the document element class relationships by using the Composite pattern.

Applying the Composite pattern introduces a common superclass for all document elements and a common superclass for all the document con-

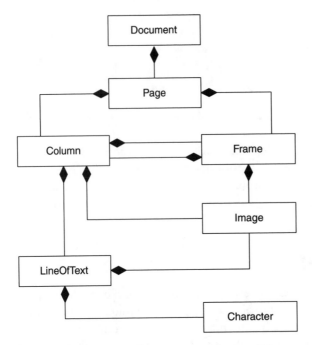

FIGURE 6.7 Document container relationships.

tainer classes. Doing so reduces the number of aggregation relationships to one. Management of the aggregation is now the responsibility of the `CompositeDocumentElement` class. The concrete container classes (`Document`, `Page`, `Column`,) now need to understand how to combine only one kind of element.

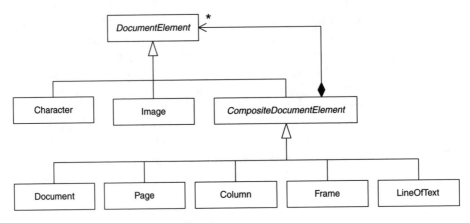

FIGURE 6.8 Document composite.

FORCES

- You have a complex object that you want to decompose into a part-whole hierarchy of objects.
- You want to minimize the complexity of the part-whole hierarchy by minimizing the number of different kinds of child objects that objects in the tree need to be aware of.

SOLUTION

Minimize the complexity of a composite object organized into part-whole hierarchies by providing an abstract superclass for all objects in the hierarchy and an abstract superclass for all composites in the hierarchy. The class relationships for such an organization look like Figure 6.9.

Here are the descriptions for the classes that participate in the Recursive Composition pattern:

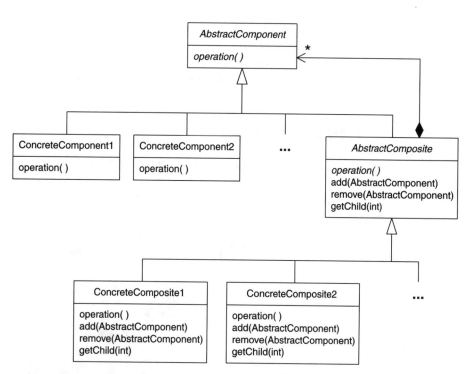

FIGURE 6.9 Composite class relationships.

AbstractComponent `AbstractComponent` is an abstract class and is the common superclass of all of the objects that are in the tree of objects that make up a composite object. Composite objects normally treat the objects that they contain as instances of `AbstractComponent`. Clients of composite objects normally treat them as instances of `AbstractComponent`.

ConcreteComponent1,ConcreteComponent2,... Instances of these classes are used as leaves in the tree organization.

AbstractComposite `AbstractComposite` is the abstract superclass of all composite objects that participate in the Composite pattern. `AbstractComposite` defines and provides default implementations for methods for managing a composite object's components. The `add` method adds a component to a composite object. The `remove` method removes a component from a composite object. The `getChild` method returns a reference to a component object of a composite object.

ConcreteComposite1,ConcreteComposite2,... Instances of these classes are composite objects that use other instances of `AbstractComponent`.

Instances of these classes can be assembled in a tree-link manner, as shown in Figure 6.10.

Note that you don't need to have an abstract composite class if there is only one concrete composite class.

CONSEQUENCES

- You can create a tree-structured composite object that treats the objects that constitute it as instances of `AbstractComponent`, whether they are simple or composite objects.

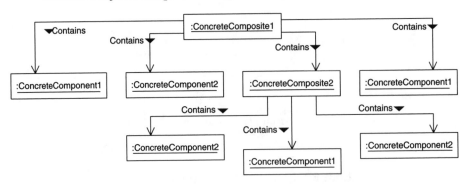

FIGURE 6.10 Composite object.

- Client objects of an `AbstractComponent` can simply treat it as an `AbstractComponent`, without having to be aware of any subclasses of `AbstractComponent`.
- If a client invokes a method of an `AbstractComponent` that is supposed to perform an operation and the `AbstractComponent` object is an `AbstractComposite` object, then it will delegate that operation to the `AbstractComponent` objects that constitute it. Similarly, if a client object calls a method of an `AbstractComponent` object that is *not* an `AbstractComposite` and the method requires some contextual information, then the `AbstractComponent` will delegate the request for contextual information to its parent.
- The Composite pattern allows any `AbstractComponent` to be a child of an `AbstractComposite`. If you need to enforce a more restrictive relationship, then you will have to add type-aware code to `AbstractComposite` or its subclasses. This reduces some of the value of the Composite pattern.
- Some components may implement operations that are unique to that component. For example, under the "Context" heading of this pattern is a design for the recursive composition of a document. At the lowest level, it has a document that consists of character and image elements. It's very reasonable for the character elements of a document to have a `getFont` method. A document's image elements have no need for a `getFont` method. The main benefit of the Composite pattern is that it allows the clients of a composite object and the objects that constitute it to remain unaware of the specific class of the objects they deal with. To allow other classes to call `getFont` without being aware of the specific class they are dealing with, all of the objects that can constitute a document can inherit the `getFont` method from `DocumentElement`. In general, when applying the Composite pattern the class in the role of the `AbstractComponent` class declares specialized methods if they are needed by any `ConcreteComponent` class.

    A principle of object-oriented design is that specialized methods should appear only in classes that need them. Normally, a class should have methods that provide related functionality and form a cohesive set. This principle is the essence of the High Cohesion pattern described in Volume 2. Putting a specialized method in a general-purpose class rather than the specialized class that needs the method is contrary to the principle of high cohesion, because it adds a method that is unrelated to the other methods of the general-purpose class. The unrelated method is inherited by subclasses of the general-purpose class that are unrelated to the method.

Because simplicity through ignorance of class is the basis of the Composite pattern, it's okay to sacrifice high cohesion for simplicity, when applying it.

IMPLEMENTATION

If classes that participate in the Composite pattern implement any operations by delegating them to their parent objects, then the best way to preserve speed and simplicity is by having each instance of `AbstractComponent` contain a reference to its parent. It is important to implement the parent pointer in a way that ensures consistency between parent and child. It must always be the case that an `AbstractComponent` identifies an `AbstractComposite` as its parent if and only if the `AbstractComposite` identifies it as one of its children. The best way to enforce this is to modify parent and child references only in the `AbstractComposite` class's add and remove methods.

Sharing components among multiple parents using the Flyweight pattern is a way to conserve memory. However, it is difficult for shared components to properly maintain parent references.

The `AbstractComposite` class may provide a default implementation of child management for composite objects. However, it is very common for concrete composite classes to override this implementation.

The Composite pattern is sometimes implemented with classes that do not share a common superclass, but do share a common interface.

If a concrete composite class delegates an operation to the objects that constitute it, then caching the result of the operation may improve performance. If a concrete composite class caches the result of an operation, then it is important that the objects that constitute the composite notify the composite object so that it can invalidate its cached values.

JAVA API USAGE

The `java.awt.swing` package contains a good example of the Composite pattern. Its `Component` class fills the `AbstractComponent` role. Its `Container` class fills the `AbstractComposite` role. It has a number of classes in the `ConcreteComponent` role, including `Label`, `TextField`, and `Button`. The classes in the `ConcreteComposite` role include `Panel`, `Frame`, and `Dialog`.

CODE EXAMPLE

The example for applying the Composite pattern is a more detailed version of the document-related classes that appear under the "Context" heading. Figure 6.11 shows a more detailed class diagram.

Figure 6.11 shows some of the methods that were left out of Figure 6.7. As you look through the following code, you will see that the `setFont` method is an example of a method that consults an object's parent object. The `getCharLength` method gathers information from an object's children and caches it for later use. The `changeNotification` method is used to invalidate cached information.

Here is the code for the `DocumentElement` class:

```
abstract class DocumentElement {
    // This is the font associated with this object. If font
    // is null, this object's font will be inherited from its parent.
    private Font font;

    CompositeDocumentElement parent; // this object's container
...
```

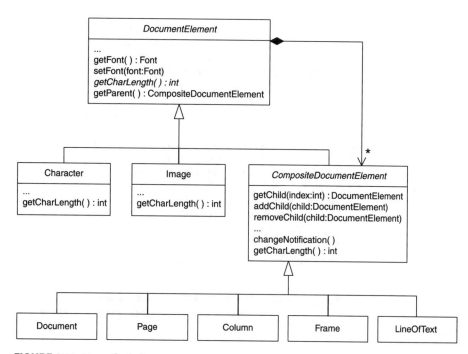

FIGURE 6.11 Detailed document composite.

```
    public CompositeDocumentElement getParent() {
        return parent;
    } // getParent()


    /**
     * Return the Font associated with this object. If there is
     * no Font associated with this object, then return the Font
     * associated with this object's parent. If there is no Font
     * associated with this object's parent then return null.
     */
    public Font getFont() {
        if (font != null)
          return font;
        else if (parent != null)
          return parent.getFont();
        else
          return null;
    } // getFont()


    /**
     * Associate a Font with this object.
     */
    public void setFont(Font font) {
        this.font = font;
    } // setFont(Font)


    /**
     * Return the number of characters that this object contains.
     */
    public abstract int getCharLength() ;
} // class DocumentElement
```

Here is the code for the CompositeDocumentElement class:

```
abstract class CompositeDocumentElement extends DocumentElement {
    // Collection of this object's children
    private Vector children = new Vector();

    // The value from the previous call to getCharLength or -1
    private int cachedCharLength = -1;

    /**
     * Return the child of this object that is at the given
     * position.
     */
    public DocumentElement getChild(int index) {
        return (DocumentElement)children.elementAt(index);
    } // getChild(int)

    /**
     * Make the given DocumentElement a child of this object.
```

```
        */
    public synchronized void addChild(DocumentElement child) {
        synchronized (child) {
            children.addElement(child);
            child.parent = this;
            changeNotification();
        } // synchronized
    } // addChild(DocumentElement)
    /**
     * Make the given DocumentElement NOT a child of this object.
     */
    public synchronized void removeChild(DocumentElement child) {
        synchronized (child) {
            if (this == child.parent)
              child.parent = null;
            children.removeElement(child);
            changeNotification();
        } // synchronized
    } // removeChild(DocumentElement)
...
    /**
     * A call to this method means a child of this object has
     * changed, invalidating any data cached in this object about
     * its children.
     */
    public void changeNotification() {
        cachedCharLength = -1;
        if (parent != null)
          parent.changeNotification();
    } // changeNotification()

    /**
     * Return the number of characters that this object contains.
     */
    public int getCharLength() {
        int len = 0;
        for (int i = 0; i < children.size(); i++) {
            DocumentElement child;
            child = (DocumentElement)children.elementAt(i);
            len += child.getCharLength();
        } // for
        cachedCharLength = len;
        return len;
    } // getCharLength()
} // class CompositeDocumentElement
```

The Character class implements `getCharLength` in the obvious way:

```
class Character extends DocumentElement {
...
    /**
```

```
        * Return the number of characters that this object contains.
        */
     public int getCharLength() {
         return 1;
     } // getCharLength()
} // class Character
```

The Image class is an example of a class that implements a method so that the other classes that constitute a document do not need to be aware of the `Image` class as requiring any special treatment. Its `getCharLength` method always returns 1, so that an image can be treated as just a big character.

```
class Image extends DocumentElement {
...
     public int getCharLength() {
         return 1;
     } // getCharLength()
} // class Image
```

The other classes in the class diagram that are subclasses of `CompositeDocumentElement` do not have any features that are interesting with respect to the Composite pattern. In the interest of brevity, just one of them is shown here:

```
class Page extends CompositeDocumentElement {
...
} // class Page
```

RELATED PATTERNS

Chain of Responsibility   The Chain of Responsibility pattern can be combined with the Composite pattern by adding child-to-parent links so that children can get information from an ancestor without having to know which ancestor the information came from.

High Cohesion   The High Cohesion pattern (described in Volume 2) discourages putting specialized methods in general-purpose classes, which is something that the Composite pattern encourages.

Visitor   You can use the Visitor pattern to encapsulate operations in a single class that would otherwise be spread across multiple classes.

C H A P T E R

Structural Patterns

The patterns in this chapter describe common ways that different types of objects can be organized to work with each other.

Adapter [GoF95]

SYNOPSIS

An Adapter class implements an interface known to its clients and provides access to an instance of a class not known to its clients. An adapter object provides the functionality promised by an interface without having to assume what class is used to implement that interface.

CONTEXT

Suppose that you are writing a method that copies an array of objects, filtering out objects that don't meet certain criteria. To promote reuse, you would like to make the method independent of the actual filtering criteria used. You can achieve this by defining an interface that declares a method that the array copier calls to find out if it should include a particular object in the new array, as shown in Figure 7.1.

In Figure 7.1, an `ArrayCopier` class uses instances of classes that implement the `CopyFilterIF` interface to decide if it should copy an element of the old array to the new array. If the `isCopyable` method returns true for an object, then that object is copied to the new array.

This solution solves the immediate problem of allowing the copy criteria used by the array copier to be encapsulated in a separate object with-

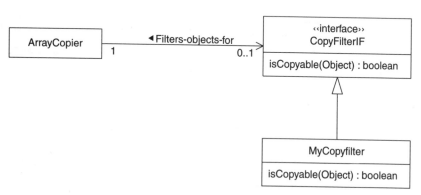

FIGURE 7.1 Simple copy filter.

out concern about what the object's class is. This solution also presents a different problem—filtering logic is in a different object than the objects that are filtered. Sometimes the logic needed for the filtering is in a method of the objects to be filtered. If those objects don't implement the CopyFilterIF interface, then there is no way for the array copier to directly ask those objects if they should be copied. However, it's possible for the array copier to indirectly ask the filtered objects if they should be copied, even if they don't implement the CopyFilterIF interface.

Suppose there's a class called Document that has a method called isValid that returns a boolean result. Suppose that you need to use the result of the isValid method to perform the filtering for a copy operation. Because Document does not implement the CopyFilterIF interface, an ArrayCopier object cannot directly use a document object for filtering. A class that implements the CopyFilterIF interface but tries to indepen-dently determine if a Document object should be copied into a new array does not work. It doesn't work because it has no way to retrieve the neces-sary information without calling the Document object's isValid method. The answer is for that object to call the Document object's isValid method, resulting in the solution shown in Figure 7.2.

In this solution, the ArrayCopier object calls the isCopyable method of an object that implements the CopyFilterIF interface, as it always does. In this case, that object is an instance of a class called DocumentCopyFilterAdapter. The DocumentCopyFilterAdapter class implements the isCopyable method by calling the Document object's isValid method.

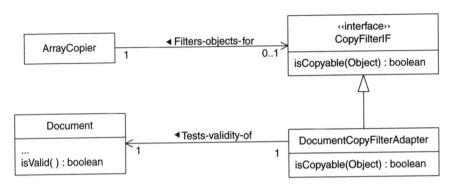

FIGURE 7.2 Copy filter adapter.

FORCES

- You want to use a class that calls a method through an interface, but you want to use it with a class that does not implement that interface. Modifying that class to implement the interface is not an option for a couple of reasons:

  1. You don't have the source code for the class.
  2. The class is a general-purpose class, and it's inappropriate for it to implement an interface for a specialized purpose.

- You want to dynamically determine which methods of another object that an object calls. You want to accomplish that without the calling object having knowledge of the other object's class.

SOLUTION

Suppose that you have a class that calls a method through an interface. You want an instance of that class to call a method of an object that does not implement the interface. You can arrange for the instance to make the call through an adapter object that implements the interface with a method that calls a method of the object that doesn't implement the interface. Figure 7.3 shows a class diagram that demonstrates this organization.

Here are the roles that the classes and the interface play in Figure 7.3:

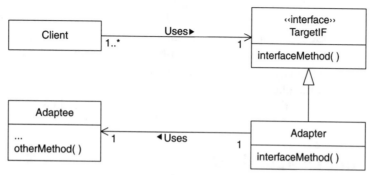

FIGURE 7.3 Adapter.

Client   This is a class that calls a method of another class through an interface in order that it need not assume that the object it calls the method through belongs to a specific class.

TargetIF   This interface declares the method that a `Client` class calls.

Adapter   This class implements the `TargetIF` interface. It implements the method that the client calls by having it call a method of the `Adaptee` class, which does not implement the `TargetIF` interface.

Adaptee   This class does not implement the `TargetIF` method but has a method that you want the Client class to call.

It's possible for an adapter class to do more than simply delegate the method call. It may perform some transformation on the arguments. It may provide additional logic to hide differences between the intended semantics of the interface's method and the actual semantics of the adaptee class's method. There is no limit to how complex an adapter class can be. So long as the essential purpose of the class is as an intermediary for method calls to one other object, you can consider it to be an adapter class.

CONSEQUENCES

- The client and adaptee classes remain independent of each other.
- The Adapter pattern introduces an additional indirection into a program. Like any other indirection, it contributes to the difficulty involved in understanding the program.
- You can use an adapter class to determine which of an object's methods another object calls. For example, suppose you have a class whose instances are GUI widgets that allow telephone numbers to be displayed and edited. This class fetches and stores telephone numbers by calling methods defined by an interface. To make use of the interface, you define adapter classes. You may have an adapter class to fetch and store a FAX number from instances of a class and another adapter class to fetch and store pager numbers from instances of the same class. The difference between the two adapter classes is that they call different methods of the `Adaptee` class.

IMPLEMENTATION

Implementation of the adapter class is rather straightforward. However, an issue that you should consider when implementing the Adapter pattern is how the adapter objects know what instance of the adaptee class to call. There are two approaches:

1. Pass a reference to the client object as a parameter to the adapter object's constructor or one of its methods. This allows the adapter object to be used with any instance or possibly multiple instances of the adaptee class. This approach is illustrated in the following example:

```
class CustomerBillToAdapter implements AddressIF {
    private Customer myCustomer;

    public CustomerBillToAdapter(Customer customer) {
        myCustomer = customer;
    } // constructor

    public String getAddress1() {
    return myCustomer.getBillToAddress1();
    } // get Address1()

    public void setAddress1(String address1) {
        myCustomer.setBillToAddress1(address1);
    } // setAddress1(String)
    ...
} // class CustomerBillToAdapter
```

2. Make the adapter class an inner class of the adaptee class. This simplifies the association between the adapter object and the adaptee object by making it automatic. It also makes the association inflexible. This approach is illustrated in the following example:

```
MenuItem exit = new MenuItem(caption);
exit.addActionListener(new ActionListener() {
    public void actionPerformed(ActionEvent evt) {
        close();
    } // actionPerformed(ActionEvent)
} );
```

JAVA API USAGE AND CODE EXAMPLE

A very common way to use adapter classes with the Java API is for event handling, like this:

```
Button ok = new Button("OK");
ok.addActionListener(new ActionListener() {
```

```
    public void actionPerformed(ActionEvent evt) {
        doIt();
    } // actionPerformed(ActionEvent)
  } );
add(ok);
```

The preceding code example creates an instance of an anonymous class that implements the `ActionListener` interface. The Button object calls that class's `actionPerformed` method when the button is pressed. This coding pattern is very common for code that handles events.

The Java API does not include any public adapter objects that are ready to use. It does include classes such as `java.awt.event.WindowAdapter` that are intended to be subclassed rather than used directly. The idea is that there are some event listener interfaces, such as `WindowListener`, that declare multiple methods. In many cases not all of the methods need to be implemented. The `WindowListener` interface declares eight methods that are called to provide notification about eight different kinds of window events. Often only one or two of those event types are of interest. The methods that correspond to the events that are not of interest typically are given do-nothing implementations. The `WindowAdapter` class implements the `WindowListener` interface and implements all eight of its methods with do-nothing implementations. An adapter class that subclasses the `WindowAdapter` class needs to implement only the methods that correspond to events that are of interest. It inherits do-nothing implementations for the rest. For example:

```
addWindowListener(new WindowAdapter() {
    public void windowClosing(WindowEvent e) {
        exit();
    } // windowClosing(WindowEvent)
  } );
```

In this code example, the anonymous adapter class is a subclass of the `WindowAdapter` class. It implements only the `windowClosing` method. It inherits do-nothing implementations for the other seven methods from the `WindowAdapter` class.

RELATED PATTERNS

Façade　The Adapter class provides an object that acts as an intermediary for method calls between client objects and *one other* object not known to the client objects. The Façade pattern provides an object that acts as an intermediary for method calls between client objects and *multiple* objects not known to the client objects.

Iterator　The Iterator pattern is a specialized version of the Adapter pattern for sequentially accessing the contents of collection objects.

Proxy　The Proxy pattern, like the Adapter pattern, uses an object that is a surrogate for another object. However, a Proxy object has the same interface as the object for which it is a surrogate.

Strategy　The Strategy pattern is structurally similar to the Adapter pattern. The difference is in the intent. The Adapter pattern allows a `Client` object to carry out its originally intended function in collaboration by calling the method of objects that implement a particular interface. The Strategy pattern provides objects that implement a particular interface for the purpose of altering or determining the behavior of a `Client` object.

Iterator [GoF95]

SYNOPSIS

The Iterator pattern defines an interface that declares methods for sequentially accessing the objects in a collection. A class that accesses a collection only through such an interface remains independent of the class that implements the interface.

CONTEXT

Suppose that you are writing some classes that will allow someone to browse the inventory of a warehouse. There will be a user interface that allows a user to see the description, quantity on hand, location, and other information about each inventory item.

The inventory browsing classes will be part of a very customizable application. For that reason, they must be independent of the actual class that provides the collections of inventory items. To provide this independence, you design an interface that allows the user interface to sequentially access a collection of inventory items without having to be aware of the actual collection class being used. The class diagram shown in Figure 7.4 shows the relevant part of the design.

In the diagram above, the user interface classes that constitute the inventory browser are shown as the composite class `InventoryBrowser`. An instance of the `InventoryBrowser` class is asked to display `InventoryItem` objects that are in the collection encapsulated by an `InventoryCollection` object. The `InventoryBrowser` object does not directly access the `InventoryCollection` object. Instead, it is given an object that implements the `InventoryIteratorIF` interface. The `InventoryIteratorIF` interface defines methods to allow an object to sequentially fetch the contents of a collection of `InventoryItem` objects.

FORCES

■ A class needs access to the contents of a collection without becoming dependent on the class that is used to implement the collection.

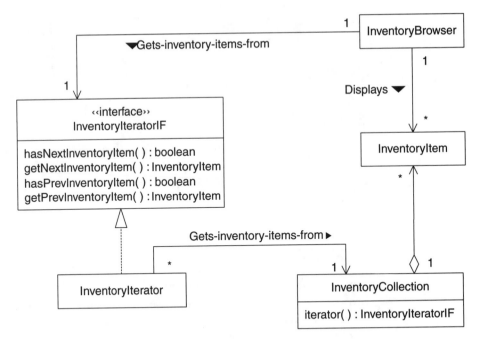

FIGURE 7.4 Inventory Iterator.

- A class needs a uniform way of accessing the contents of multiple collections.

SOLUTION

The class diagram in Figure 7.5 shows the organization of the classes and interfaces that participate in the Iterator pattern.

Here are descriptions of the roles that classes and interfaces play in the above organization:

Collection   A class in this role encapsulates a collection of objects or values.

IteratorIF   An interface in this role defines methods to sequentially access the objects that are encapsulated by a `Collection` object.

Iterator   A class in this role implements an `IteratorIF` interface. Its instances provide sequential access to the contents of the `Collection` object associated with `Iterator` object.

CollectionIF   `Collection` classes normally take responsibility for creating their own iterator objects. It is convenient to have a consistent way

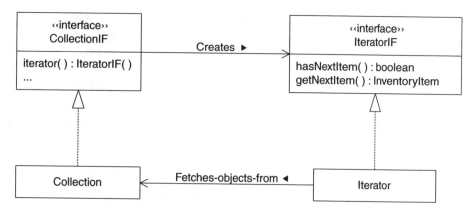

FIGURE 7.5 Iterator Pattern.

to ask a `Collection` object to create an iterator object for itself. To provide that consistency, all `Collection` classes implement a `CollectionIF` interface that declares a method for creating `Iterator` objects.

CONSEQUENCES

It is possible to access a collection of objects without knowing the source of the objects.

By using multiple iterator objects, it is simple to have and manage multiple transversals at the same time.

It is possible for a collection class to provide different kinds of iterator object that traverse the collection in different ways. For example, a collection class that maintains an association between key objects and value objects may have different methods for creating iterators that traverse just the key objects and for creating iterators that traverse just the value objects.

IMPLEMENTATION

The iterator interface shown in Figure 7.5 contains a minimal set of methods. It is common for iterator interfaces to define additional methods when they are useful and are supported by the underlying collection classes. In addition to methods for testing the existence of and fetching the next collection element, the following methods are common:

- Test for the existence of and fetch the previous collection element.
- Move to the first or last collection element.
- Get the number of elements in the traversal.

In many cases, an iterator class' traversal algorithm requires access to a collection class' internal data structure. For that reason, iterator classes are often implemented as a private inner class of a collection class.

A *null iterator* is an iterator that returns no objects. Its hasNext method always returns false. Null iterators are usually implemented as a simple class that implements the appropriate iterator interface. The use of null iterators can simplify the implementation of collection classes and other iterator classes by removing the need for some code that would otherwise be needed to handle the special case of a null traversal.

Modifications to a collection object while an iterator is traversing its contents can cause problems. If no provisions are made for dealing with such modifications, an iterator may return an inconsistent set of results. Such potential inconsistencies include skipping objects or returning the same object twice.

The simplest way of handling modifications to an underlying collection during a traversal by an iterator is to consider the iterator to be invalid after the modification. You can implement this by having each of a collection class' methods that modifies a collection increment a counter when they modify the collection. Iterator objects can then detect a change to their underlying collection by noticing a change in its change count. If one of the iterator object's methods is called and it notices that the underlying collection has changed, then it can throw an exception.

A more robust way to handling modifications to an underlying collection during a traversal by an iterator is to ensure that the iterator does return a consistent set of results. There are a number of ways to accomplish this. Though making a full copy of the underlying collection works in most cases, it is usually the least desirable technique because it is the most expensive in both time and memory.

JAVA API USAGE

The collection classes in the java.util package follow the Iterator pattern. The interface java.util.Collection plays the ConnectionIF role. The package includes a number of classes that implement java.util.Collection.

The `java.util.Iterator` interface plays the `IteratorIF` role. The classes in the package that implement `java.util.Collection` define private inner classes that implement `java.util.Iterator` and play the Iterator role.

CODE EXAMPLE

For a code example, we will look at some skeletal code that implements the design discussed under the "Context" heading. Below is a listing of the `InventoryIteratorIF` interface.

```
public interface InventoryIteratorIF {
    public boolean hasNextInventoryItem() ;
    public InventoryItem getNextInventoryItem() ;
    public boolean hasPrevInventoryItem() ;
    public InventoryItem getPrevInventoryItem() ;
} // interface InventoryIterator
```

Below is a skeletal listing of the `InventoryCollection` class. The listing includes the `iterator` method that other classes will use to get an object to iterate over the contents of an `InventoryCollection` object. It also includes the private class that the `iterator` method instantiates.

```
public class InventoryCollection {
    ...
    public InventoryIteratorIF iterator() {
        return new InventoryIterator();
    } // iterator()

    private class InventoryIterator implements InventoryIteratorIF {
        public boolean hasNextInventoryItem() {
            ...
        } // hasNextInventoryItem()

        public InventoryItem getNextInventoryItem() {
            ...
        } // getNextInventoryItem()

        public boolean hasPrevInventoryItem() {
            ...
        } // hasPrevInventoryItem()

        public InventoryItem getPrevInventoryItem() {
            ...
        } // getPrevInventoryItem()
```

```
        } // class InventoryIterator
    ...
} // class InventoryCollection
```

RELATED PATTERNS

Adapter   The Iterator pattern is a specialized form of the Adapter pattern for sequentially accessing the contents of collection objects.

Factory Method   Some collection classes may use the Factory Method pattern to determine what kind of iterator to instantiate.

Null Object   Null iterators are sometimes used to implement the Null Object pattern.

Bridge [GoF95]

SYNOPSIS

The Bridge pattern is useful when there is a hierarchy of abstractions and a corresponding hierarchy of implementations. Rather than combining the abstractions and implementations into many distinct classes, the Bridge pattern implements the abstractions and implementations as independent classes that can be combined dynamically.

CONTEXT

Suppose that you need to supply Java classes that provide access to sensors for control applications. These are devices such as scales, speed-measuring devices, and location-sensing devices. What these devices have in common is that they perform a physical measurement and produce a number at the request of a computer. One way that these devices differ is in the type of measurements that they produce.

- The scale produces a single number based on a measurement at a single point in time.
- The speed-measuring device produces a single measurement that is an average over a period of time.
- The location-sensing device produces a stream of measurements.

This suggests that these devices can be supported by three classes that support these different measurement techniques, as shown in Figure 7.6.

The three classes shown in Figure 7.6 provide clean abstractions that can apply to many other types of sensors in addition to the three that inspired them. Since there are other kinds of sensors that produce simple measurements, time-averaged measurements, and streams of measurements, you want to be able to reuse these three classes for those kinds of sensors as well. A difficulty in achieving such reuse is that the details for communicating with sensors from different manufacturers

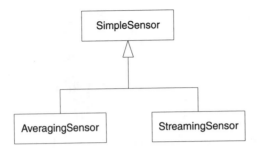

FIGURE 7.6 Sensor classes.

vary. Suppose the software that you are writing needs to work with sensors from two manufacturers called Eagle and Hawk. You can handle this problem by having manufacturer-specific classes like those shown in Figure 7.7.

The problem with this solution is not just that it doesn't reuse classes for simple, averaging, and streaming sensors. It also exposes the differences between manufacturers to other classes. In other words, it forces other classes to recognize the differences between manufacturers, which makes them less reusable. The challenge here is to represent a hierarchy of abstractions in a way that keeps the abstractions independent of their implementations.

A way to accomplish this is to shield a hierarchy of classes that support abstractions from classes that implement those abstractions by having the abstraction classes access implementation classes through a hierarchy of implementation interfaces that parallels the abstraction hierarchy (see Figure 7.8).

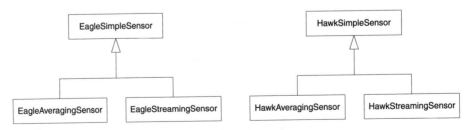

FIGURE 7.7 Manufacturer-specific sensor classes.

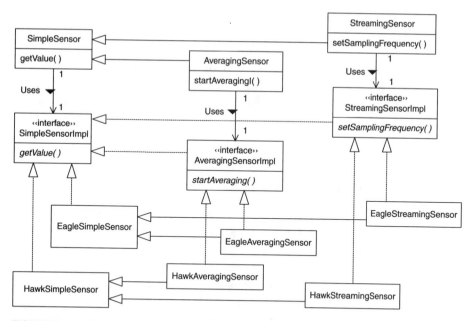

FIGURE 7.8 Independent sensor and sensor manufacturer classes.

The solution shown in Figure 7.8 divides the problem into three hierarchies:

1. There is a hierarchy for manufacturer-independent sensor classes shown with bold boxes—SimpleSensor, AveragingSensor, and StreamingSensor.
2. There is a parallel hierarchy of manufacturer-specific classes shown in dark gray boxes—SimpleSensorImpl, AveragingSensorImpl, and StreamingSensorImpl.
3. There is a parallel hierarchy of interfaces, shown in light gray boxes, that allow the manufacturer-independent classes to remain independent of any manufacturer-specific classes.

Any logic that is common to the type of sensor goes in a manufacturer-independent class. Logic that is specific to a manufacturer goes in a manufacturer-specific class.

Most of the logic that we're talking about in this example is for handling exceptional conditions. An example of such a condition is when a simple sensor detects an out-of-range value that is too large for it to measure. Manufacturer-independent handling for that condition could be to translate the value to a predetermined maximum value for the application. Manufacturer-specific handling for that condition might require not considering any readings from the sensor to be valid until a certain amount of time has elapsed after the end of the out-of-range condition.

FORCES

- When you combine hierarchies of abstractions and hierarchies of their implementations into a single class hierarchy, classes that use those classes become tied to a specific implementation of the abstraction. Changing the implementation used for an abstraction should not require changes to the classes that use the abstraction.
- You want to reuse logic common to different implementations of an abstraction. The usual way to make logic reusable is to encapsulate it in a separate class.
- You want to create a new implementation of an abstraction without having to reimplement the common logic of the abstraction.
- You want to extend the common logic of an abstraction by writing one new class rather than writing a new class for each combination of the base abstraction and its implementation.
- When appropriate, multiple abstractions should share the same implementation.

SOLUTION

The Bridge pattern allows classes that correspond to abstractions to be separate from classes that implement those abstractions. You can maintain a clean separation by having the abstraction classes access the implementation classes through interfaces that are in a hierarchy that parallels the inheritance hierarchy of the abstraction classes, as shown in Figure 7.9.

Here are descriptions of the roles the classes and interfaces play in the Bridge pattern class diagram shown in Figure 7.9:

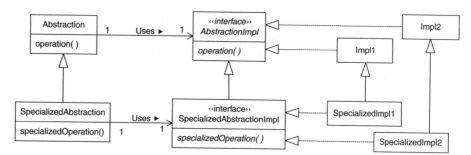

FIGURE 7.9 Bridge pattern.

Abstraction This class represents the top-level abstraction. It is responsible for maintaining a reference to an object that implements the `AbstractionImpl` interface, so that it can delegate operations to its implementation. If an instance of the `Abstraction` class is also an instance of a subclass of the `Abstraction` class, then the instance will refer to an object that implements the corresponding subinterface of the `AbstractionImpl` interface.

SpecializedAbstraction This role corresponds to any subclass of the `Abstraction` class. For each such subclass of the `Abstraction` class there is a corresponding subinterface of the `AbstractionImpl` interface. Each `SpecializedAbstraction` class delegates its operations to an implementation object that implements the interface that corresponds to the `SpecializedAbstraction` class.

AbstractionImpl This interface declares methods for all of the low-level operations that an implementation for the `Abstraction` class must provide.

SpecializedAbstractionImpl This corresponds to a subinterface of `AbstractionImpl`. Each `SpecializedAbstractionImpl` interface corresponds to a `SpecializedAbstraction` class and declares methods for the low-level operations needed for an implementation of that class.

Impl1, Impl2 These classes implement the `AbstractionImpl` interface and provide different implementations for the `Abstraction` class.

SpecializedImpl1, SpecializedImpl2 These classes implement one of the `SpecializedAbstractionImpl` interfaces and provide different implementations for a `SpecializedAbstraction` class.

In the diagrams shown in Figures 7.8 and 7.9, the abstraction implementation interfaces have the same methods as the corresponding abstraction classes. This is just a convenience for presentation purposes. It's possible for abstraction implementation interfaces to have different methods than the corresponding abstraction classes

CONSEQUENCES

The Bridge pattern keeps the classes that represent an abstraction independent of the classes that supply an implementation for the abstraction. The abstraction and its implementations are organized into separate class hierarchies. You can extend each class hierarchy without directly impacting another class hierarchy. It is also possible to have multiple implementation classes for an abstraction class or multiple abstraction classes using the same implementation class.

Classes that are clients of the abstraction classes don't possess any knowledge of the implementation classes, so an abstraction object can change its implementation without any impact on its clients.

IMPLEMENTATION

One issue that you always must decide when implementing the Bridge pattern is how to create implementation objects for each abstraction object. The most basic decision is whether abstraction objects create their own implementation objects or delegate the creation of their implementation objects to another object.

The best choice is usually to have the abstraction objects delegate the creation of implementation objects. It preserves the independence of the abstraction and implementation classes. If abstraction classes are designed to delegate the creation of implementation objects, then the design usually uses the Abstract Factory pattern to create the implementation objects.

However, if there are only a small number of implementation classes for an abstract class and the set of implementation classes is not expected to change, then a reasonable optimization is to have the abstraction classes create their own implementation objects.

A related decision is whether an abstraction object will use the same implementation object during its lifetime. As usage patterns or other conditions change, it may be appropriate to change the implementation object that an abstraction object uses. If an abstraction class directly creates its own implementation objects, then it's reasonable to directly embed the logic for changing the implementation object in the abstraction class. Otherwise, you can use the Decorator pattern to encapsulate the logic for switching implementation objects in a wrapper class.

JAVA API USAGE

The Java API includes the package `java.awt`. That package contains the `Component` class. The `Component` class is an abstract class that encapsulates logic common to all GUI components. The `Component` class has subclasses such as `Button`, `List`, and `TextField` that encapsulate the logic for those GUI components that are platform independent. The package `java.awt.peer` contains interfaces such as `ComponentPeer`, `ButtonPeer`, `ListPeer`, and `TextFieldPeer` that declare methods required for implementation classes that provide platform specific support for the subclasses of the `Component` class.

The subclasses of the `Component` class use the Abstract Factory pattern to create their implementation objects. The `java.awt.Toolkit` class is an abstract class that plays the role of abstract factory. The platform supplies the concrete factory class used to instantiate the implementation classes and the implementation classes.

CODE EXAMPLE

For an example of the Bridge pattern, let's look at some code to implement the sensor-related classes that we discussed under the "Context" heading. Assume that the objects that represent sensors and their implementations are created with a Factory Method. The Factory Method object knows what sensors are available, knows what objects to create to provide access to a sensor, and creates those objects when access to a sensor is first requested.

Here is the code for the `SimpleSensor` class that plays the role of abstraction class:

```
public class SimpleSensor {
    // The object that implements operations specific to
    // the actual sensor device that this object represents.
    private SimpleSensorImpl impl;
    /**
     * @param impl Object that implements type-specific operations.
     */
    SimpleSensor(SimpleSensorImpl impl) {
        this.impl = impl;
    } // constructor(SimpleSensorImpl)


    protected SimpleSensorImpl getImpl() {
        return impl;
    } // getImpl()
...
    /**
     * Return the value of the sensor's current measurement.
     */
    public int getValue() throws SensorException {
        return impl.getValue();
    } // getValue()
} // class SimpleSensor
```

As you can see, the `SimpleSensor` class is simple in that it does little more than delegate its operations to an object that implements the `SimpleSensorImpl` interface. Here is the code for the `SimpleSensorImpl` interface:

```
interface SimpleSensorImpl {
    /**
     * Return the value of the sensor's current measurement.
     */
    public int getValue() throws SensorException;
} // interface SimpleSensorImpl
```

Some subclasses of the `SimpleSensor` class maintain the same simple structure. Following is code for the `AveragingSensor` class. Instances of the `SimpleSensor` class represent sensors that produce values that are the average of measurements made over a period of time.

```
public class AveragingSensor extends SimpleSensor {
    /**
     * @param impl Object that implements sensor type-specific
     * operations.
     */
    AveragingSensor(AveragingSensorImpl impl) {
        super(impl);
    } // constructor(AveragingSensorImpl)
...
    /**
     * Averaging sensors produce a value that is the average of
     * measurements made over a period of time. That period of time
     * begins when this method is called.
     */
    public void beginAverage() throws SensorException {
        ((AveragingSensorImpl)getImpl()).beginAverage();
    } // beginAverage()
} // class AveragingSensor
```

As you can see, the AveragingSensor class is also very simple, delegating its operations to the implementation objects that it is using. Here is its corresponding implementation interface:

```
interface AveragingSensorImpl extends SimpleSensorImpl {
    /**
     * Averaging sensors produce a value that is the average of
     * measurements made over a period of time. That period of time
     * begins when this method is called.
     */
    public void beginAverage() throws SensorException;
} // interface AveragingSensorImpl
```

It's reasonable for subclasses of the SimpleSensorImpl class to be more complex and provide additional services of their own. The StreamingSensor class delivers a stream of measurements to objects that have registered to receive those measurements. It delivers those measurements by calling a method of the object it is delivering the measurement to. It does not place any requirements on how long that method may take before it returns. There is merely an expectation that the method will return in a reasonable amount of time. On the other hand, the implementation objects used with instances of the StreamingSensor class may need to deliver measurements at a steady rate or lose them. In order to avoid losing measurements, instances of the StreamingSensor class buffer measurements that are delivered to it, while it asynchronously delivers those measurements to other objects. Here is the code for the StreamingSensor class:

```
public class StreamingSensor extends SimpleSensor
                             implements StreamingSensorListener,
                                 Runnable


    // These objects are used to provide a buffer that allows the
    // implementation object to asynchronously deliver measurement values
    // while this object is delivering value it has already received
    // to its listeners.
    private DataInputStream consumer;
    private DataOutputStream producer;


    private Vector listeners = new Vector(); // aggregate listeners
    /**
     * @param impl The object that implements the sensor
     *              type-specific operations this object provides.
     */
    StreamingSensor(StreamingSensorImpl impl)
                    throws SensorException
    {
        super(impl);


        // Create pipe stream that supports this object's ability
        // to deliver measurement values at the same time it is
        // receiving them.
        PipedInputStream pipedInput = new PipedInputStream();
        consumer = new DataInputStream(pipedInput);
        PipedOutputStream pipedOutput;
        try {
            pipedOutput = new PipedOutputStream(pipedInput);
        } catch (IOException e) {
            throw new SensorException("pipe creation failed");
        } // try
        producer = new DataOutputStream(pipedOutput);


        // start a thread to deliver measurement values
        new Thread(this).start();
    } // constructor(StreamingSensorImpl)
    ...
    /**
     * Streaming sensors produce a stream of measurement values.
```

```
 * The stream of values is produced with a frequency no greater
 * than the given number of times per minute.
 * @param freq The maximum number of times per minute that this
 *              streaming sensor produces a measurement.
 */
public void setSamplingFrequency(int freq)
            throws SensorException {
    // delegate this to the implementation object
    ((StreamingSensorImpl)getImpl()).setSamplingFrequency(freq);
} // setSamplingFrequency(int)



/**
 * StreamingSensor objects deliver a stream of values to
 * interested objects by passing each value to the object's
 * processMeasurement method. The delivery of values is done
 * using its own thread and is asynchronous of everything else.
 * @param value The measurement value being delivered.
 */
public void processMeasurement(int value) {
    try {
        producer.writeInt(value);
    } catch (IOException e) {
        // If the value cannot be delivered, just discard it.
    } // try
} // processMeasurement(int)



/**
 * This method registers its argument as a recipient of future
 * measurement values from this sensor.
 */
public void
addStreamingSensorListener(StreamingSensorListener
                        listener) {
    listeners.addElement(listener);
} // addStreamingSensorListener(StreamingSensorListener)



/**
 * This method unregisters its argument as a recipient of future
 * measurement values from this sensor.
 */
public void
removeStreamingSensorListener(StreamingSensorListener listener) {
    listeners.removeElement(listener);
} // addStreamingSensorListener(StreamingSensorListener)



/**
 * This method asynchronously removes measurement values from
```

```
    * the pipe and delivers them to registered listeners.
    */
   public void run() {
      ...
   } // run()
} // class StreamingSensor
```

In order for the StreamingSensor class to deliver a measurement to an object, it requires that object to implement the StreamingSensorListener interface. It delivers measurements by passing them to the processMeasurement method that the StreamingSensorListener interface declares. The StreamingSensor class also implements the StreamingSensorListener interface. Implementation objects deliver measurements to instances of the StreamingSensor class by calling its processMeasurement method.

Finally, here is the implementation interface that corresponds to the StreamingSensor class:

```
interface StreamingSensorImpl extends SimpleSensorImpl {
   /**
    * Streaming sensors produce a stream of measurement values.
    * The stream of values is produced with a frequency no greater
    * than the given number of times per minute.
    * @param freq The maximum number of times per minute that this
    *             streaming sensor produces a measurement.
    */
   public void setSamplingFrequency(int freq)
            throws SensorException;


   /**
    * This method is called by an object that represents the
    * streaming sensor abstraction so this object can perform a
    * call-back to that object to deliver measurement values to it.
    * @param abstraction The abstraction object to deliver
    *                     measurement values to.
    */
   public void
   setStreamingSensorListener(StreamingSensorListener
listener);
} // interface StreamingSensorImpl
```

RELATED PATTERNS

Layered Architecture Analysis   The Bridge design pattern is a way of organizing the entities identified using the Layered Architecture pattern (described in Volume 2) into classes.

Abstract Factory/Toolkit   The Abstract Factory pattern can be used by the Bridge pattern to decide which implementation class to instantiate for an abstraction object.

Façade [GoF95]

SYNOPSIS

The Façade pattern simplifies access to a related set of objects by providing one object that all objects outside the set use to communicate with the set.

CONTEXT

Consider the organization of a set of classes that supports creating and sending e-mail messages. A set of classes for sending e-mail messages might include the following classes:

- A `MessageBody` class whose instances contain message bodies.
- An `Attachment` class whose instances contain message attachments that can be attached to a message body object.
- A `MessageHeader` class whose instances contain the header information (to, from, subject . . .) for an e-mail message.
- A `Message` class whose instances tie together a `MessageHeader` object and a `MessageBody` object.
- A `Security` class whose instances are used to add a digital signature to a message.
- A `MessageSender` class whose instances are responsible for sending `Message` objects to a server that is responsible for delivering the e-mail to its destination or another server.

Figure 7.10 shows a class diagram that demonstrates the relationships between these classes and a client class.

As you can see, working with these e-mail classes adds complexity to a client class. To work with these classes, a client must know about at least these six classes, the relationship between them, and the order in which it must create instances of those classes. If every client of these classes must take on that additional complexity, it will make the e-mail classes more difficult to reuse. The Façade pattern provides a way to shield clients of a set of classes—such as the e-mail classes—from the complexity of using those classes. The way that it does this is to provide an additional reusable object that hides most of the complexity of working with the other classes from

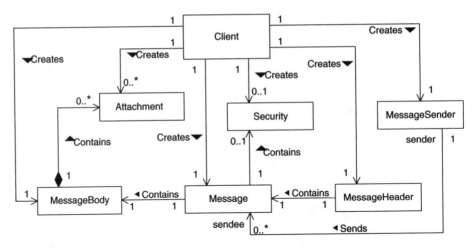

FIGURE 7.10 E-mail creation.

client classes. Figure 7.11 shows a class diagram that demonstrates this more reusable organization.

Client classes now have to be aware of only the `MessageCreator` class. Furthermore, the internal logic of the `MessageCreator` class can shield client classes from having to create the parts of an e-mail message in any particular order.

FORCES

- There are many dependencies between classes that implement an abstraction and their client classes. The dependencies add noticeable complexity to clients.
- You want to simplify the client classes. Simpler classes result in fewer bugs. Simpler clients also mean that less work is required to reuse the classes that implement the abstraction.
- Interposing a façade class between the classes that implement an abstraction and their clients simplifies client classes by moving dependencies from client classes to the façade class.
- It is not necessary for a façade class to be an impenetrable barrier separating the client classes from the classes that implement an abstraction. It is sufficient, and sometimes better, for a façade class to

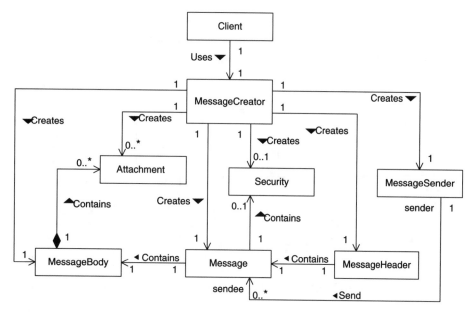

FIGURE 7.11 Reusable e-mail creation.

merely be a default way of accessing the functionality of the classes that implement an abstraction. If some clients need to access abstraction-implementing classes directly, then the façade class should facilitate that with a method that returns a reference to the appropriate implementation object. The point of the façade class is to allow simple clients, not require them.

SOLUTION

Figure 7.12 shows a class diagram that demonstrates the general structure of the Façade pattern.

The client object interacts with a façade object that provides the necessary functionality by interacting with the rest of the objects. If there is some additional functionality that is needed by only some clients, then instead of providing it directly, the façade object provides a method to access another object that does provide the functionality.

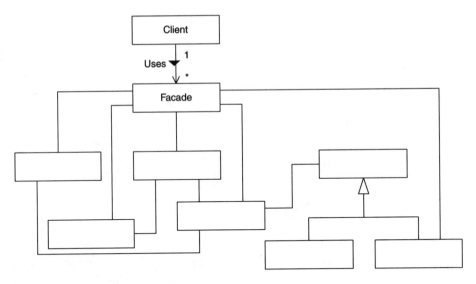

FIGURE 7.12 Façade pattern.

CONSEQUENCES

Clients of façade objects don't need to know about any of the classes behind the façade.

Because the Façade pattern reduces or eliminates the coupling between a client class and the classes that implement an abstraction, it may be possible to change the classes that implement the abstraction without any impact on the client class.

Client objects that need direct access to abstraction-implementing objects can access those objects.

IMPLEMENTATION

A façade class should provide a way for client objects to obtain a direct reference to an instance of some abstraction-implementing classes. However, there may be abstraction-implementing classes that client classes have no legitimate reason to know about. The façade class should hide those classes from client classes. One way to do this is to make those classes private inner classes of the façade class.

Sometimes you want to vary the implementation classes that a façade object uses to accommodate variations on the abstraction being implemented. For example, returning to the e-mail example under the context heading, you may need a different set of classes to create MIME-, MAP-, or Notes-compliant messages. Different sets of implementation classes usually require different façade classes. You can hide the use of different façade classes from client classes by applying the Interface pattern. Define an interface that all facade classes for e-mail creation must implement. Then have client classes access the façade class through an interface rather than directly.

JAVA API USAGE

The `java.net URL` class is an example of the Façade pattern. It provides access to the contents of URLs. A class can be a client of the URL class and use it to get the contents of a URL without being aware of the many classes that operate behind the façade provided by the URL class. On the other hand, to send data to a URL, the client of a URL object may call its `openConnection` method that returns the `URLConnection` object that the URL object uses.

CODE EXAMPLE

Following is the code for the `MessageCreator` class shown in the class diagram under the "Context" heading. Instances of the `MessageCreator` class are used to create and send e-mail messages. It is shown here as a typical example of a façade class.

```
public class MessageCreator {
    // Constants to indicate the type of message to create
    public final static int MIME = 1;
    public final static int MAPI = 2;
...
    private Hashtable headerFields = new Hashtable();
    private RichText messageBody;
    private Vector attachments = new Vector();
    private boolean signMessage;

    public MessageCreator(String to, String from, String subject) {
        this(to, from , subject, inferMessageType(to));
    } // Constructor(String, String, String)
```

```java
public MessageCreator(String to, String from, String subject,
            int type) {
    headerFields.put("to", to);
    headerFields.put("from", from);
    headerFields.put("subject", subject);
    ...
} // Constructor(String, String, String, int)


/**
 * Set the contents of the message body.
 */
public void setMessageBody(String messageBody) {
    setMessageBody(new RichTextString(messageBody));
} // setMessageBody(String)


/**
 * Set the contents of the message body.
 */
public void setMessageBody(RichText messageBody) {
    this.messageBody = messageBody;
} // setMessageBody(RichText)


/**
 * Add an attachment to the message
 */
public void addAttachment(Object attachment) {
    attachments.addElement(attachment);
} // addAttachment(Object)
/**
 * Set whether this message should be signed
 * The default is
false.
 */
public void setSignMessage(boolean signFlag) {
    signMessage = signFlag;
} // setSignMessage(boolean)


/**
 * Set the value of a header field.
 */
public void setHeaderField(String name, String value) {
    headerFields.put(name.toLowerCase(), value);
} // setHeaderField(String, String)


/**
 * Send the message.
 */
public void send() {
    ...
} // send()
```

```
      /**
       * Infer a message type from a destination e-mail address.
       */
      private static int inferMessageType(String address) {
          int type = 0;
...
          return type;
      } // inferMessageType(String)

      /**
       * Create a Security object for signing this message.
       */
      private Security createSecurity() {
          Security s = null;
...
          return s;
      } // createSecurity()

      /**
       * Create a MessageSender object appropriate for the type of
       * message being sent.
       */
      private void createMessageSender(Message msg) {
...
      } // createMessageSender(Message)
...} // class MessageCreator
```

The Façade pattern places no demands on the classes that the façade class uses. Since they contain nothing that contributes to the Façade pattern, their code is not shown here.

RELATED PATTERNS

Interface   You can use Interface pattern with the Façade pattern to allow using different sets of façade and implementation classes without having client classes be aware of the different classes.

Don't Talk to Strangers   A conceptual model that uses the Don't Talk to Strangers pattern (discussed in Volume 2) often gives rise to a design that follows the Façade pattern.

Flyweight [GoF95]

SYNOPSIS

If instances of a class that contain the same information can be used inter-changeably, the Flyweight pattern allows a program to avoid the expense of multiple instances that contain the same information by sharing one instance.

CONTEXT

Suppose that you are writing a word processor. Figure 7.13 presents a class diagram that shows the basic classes you might use to represent a document.

The class organization shown in Figure 7.13 includes the following classes:

- The DocumentElement class is the ultimate superclass for all classes used to represent a document. All subclasses of the DocumentElement class inherit methods to set and fetch their font.
- An instance of the DocChar class represents each character in a document.
- The DocumentContainer class is the superclass for container classes Document, Page, Paragraph, and LineOfText.

You can specify the font of each character by calling the setFont method of the DocChar object that represents it. If the character's font is unspecified, then it uses its container's font.

Given the structure shown in Figure 7.13, one document that is a few pages long can contain tens of Paragraph objects that contain a few hundred LineOfText objects and thousands or tens of thousands of DocChar objects. Clearly, using this design will result in a program that uses a lot of memory to store characters.

It's possible to avoid the memory overhead of those many character objects by having only one instance for each distinct Docchar object. The classes in Figure 7.13 use a DocChar object to represent each character in

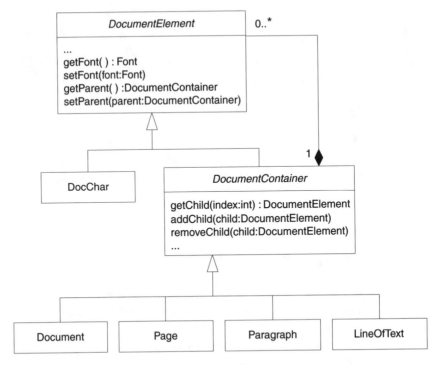

FIGURE 7.13 Document representation classes.

a document. To represent "She saw her father," a `LineOfText` object uses `DocChar` objects, as shown in Figure 7.14.

As you can see, the line uses the characters 'h', 'e', ' ', 'a' and 'e' a number of times. In an entire document, all of the characters typically occur many times. It's possible to reorganize the objects so that one `DocChar` object represents all occurrences of the same character, as shown in Figure 7.15.

In order to make the sharing of `DocChar` objects work, the `DocChar` objects cannot possess any intrinsic attributes that are not common to every place the object is referenced. An *intrinsic attribute* is an attribute whose value is stored within the object. This is distinct from an *extrinsic attribute,* whose value is stored outside of the object that it applies to.

The class organization shown in Figure 7.13 presents a `DocChar` class whose instances can have an intrinsic font attribute. Those `Character` objects that don't have a font stored intrinsically use the font of their paragraph.

To make the sharing of `DocChar` objects work, the classes need to be reorganized so that `DocChar` objects with their own font store them extrin-

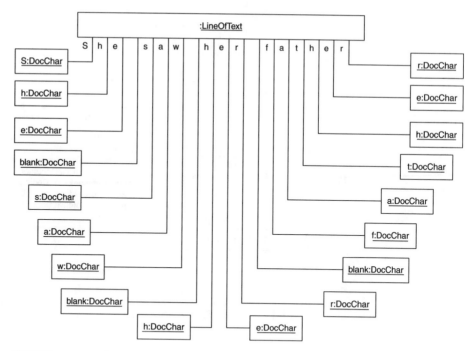

FIGURE 7.14 Unshared character objects.

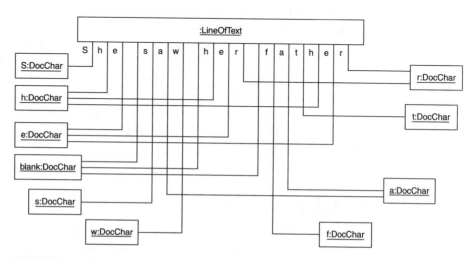

FIGURE 7.15 Shared character objects.

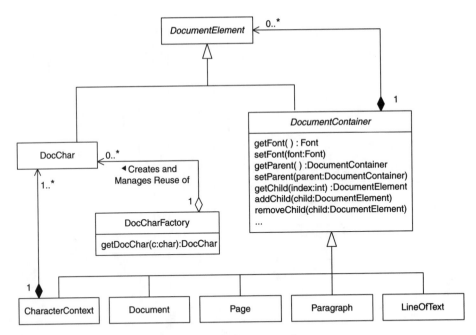

FIGURE 7.16 Document shared representation classes.

sically. Figure 7.16 includes a `CharacterContext` class whose instances store extrinsic attributes for a range of characters.

In this organization, the `DocCharFactory` class is responsible for providing a `DocChar` object that represents a given character. Given the same character to represent, a `DocCharFactory` object's `getDocChar` method will always return the same `DocChar` object. Also, the `DocumentContainer` class defines the font methods rather than the `DocumentElement` class. All the concrete classes are subclasses of the `DocumentContainer` class, except for the `DocChar` class. This means that the `DocChar` class does not have an intrinsic font attribute. If the user wants to associate a font with a character or range of characters, then the program creates a `CharacterContext` object that looks like Figure 7.17.

FORCES

- The primary motivation for using the Façade pattern is as an optimization for an application that uses a large number of similar objects.

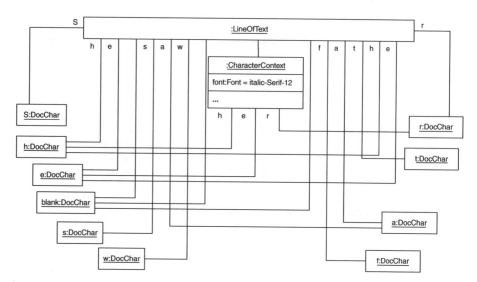

FIGURE 7.17 Font in CharacterContext.

- The program does not rely on the object identity of any of the objects that you want it to share. When a program uses different objects in different contexts, it is possible to distinguish between the contexts by the object identities of the objects. When different contexts share objects, then their object identities are no longer useful for distinguishing between contexts.
- It is possible, through object sharing, to reduce a large number of similar objects to a small number of shared unique objects.
- It is possible to further increase the level of sharing and reduce the number of objects by changing some of the intrinsic attributes of the unique shared object to extrinsic attributes.

SOLUTION

Figure 7.18 shows the general organization of classes for the Flyweight pattern.

Here are the descriptions of the roles that classes that participate in the Flyweight pattern play:

AbstractFlyweight   The `AbtractFlyweight` class is the superclass of all other flyweight classes. It defines the operations common to flyweight

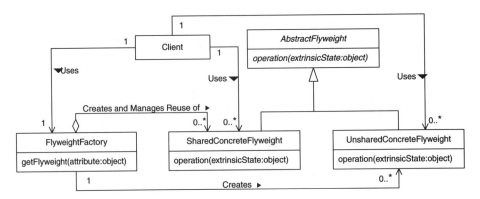

FIGURE 7.18 Flyweight pattern.

classes. Those operations that require access to extrinsic state information obtain it through parameters.

SharedConcreteFlyweight   Instances of classes in this role are sharable objects. If they contain any intrinsic state, it must be common to all of the entities that they represent. For example, the sharable DocChar objects from the example under the "Context" heading have the character that they represent as their intrinsic state.

UnsharedConcreteFlyweight   Instances of classes that participate in the UnsharedConcreteFlyweight are not sharable. The Flyweight pattern does not require the sharing of objects. It simply allows the sharing of objects. If there are unsharable objects that are instances of the AbstractFlyweight class, then they will typically be instances of different subclasses of the AbstractFlyweight class than objects that are sharable.

FlyweightFactory   Instances of FlyweightFactory classes provide instances of the AbstractFlyweight class to client objects. If a client object asks a FlyweightFactory object to provide an instance of an UnsharedConcreteFlyweight class, then it simply creates the instance. However, if a client object asks a FlyweightFactory object to provide an instance of a SharedConcreteFlyweight class, it first checks to see if it previously created a similar object. If it did previously create a similar object, then it provides the same object to the client object. Otherwise, it creates a new object and provides that to the client.

Client   Instances of Client classes are objects that use flyweight objects.

If there is only one class in the `SharedConcreteFlyweight` role, then it may be unnecessary to have any classes in the roles of `AbstractFlyweight` or `UnsharedConcreteFlyweight`.

CONSEQUENCES

The use of shared flyweight objects can drastically reduce the number of objects in memory. However, there is a price to pay for the reduced memory consumption, as listed here:

- The Flyweight pattern makes a program more complex. The major sources of additional complexity are providing flyweight objects with their extrinsic state and managing the reuse of flyweight objects.
- The Flyweight pattern can increase the runtime of a program because it takes more effort for an object to access extrinsic state than intrinsic state.

Usually it's possible to distinguish between entities by the objects that represent them. The Flyweight pattern makes this impossible, because it results in representing multiple entities by the same object.

Shared flyweight objects cannot contain parent pointers.

Because of the complexity that the Flyweight pattern adds and the constraints it places on the organization of classes, you should consider the Flyweight pattern an optimization for use only after the rest of a design is worked out.

IMPLEMENTATION

There is a trade-off to make between the number of attributes you make extrinsic and the number of flyweight objects needed at runtime. The more attributes you make extrinsic, the fewer flyweight objects will be needed. The more attributes you make intrinsic, the less time it will take objects to access their attributes.

For example, in the document representation example, if the user makes a range of characters italic, the program creates a separate `CharacterContext` object to contain the extrinsic font attribute for the `DocChar` objects that represent those characters. An alternative would be to allow the font attribute to be intrinsic to the `DocChar` objects. If the font attribute is intrinsic then `DocChar` objects will spend less time accessing their font attribute. Letting the font attribute be intrinsic also means that the program will need a `DocChar` object for each combination of character and font that it has to represent.

JAVA API USAGE

Java uses the Flyweight pattern to manage `String` objects used to represent string literals. If there is more than one string literal in a program that consists of the same sequence of characters, a Java virtual machine uses the same `String` object to represent all of those string literals.

The `String` class's intern method is responsible for managing the `String` objects used to represent string literals.

CODE EXAMPLE

Here is some of the code that implements the class diagram shown in Figure 7.13. Some of the classes don't contain any code that is of interest with respect to the Flyweight pattern, so code for those classes is not presented. For example, there is no code of interest in the `DocumentElement` class. On the other hand, the `DocumentContainer` class defines some methods that all of the container classes that are used to represent a document inherit:

```
abstract class DocumentContainer extends DocumentElement {
    // Collection of this object's children
    private Vector children = new Vector();

    // This is the font associated with this object. If the font
    // variable is null, then this object's font will be inherited
    // through the container hierarchy from an enclosing object.
    private Font font;

    DocumentContainer parent; // this object's container

    /**
     * Return the child of this object that is at the given
     * position.
     */
    public DocumentElement getChild(int index) {
        return (DocumentElement)children.elementAt(index);
    } // getChild(int)
```

```
/**
 * Make the given DocumentElement a child of this object.
 */
public synchronized void addChild(DocumentElement child) {
    synchronized (child) {
        children.addElement(child);
        if (child instanceof DocumentContainer)
          ((DocumentContainer)child).parent = this;
    } // synchronized
} // addChild(DocumentElement)

/**
 * Make the given DocumentElement NOT a child of this object.
 */
public synchronized void removeChild(DocumentElement child) {
    synchronized (child) {
        if (child instanceof DocumentContainer
            && this == ((DocumentContainer)child).parent)
          ((DocumentContainer)child).parent = null;
        children.removeElement(child);
    } // synchronized
} // removeChild(DocumentElement)

/**
 * Return this object's parent or null if it has no parent.
 */
public DocumentContainer getParent() {
    return parent;
} // getParent()

/**
 * Return the Font associated with this object. If no Font
 * is associated with this object, return its parent's Font. If
 * no Font is associated with this object's parent then return
 * null.
 */
public Font getFont() {
    if (font != null)
      return font;
    else if (parent != null)
      return parent.getFont();
    else
      return null;
} // getFont()

/**
 * Associate a Font with this object.
 */
public void setFont(Font font) {
    this.font = font;
} // setFont(Font)
```

```
...
} // class DocumentContainer
```

The methods shown for the `DocumentContainer` class manage the state of all of the document container classes, including the `CharacterContext` class. Using those inherited methods, the `CharacterContext` class is able to manage the extrinsic state of `DocChar` objects even though it doesn't declare any of its own methods for that purpose. Here is the code for the `DocChar` class that represents characters in a document:

```java
class DocChar extends DocumentElement {
    private char character;

    DocChar (char c) {
        character = c;
    } // Constructor(char)
    ...
    /**
     * Return the character that this object represents
     */
    public char getChar() {
        return character;
    } // getChar()

    /**
     * This method returns a unique value that determines where it
     * is stored internally in a hash table.
     */
    public int hashCode() {
        return getChar();
    } // hashCode()

    /**
     * Redefine equals so that two DocChar objects are considered
     * equal if they represent the same character.
     */
    public boolean equals(Object o) {
        // Call getChar rather than access character directly so
        // that this method will respect any alternate way a
        // subclass has of providing the character it represents.
        return (o instanceof DocChar
                && ((DocChar)o).getChar() == getChar());
    } // equals(Object)
} // class DocChar
```

Last, here is the code for the `DocCharFactory` class, which is responsible for the sharing of `DocChar` objects:

```
class DocCharFactory {
    private MutableDocChar myChar = new MutableDocChar();
    private Hashtable docCharPool = new Hashtable();

    /**
     * Return a DocChar object that represents the given character.
     */
    DocChar getDocChar(char c) {
        myChar.setChar(c);
        DocChar thisChar = (DocChar)docCharPool.get(myChar);
        if (thisChar == null) {
            thisChar = new DocChar(c);
            docCharPool.put(thisChar, thisChar);
    } // if
    return thisChar;
} // getDocChar(char)
```

To allow lookups of DocChar objects in a HashSet or similar collection, you would need to present to the collection a DocChar object that represents the same character as the DocChar object you want to find in the collection. Creating a DocChar object to perform each lookup would largely defeat the purpose of putting DocChar objects into the collection— that is, to avoid creating a DocChar object for each character and instead use only one DocChar object to represent every occurrence of a character.

An alternative to creating a DocChar object for each lookup would be to reuse the same DocChar object, changing the character that it represents for each lookup. The problem with changing the character a DocChar object represents is that DocChar objects are immutable. There is no way to change the character that a DocChar object represents.

A way the DocCharFactory class gets around that problem is by using this private subclass of DocChar that does provide a way to change the character that it represents:

```
private class MutableDocChar extends DocChar {
    private char character;

    MutableDocChar() {
        super('\u0000');               // Don't care what we pass to super.
    } // Constructor(char)

    /**
     * Return the character that this object represents.
     */
    public char getChar() {
        return character;
    } // getChar()
```

```
    /**
     * Set the character that this object represents.
     */
    public void setChar(char c) {
        character = c;
    } // setChar(char)
  } // class MutableDocChar
} // class DocCharFactory
```

RELATED PATTERNS

Composite   The Flyweight pattern is often combined with the Composite
pattern to represent the leaf nodes of a hierarchical structure with
shared objects.

Factory Method   The Flyweight pattern uses the factory method pattern
to create new flyweight objects.

Immutable Object   Shared flyweight objects are often immutable.

Dynamic Linkage [Grand98]

SYNOPSIS

Allow a program, upon request, to load and use arbitrary classes that implement a known interface.

CONTEXT

Suppose that you are writing software for a new kind of smart food processor that can be fed raw ingredients and by slicing, dicing, mixing, boiling, baking, frying, and stirring is able to produce cooked, ready-to-eat food. On a mechanical level, the new food processor is a very sophisticated piece of equipment. However, a crucial part of the food processor is a selection of programs to prepare different kinds of foods. A program that can turn flour, water, yeast, and other ingredients into different kinds of bread is very different from a program that can stir-fry shrimp to exactly the right texture. The food processor is required to run a great variety of programs that allow it to produce a great variety of foods. Because of the large variety of programs that are required, it's not possible to build all of the necessary programs into the food processor. Instead, the food processor can load its programs from a CD-ROM or similar media.

In order for these dynamically loaded programs and the food processor's operating environment to work with each other, they need a way to call each other's methods. Figure 7.19 presents a class diagram that shows an arrangement of classes and interfaces that allows for this capability.

The organization shown in Figure 7.19 allows an object in the food processor environment to call methods of the top-level object in a food processor program by calling the methods of its superclass. It also allows that top-level object to call the methods of the food processor environment object through the `FoodProcessorEnvironmentIF` interface that it implements.

Figure 7.20 shows a collaboration diagram that demonstrates how these classes work together.

Figure 7.20 shows the initial steps that occur when the food processor's operating environment is asked to run a program. The steps are described in more detail below.

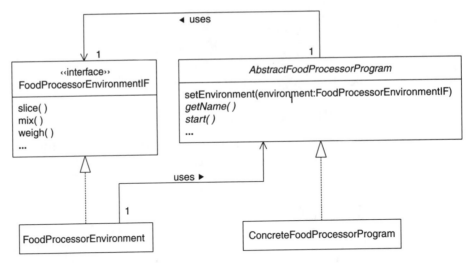

FIGURE 7.19 Food processor program class diagram.

1. The food processor environment is asked to run a program with a given name.

   1.1 The environment calls the `Class` class's `forName` method, passing it the name of the program to run. The `forName` method finds the `Class` object with the same name as the program. If necessary, it loads the class from the CD-ROM. The `forName` method concludes by returning the `Class` object that encapsulates the top-level class of the program.

   1.2 The environment creates an instance of the class that is the top-level class for the program. The diagram names that instance `program`.

   1.3 The environment passes a reference to itself to the `program` object's `setEnvironment` method. Passing that reference to the program allows the program to call the environment's methods.

   1.4 The environment gets the program's name from the program.

   1.5 The environment displays the program's name.

   1.6 The environment starts the program running.

      1.6.1 The program weighs its ingredients.

      1.6.2 The program mixes its ingredients.

The program continues as it executes additional steps that are beyond the scope of the drawing.

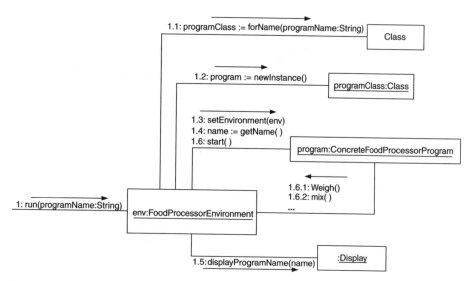

FIGURE 7.20 Food processor collaboration.

FORCES

- A program must be able to load and use arbitrary classes that it has no prior knowledge of.
- An instance of a loaded class must be able to call back to the program that loaded it.

SOLUTION

Figure 7.21 shows a class diagram that demonstrates the interfaces and classes that participate in the Dynamic Linkage pattern.

Here are the descriptions of the roles these classes play in the Dynamic Linkage pattern:

EnvironmentIF   An interface in this role declares the methods provided by an environment object that a loaded class can call.

Environment   A class in this role is the part of the environment that loads a `ConcreteLoadableClass` class. It implements the `EnvironmentIF` class. It implements the `EnvironmentIF` interface. A reference to an instance of this class is passed to instances of the `ConcreteLoadableClass` class, so that they can call the methods of the `Environment` object that are declared by the `EnvironmentIF` interface.

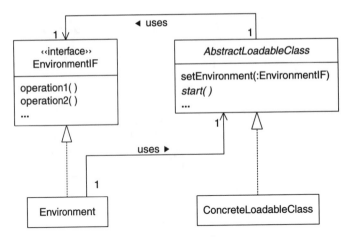

FIGURE 7.21 Dynamic Linkage pattern.

AbstractLoadableClass Any class that is the top-level class of a food processor program must be a subclass of AbstractLoadableClass. A class in this role is expected to declare a number of other, usually abstract, methods in addition to the two that are shown. Here is a description of those methods:

- There should be a method with a name like setEnvironment that allows instances of subclasses of AbstractLoadableClass to be passed a reference to an instance of a class that implements the EnvironmentIF interface. The purpose of this method is to allow AbstractLoadableClass objects to call the methods of an Environment object.
- The environment calls another method, typically named start, to tell an instance of a loaded class to start doing whatever it is supposed to be doing.

ConcreteLoadableClass Classes in this role are classes and subclasses of AbstractLoadableClass that can be dynamically loaded.

CONSEQUENCES

- Subclasses of the AbstractLoadableClass class can be dynamically loaded.

- The operating environment and the loaded classes do not need any specific foreknowledge of each other.
- Dynamic linkage increases the total amount of time it takes for a program to load all of the classes that it uses. However, it does have the effect of spreading out, over time, the overhead of loading. This can make an interactive program seem more responsive. The Virtual Proxy pattern can be used for that purpose.

IMPLEMENTATION

The Dynamic Linkage pattern, as presented, requires that the environment knows about the `AbstractLoadableClass` class and that the loaded class knows about the `EnvironmentIF` interface. In cases where less structure than this is needed, other mechanisms for interoperation are possible. For example, JavaBeans uses a combination of reflection classes and naming conventions to allow other classes to infer how to interact with a bean.

Another requirement of the Dynamic Linkage pattern is that the `Environment` class must somehow know the name of a class that it wants to load. The mechanism used for this varies with the application. In some cases, names may be hardwired. For the food processor example, a reasonable mechanism would be for the CD-ROM or other distribution medium to contain a directory of programs. The food processor would display the directory of programs as a menu, allowing the user to pick one.

Some implementations of the Dynamic Linkage pattern may need to deal with the possibility that different dynamically loaded classes use incompatible versions of the same class. For example, suppose that those programs for making lasagna sheets and wonton wrappers come on different CD-ROMs and both use a helper class named `Fu`. However, the two classes named `Fu` are incompatible with each other. Suppose the food processor first runs the lasagna program and then tries to run the wonton wrapper program. If the wonton wrapper class is given the lasagna `Fu` class when it's loaded, it will not work.

A strategy for avoiding this problem is to ensure that all of the supporting classes that are implicitly dynamically loaded along with an explicitly dynamically loaded class are not used by any other explicitly dynamically loaded class. You can implement this strategy by using a different `ClassLoader` object for each dynamically loaded class.

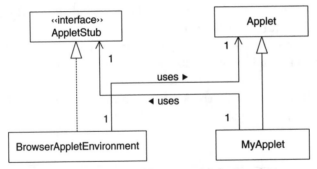

FIGURE 7.22 Applets and browsers relationship.

JAVA API USAGE

Web browsers use the Dynamic Linkage pattern to run applets. Figure 7.22 presents a class diagram that shows the relationship between applet and browser.

The browser environment accesses a subclass of `Applet` that it loads through the `Applet` class. Loaded applet subclasses access the browser environment through the `AppletStub` interface.

CODE EXAMPLE

For our example we provide the code that implements the food processor design shown under the "Context" heading for this pattern. First, here is the interface for the food processor environment:

```
public interface FoodProcessorEnvironmentIF {
    /**
     * Make a slice of food of the given width.
     */
    public void slice(int width) ;

    /**
     * Weigh food.
     * @return the weight in ounces.
     */
    public double weight() ;
...
} // interface FoodProcessorEnvironmentIF
```

Here is the abstract class that is the superclass for all top-level program classes:

```
public abstract class AbstractFoodProcessorProgram {
    private FoodProcessorEnvironmentIF environment;

    /**
     * The food processor environment passes a self-reference to
     * this method. That allows instances of subclasses of this
     * class to call methods of the environment object
     * that implements the FoodProcessorEnvironmentIF interface.
     */
    public
    void setEnvironment(FoodProcessorEnvironmentIF environment) {
        this.environment = environment;
    } // setEnvironment(FoodProcessorEnvironmentIF)

    /**
     * Allow subclasses to fetch the reference to the environment.
     */
    protected FoodProcessorEnvironmentIF getEnvironment() {
        return environment;
    } // getEnvironment()

    /**
     * Return the name of this food processing program object.
     */
    public abstract String getName() ;

    /**
     * A call to this method tells a food processing program to
     * start doing whatever it is supposed to be doing.
     */
    public abstract void start() ;
...
} // class AbstractFoodProcessorProgram
```

Here is the class that enables the food processor environment to run programs. It uses a `ClassLoader` object to manage the classes that it loads.

```
public class FoodProcessorEnvironment
        implements FoodProcessorEnvironmentIF {
    private static final URL[] classPath; // URL to load programs.
    static {
        try {
            classPath = new URL[]{new URL("file:///bin")};
        } catch (java.net.MalformedURLException e) {
            throw new ExceptionInInitializerError(e);
        } // try
    } // static
```

```
        /**
         * Make a slice of food of the given width.
         */
        public void slice(int width) {
...
        } // slice(int)

        /**
         * Weigh food.
         * @return the weight in ounces.
         */
        public double weigh() {
            double weight = 0.0;
...
            return weight;
        } // weight()
...
        /**
         * Run the named program.
         */
        void run(String programName) {
            // Create a ClassLoader to load program classes. When those
            // classes are no longer used, they can be garbage collected
            // when their ClassLoader is garbage collected.
            URLClassLoader classLoader = new URLClassLoader(classPath);
            Class programClass;
            try {
                programClass = classLoader.loadClass(programName);
            } catch (ClassNotFoundException e) {
                // Not found
...
                return;
            } // try
            AbstractFoodProcessorProgram program;
            try {
                program = (AbstractFoodProcessorProgram)
                programClass.newInstance();
            } catch (Exception e) {
                // Unable to run
                ...
                return;
            } // try
            program.setEnvironment(this);
            display(program.getName());
            program.start();
        } // run(String)
...
} // class FoodProcessorEnvironment
```

Finally, here is the sample code for a top-level program class:

```
public class ConcreteFoodProcessorProgram
            extends AbstractFoodProcessorProgram {
    /**
     * Return the name of this food processing program object.
     */
    public String getName() { return "Chocolate Milk"; }

    /**
     * A call to this method tells a food processing program to
     * start doing whatever it is supposed to be doing.
     */
    public void start() {
        double weight = getEnvironment().weigh();
        if (weight > 120.0 && weight < 160.0)
            getEnvironment().mix(4);
    ...
    } // start()
...
} // class ConcreteFoodProcessorProgram
```

RELATED PATTERNS

Virtual Proxy   The Virtual Proxy sometimes uses the Dynamic Linkage pattern to load the class that it needs to create its underlying object.

Virtual Proxy [Larman98]

SYNOPSIS

If an object is expensive to instantiate and may not be needed, it may be advantageous to postpone its instantiation until it is clear that the object is required. The Virtual Proxy pattern hides the fact that an object may not yet exist from its clients, by having them access the object indirectly through a proxy object that implements the same interface as the object that may not exist. The technique of delaying the instantiation of an object until it is actually needed is sometimes called *lazy instantiation*.

CONTEXT

Suppose that you are part of a team that has written a large Java applet for a company that operates a chain of home improvement warehouses. The applet allows people to buy everything that the warehouses sell through a web page. In addition to offering a catalog, it includes a variety of assistants to allow customers to decide just what they need. These aides include:

- A kitchen cabinet assistant that allows a customer to design a set of kitchen cabinets and then automatically order all of the pieces necessary to assemble the cabinets.
- An assistant to determine how much lumber a customer needs to build a deck.
- An assistant to determine the quantity of broadloom carpet needed for a particular floor plan and the best way to cut it.

There are more of these assistants, but they are not the point of this discussion. The point here is that the applet is very large. Due to its size, it takes an unacceptably long time for a browser to download the applet over a modem connection.

One way to reduce the time needed to download the applet is to not download any of the assistants until they are needed. The Virtual Proxy pattern provides a way to postpone the downloading part of an applet in a way that is transparent to the rest of the applet. The idea is that instead of having the rest of the applet directly access the classes that comprise an assistant, they access those classes indirectly through a proxy class. The proxy classes are specially coded so that they don't contain any static reference to the class that they act as a proxy for. This means that when the proxy classes are loaded, the Java virtual machine does not see any reference to the class that those classes are a proxy for. If the rest of the applet refers only to the proxies and not to the classes that implement assistants, Java won't automatically load the assistants.

When a method of a proxy is called, it first ensures that the classes that implement the assistant are loaded and instantiated. It then calls the corresponding method through an interface. Figure 7.23 shows a class diagram that demonstrates this organization.

Figure 7.23 shows the main portion of the applet that refers to a `CabinetAssistantProxy` class that implements the `CabinetAssistantIF` interface. The main portion of the applet contains no references to the classes that implement the cabinet assistant. When it's needed, the `CabinetAssistantProxy` class ensures that the classes that implement the cabinet assistant are loaded and instantiated. The code that accomplishes this is found later on in this pattern under the "Code Example" heading.

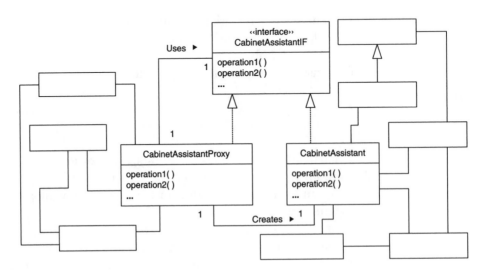

FIGURE 7.23 Cabinet assistant proxy.

FORCES

- It is very time consuming to instantiate a class.
- It may not be necessary to instantiate the class.
- If there are a number of classes whose instances are not needed until an indefinite amount of time has passed, instantiating them all at once may introduce a noticeable delay in the program's response. Postponing their instantiation until they are needed may spread out the time that the program spends instantiating them and appear to make the program more responsive.
- Managing the delayed instantiation of classes should not be a burden placed on the class's clients. Therefore, the delayed instantiation of a class should be transparent to its clients.

SOLUTION

Figure 7.24 presents a class diagram that shows the organization of classes that participate in the Virtual Proxy pattern.

Here is an explanation of the roles played by the interface and classes of the Virtual Proxy pattern:

Service   A `Service` class provides the top-level logic for a service that it provides. When you create an instance of it, it creates instances of the rest of the classes that it needs. Those classes are indicated in the diagram as `ServiceHelper1`, `ServiceHelper2` . . .

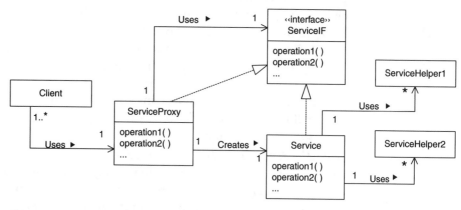

FIGURE 7.24 Virtual Proxy pattern.

Client   The `Client` class is any class that uses the service provided by the `Service` class. `Client` classes never directly use a `Service` class. Instead, they use a `ServiceProxy` class that provides the functionality of the `Service` class. Not directly using a `Service` class keeps client classes insensitive to whether the instance of the `Service` class that `Client` objects indirectly use already exists.

ServiceProxy   The purpose of the `ServiceProxy` class is to delay creating instances of the `Service` class until they are actually needed.

A `ServiceProxy` class provides indirection between `Client` classes and a `Service` class. The indirection hides from `Client` objects the fact that when a `ServiceProxy` object is created, the corresponding `Service` object does not exist and the `Service` class may not even have been loaded.

A `ServiceProxy` object is responsible for creating the corresponding `Service` object. A `ServiceProxy` object creates the corresponding `Service` object the first time that it is asked to perform an operation that requires the existence of the `Service` object.

A `ServiceProxy` class is specially coded to obtain access to the `Service` class through a dynamic reference. Usually, classes reference other classes through static references. A static reference simply consists of the name of a class appearing in an appropriate place in some source code. When a compiler sees that kind of reference, it generates output that causes the other class to automatically be loaded along with the class that contains the reference.

The Virtual Proxy pattern prevents the loading of the `Service` class and related classes along with the rest of the program by ensuring that the rest of the program does not contain any static references to the `Service` class. Instead, the rest of the program refers to the `Service` class through the `ServiceProxy` class and the `ServiceProxy` class refers to the `Service` class through a dynamic reference.

A dynamic reference consists of a method call that passes a string, containing the name of a class, to a method that loads the class if it isn't loaded and returns a reference to the class. Because the name of the class appears only inside of a string, compilers are not aware that the class will be referenced and so they do not generate any output that causes that class to be loaded.

ServiceIF   A `ServiceProxy` class creates an instance of the `Service` class through method calls that do not require any static references to the `Service` class. A `ServiceProxy` class generally also needs to call methods of the `Service` class without having any static references to the `Service` class. It is able to do this by taking advantage of the fact that the `Service` class implements the `ServiceIF` interface.

The `ServiceIF` interface is an interface that declares all of the methods that the `Service` class implements that are needed by the `ServiceProxy` class. Because of this, a `ServiceProxy` object can treat the reference to the `Service` object that it creates as a reference to a `ServiceIF` object. This means that the `Service` class can use static references to the `ServiceIF` interface to call methods of `Service` objects. No static references to the `Service` class are required.

CONSEQUENCES

- Classes accessed by the rest of a program exclusively through a virtual proxy are not loaded until they are needed.
- Instances of classes accessed by the rest of a program exclusively through a virtual proxy are not created until they are needed.
- All classes other than the proxy class must access the services of the `Service` class indirectly through the proxy. This is critical. If just one class accesses the `Service` class directly, then the `Service` class will be loaded before it is needed. This is a quiet sort of bug; it generally affects performance but not function.
- Classes that use the proxy do not need to be aware of whether the `Service` class is loaded, whether an instance of it exists, or whether the class even exists.

IMPLEMENTATION

In many cases, the class accessed through a virtual proxy uses other classes that the rest of the program does not use. Because of this relationship, those classes are not loaded until the class accessed by the virtual proxy is loaded. If it is important that those classes not be loaded until the class accessed by the virtual proxy is loaded, then a problem may occur when the program is in the maintenance phase of its life cycle. A maintenance programmer may add a direct reference to one of those classes without realizing the performance implications. You can lessen the likelihood of this happening by making the relationship explicit. You can make the relationship explicit by putting the classes in question in a package with only the class used by the proxy visible outside the package, as shown in Figure 7.25.

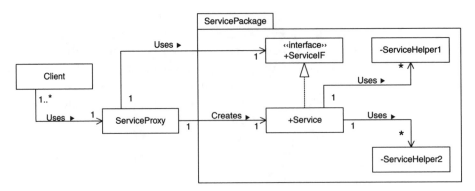

FIGURE 7.25 Relationship made explicit by the use of a package.

CODE EXAMPLE

To conclude the example started under the "Context" heading, here is some of the code that implements the cabinet assistant and its proxy. First, the relevant code for the CabinetAssistant class is:

```java
/**
 * This is a service class that is used by a virtual proxy. The
 * noteworthy aspect of this class is that it implements an interface
 * written to declare the methods of this class rather than the
 * other way around.
 */
public class CabinetAssistant implements CabinetAssistantIF {
    public CabinetAssistant(String s) {
        ...
    } // Constructor(String)
...
    public void operation1() {
        ...
    } // operation 1()

    public void operation2() {
        ...
    } // operation2()
} // class CabinetAssistant
```

The CabinetAssistantIF interface simply declares the methods defined by the CabinetAssistant class:

```java
public interface CabinetAssistantIF {
    public void operation1();
```

```
    public void operation2();
...
} // interface CabinetAssistantIF
```

Finally, here is the code for the `CabinetAssistantProxy` class where all of the interesting things happen:

```
public class CabinetAssistantProxy {
    private CabinetAssistantIF assistant = null;
    private String myParam; // for assistant object's constructor

    public CabinetAssistantProxy(String s) {
        myParam = s;
    } // constructor(String)
```

The private method that appears below is where the proxy actually creates a `CabinetAssistant` object if it hasn't already done so. Notice how it avoids any static references to the `CabinetAssistant` class that would cause the `CabinetAssistant` class to be loaded before it is needed.

```
    private CabinetAssistantIF getCabinetAssistant() {
        if (assistant == null) {
            try {
                // Get class object that represents the Assistant
                // class.
                Class clazz = Class.forName("CabinetAssistant");

                // Get a constructor object to access the
                // CabinetAssistant class' constructor that takes a
                // single string argument.
                Constructor constructor;

                // Get the constructor object to create the
                // CabinetAssistant object.
                Class[] formalArgs = new Class [] { String.class };
                constructor = clazz.getConstructor(formalArgs);

                // Use the constructor object.
                Object[] actuals = new Object[] { myParam };
                assistant = (CabinetAssistantIF)
                constructor.newInstance(actuals);
            } catch (Exception e) {
            } // try
            if (assistant == null) {
                // handle failure creating CabinetAssistant object
                throw new RuntimeException();
            } // if
        } // if
        return assistant;
```

```
        } // getCabinetAssistant()

        public void operation1() {
            getCabinetAssistant().operation1();
        } // operation1()
        public void operation2() {
            getCabinetAssistant().operation2();
        } // operation2()
...
} // class CabinetAssistantProxy
```

RELATED PATTERNS

Façade   The Façade pattern can be used with the Virtual Proxy pattern to minimize the number of proxy classes needed.

Proxy   The Virtual Proxy pattern is a specialized version of the Proxy pattern.

Double Checked Locking   If multiple threads will be getting the instance of a singleton class, you can use the Double Checked Locking coding pattern (described in Volume 2) to ensure that only one instance is created while avoiding the overhead of unnecessary thread synchronization after the instance is created.

Decorator [GoF95]

The Decorator pattern is also known as the Wrapper pattern.

SYNOPSIS

The Decorator pattern extends the functionality of an object in a way that is transparent to its clients, by using an instance of a subclass of the original class that delegates operations to the original object.

CONTEXT

Suppose that you have become responsible for maintaining the software that runs the portion of a security system responsible for controlling physical access to a building. Its basic architecture is that of a card reader or other data entry device that captures some identifying information and passes it to an object that controls a door. If the object that controls the door is satisfied with the information, it unlocks the door. Figure 7.26 shows a collaboration diagram that demonstrates just that.

Now suppose that you need to integrate this access control mechanism with a surveillance system. A surveillance system typically has many more cameras than TV monitors. Most of the TV monitors cycle through the images of different cameras, showing the picture from each camera for a few seconds and then moving on to the next camera for which that monitor is responsible. There are some rules about how the surveillance system is set up to ensure its effectiveness. For this discussion, the relevant rules are:

- At least one camera covers each doorway connected to the access control system.
- Each monitor is responsible for not more than one camera that covers an access-controlled doorway. The reason for this is that if there are

FIGURE 7.26 Basic physical access control.

multiple cameras covering a doorway, then the failure of a single monitor should not prevent the viewing of images from all of the cameras on that doorway.

The specific integration requirement is that when an object that controls a door receives a request to open the door, the monitors responsible for the cameras pointed at the doorway display that doorway. Your first thought about satisfying this requirement is probably to enhance a class or write some subclasses. Then you discover the relationships shown in Figure 7.27.

There are three different kinds of doors installed and two different kinds of surveillance monitors in use. You can resolve the situation by writing two subclasses of each of the door controller classes, but it's best not to have to write six classes. Instead, use the Decorator pattern, which solves this problem with delegation rather than inheritance.

You need to write two new classes, called `DoorControllerA` and `DoorControllerB`. Both of these classes implement the `DoorControllerIF` interface, as shown in Figure 7.28.

The new class, `AbstractDoorControllerWrapper`, is an abstract class that implements all of the methods of the `DoorController` interface with implementations that simply call the corresponding method of another object that implements the `DoorController` interface. The classes `DoorControllerA` and `DoorControllerB` are concrete wrapper classes. They extend the behavior of the `requestOpen` implementation that they inherit to also ask a surveillance monitor to display its view of that doorway (see Figure 7.29).

This approach allows doorways viewed by multiple cameras to be handled by simply putting multiple wrappers in front of the `DoorControllerIF` object.

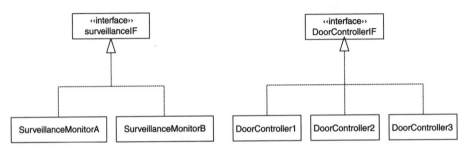

FIGURE 7.27 Security system classes.

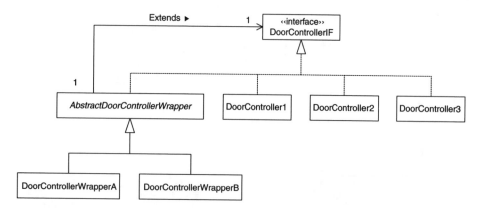

FIGURE 7.28 Door controller classes.

FORCES

- There is a need to extend the functionality of a class, but there are reasons not to extend it through inheritance.
- There is the need to dynamically extend the functionality of an object and possibly to withdraw the extended functionality.

SOLUTION

Figure 7.30 presents a class diagram that shows the general structure of the Decorator pattern.

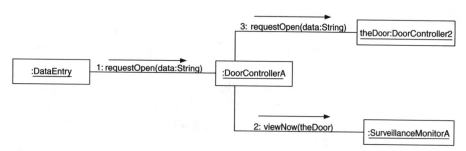

FIGURE 7.29 Door surveillance collaboration.

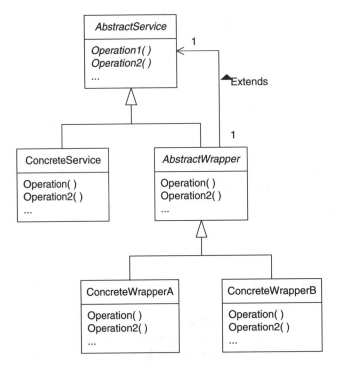

FIGURE 7.30 Decorator pattern.

Here are descriptions of the roles that the classes shown in Figure 7.30 play in the Decorator pattern.

AbstractService   An abstract class in this role is the common superclass of all of the service objects that may potentially be extended through the Decorator pattern. In some cases the service objects to be extended do not have a common superclass but do implement a common interface. In this case, the common interface takes the place of the abstract class.

ConcreteService   The Decorator pattern extends classes in this role by using objects that delegate to instances of a `ConcreteService` class.

AbstractWrapper   The abstract class in this role is the common superclass for wrapper classes. Instances of this class take responsibility for maintaining a reference to the service object that wrapper objects delegate to.

This class also normally overrides all of the methods it inherits from the `AbstractService` class so that instances simply call the like-named method of the service object that the wrapper object delegates to. This default implementation provides exactly the behavior needed for methods whose behavior is not being extended.

ConcreteWrapperA, ConcreteWrapperB, . . .   These concrete wrapper classes extend the behavior of the methods they inherit from the AbstractWrapper class in whatever way is needed.

CONSEQUENCES

The Decorator pattern provides more flexibility than inheritance. It allows you to dynamically alter the behavior of individual objects by adding and removing wrappers. Inheritance, on the other hand, determines the nature of all instances of a class statically.

By using different combinations of a few different kinds of wrapper objects, you can create many different combinations of behavior. To create that many different kinds of behavior with inheritance requires that you define that many different classes.

The flexibility of wrapper objects makes them more error prone than inheritance. For example, it is possible to combine wrapper objects in ways that do not work, or to create circular references between wrapper objects.

Using the Decorator pattern generally results in fewer classes than using inheritance. Having fewer classes simplifies the design and implementation of programs. On the other hand, using the Decorator pattern usually results in more objects. The larger number of objects can make debugging more difficult, especially since the objects tend to look mostly alike.

One last difficulty associated with using the Decorator pattern is that it makes using object identity to identify service objects difficult, since it hides service objects behind wrapper objects.

IMPLEMENTATION

Most implementations of the Decorator pattern are simpler than the general case. Here are some of the common simplifications:

- If there is only one ConcreteService class and no AbstractService class, then the AbstractWrapper class is usually a subclass of the ConcreteService class.

- Often the Decorator pattern is used to delegate to a single object. In that case, there is no need for the `AbstractWrapper` class to maintain a collection of references. Just keeping a simple reference is sufficient.
- If there is only one concrete wrapper class, then there is no need for a separate `AbstractWrapper` class. You can merge the `AbstractWrapper` class's responsibilities with those of the concrete wrapper class. It may also be reasonable to dispense with the `AbstractWrapper` class if there are two concrete wrapper classes, but no more than that.

CODE EXAMPLE

Here is some code that implements part of the door controller classes shown in Figures 7.26 to 7.29. Here is the `DoorControllerIF` interface:

```
interface DoorControllerIF {
    /**
     * Ask the door to open if the given key is acceptable.
     */
    public void requestOpen(String key);

    /**
     * close the door
     */
    public void close();
    ...
} // interface DoorControllerIF
```

Here is the `AbstractDoorControllerWrapper` class that provides default implementations to its subclasses for the methods declared by the `DoorControllerIF` interface:

```
abstract class AbstractDoorControllerWrapper
        implements DoorControllerIF {
    private DoorControllerIF wrappee;
    /**
     * Constructor
     * @param wrappee The object this object will delegate to.
     */
    AbstractDoorControllerWrapper (DoorControllerIF wrappee) {
        this.wrappee = wrappee;
    } // constructor(wrappee)
```

```
/**
 * Ask the door to open if the given key is acceptable.
 */
public void requestOpen(String key) {
    wrappee.requestOpen(key);
} // requestOpen(String)


/**
 * close the door
 */
public void close() {
    wrappee.close();
} // close()
...
} // class AbstractDoorControllerWrapper
```

Finally, here is a subclass of the `AbstractDoorControllerWrapper` class that extends the default behavior by asking a monitor to display the image from a named camera:

```
class DoorControllerWrapperA extends AbstractDoorControllerWrapper {
    private String camera;        // name of camera viewing doorway
    private SurveillanceMonitorIF monitor; // monitor for camera.

    /**
     * Constructor
     * @param wrappee The DoorController object that this object
     *          will delegate to.
     * @param camera The name of a camera that views this door
     * @param monitor The monitor to ask to view camera's image.
     */
    DoorControllerWrapperA(DoorControllerIF wrappee,
                           String camera,
                           SurveillanceMonitorIF monitor) {
        super(wrappee);
        this.camera = camera;
        this.monitor = monitor;
    } // constructor(wrappee)


    /**
     * Ask the door to open if the given key is acceptable.
     */
    public void requestOpen(String key) {
        monitor.viewNow(camera);
        super.requestOpen(key);
    } // requestOpen(String)
} // class DoorControllerWrapperA
```

RELATED PATTERNS

Delegation   The Decorator pattern is a structured way of applying the Delegation pattern.

Filter   The Filter pattern is a specialized version of the Decorator pattern that focuses on manipulating a data stream.

Strategy   The Decorator pattern is useful for arranging for things to happen before or after the methods of another object are called. If you want to arrange for different things to happen in the middle of calls to a method, consider using the Strategy pattern.

Template Method   The Template Method pattern is another alternative to the Decorator pattern that allows variable behavior in the middle of a method call instead of before or after it.

Cache Management [Grand98]

SYNOPSIS

The Cache Management pattern allows fast access to objects that would otherwise take a long time to access. It involves retaining a copy of objects that are expensive to construct after the immediate need for the object is over. The object may be expensive to construct for any number of reasons, such as requiring a lengthy computation or being fetched from a database.

CONTEXT

Suppose that you are writing a program that allows people to fetch information about products in a catalog. Fetching all of the information for a product can take a few seconds, because it may need to be gathered from multiple sources. Keeping the information for a product in the program's memory can speed things up the next time that information for that product is requested, since it won't be necessary to spend the time to gather the information.

The technique of keeping information that takes a relatively long time to fetch into memory in memory for quick access the next time it is needed is called *caching*. Because there are a few hundred thousand products in the catalog, it is not feasible to cache information for all of the products in memory. What can be done is to keep information for as many of the products as feasible in memory, trying to ensure that those products guessed to be the most likely to be used are in memory when they are needed. Deciding which and how many objects to keep in memory is called *cache management*.

Figure 7.31 is a collaboration diagram that shows how cache management works for the product information example:

1. A product ID is passed to a `ProductCacheManager` object's `getProductInfo` method.

   1.1 The `ProductCacheManager` object's `getProductInfo` method attempts to retrieve the product information from a `Cache` object. If it successfully retrieves the information from the cache, then it returns that information.

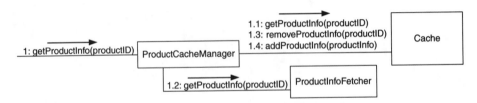

FIGURE 7.31 Product cache management collaboration.

1.2 If it is not able to retrieve the information from the cache, then it calls a `ProductInfoFetcher` object's `getProductInfo` method to fetch the product information.

1.3 Cache managers generally implement a policy to limit the number of objects in a cache because keeping too many objects in the cache can be wasteful or even counterproductive. If the cache manager decides that the retrieved information should be stored in the cache and the cache already contains as many objects as it should, the cache manager will avoid increasing the number of objects in the cache. It does this by picking a product's information to remove from the cache and passes its product ID to the `Cache` object's `removeProductInfo` method.

1.4 Finally, if the cache manager has decided that the fetched product information should be stored in the cache, it now calls the `Cache` object's `addProductInfo` method.

FORCES

- There is a need for access to an object that takes a long time to construct. Typical reasons why the construction of an object is expensive are that its contents must be fetched from external sources or that it requires a lengthy computation. The point is that it takes substantially longer to construct the object than to access the object once it is cached in internal memory.

- When the number of expensive-to-construct objects to be constructed is small enough that they can all fit comfortably in local memory, then keeping all of the objects in local memory will provide the best results. This guarantees that if access to one of those objects is needed again, it will not be necessary to incur the expense of constructing the object again.

If very many expensive-to-construct objects will be constructed, then they may not all fit in memory at the same time. If they do fit in memory, they may use memory that will later be needed for other purposes. Therefore, it may be necessary to set an upper bound on the number of objects cached in local memory.

■ An upper bound on the number of objects in a cache requires an enforcement policy. The enforcement policy will determine which fetched objects to cache and which to discard when the number of objects in the cache reaches the upper bound. Such a policy should attempt to predict which objects are the most and least likely to be used in the near future.

SOLUTION

Figure 7.32 shows the general structure of the Cache Management pattern.

Here are the descriptions of the classes that participate in the Cache Management pattern and the roles that they play:

ObjectKey   Instances of the ObjectKey class identify the content of an object to be fetched from the cache or be created.

CacheManager   All requests for objects from classes that do not participate in the Cache Management pattern are presented to a CacheManager object by calling its fetchObject method. The argument to the fetchObject method is an ObjectKey object that identifies

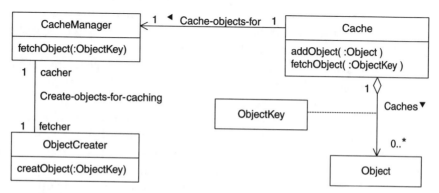

FIGURE 7.32   Cache Management pattern.

the object to fetch. The `fetchObject` method works by first calling the `Cache` object's `fetchObject` method. If this fails, it calls the `ObjectCreater` object's `createObject` method.

ObjectCreater   `ObjectCreater` objects are responsible for creating objects that are not in the cache.

Cache   A `Cache` object is responsible for managing the collection of objects in the cache so that given an `ObjectKey` object, it quickly finds the corresponding object. The `CacheManager` object passes an `ObjectKey` object to the `Cache` object's `fetchObject` method to try to get an object from the cache. If the `CacheManager` object does not get the object it requested from the `fetchObject` method, then it requests the object from the `ObjectCreater` object. If the `ObjectCreater` object returns the object that it requested, then it will pass the fetched object to this object's `addObject` method. The `addObject` method adds the object to the cache if this is consistent with its cache management policy. The `addObject` method may remove an object from the cache to make room for the object that it is adding to the cache.

CONSEQUENCES

The impact of the Cache Management pattern on the rest of a program is minimal. If the `CacheManager` class is implemented as a subclass of the `ObjectFetcher` class, then, using the Virtual Proxy pattern, an implementation of the Cache Management pattern can be inserted into a working program with minimal modification to existing code.

The primary consequence of using the Cache Management pattern is that a program spends less time creating objects that are expensive to create. The simplest way of measuring the effectiveness of caching is by computing a statistic called its *hit rate*. The hit rate is the percentage of object fetch requests that the cache manager is able to satisfy with objects stored in the cache. If every request is satisfied with an object from the cache, then the hit rate is 100 percent. If no request is satisfied, then the hit rate is 0 percent.

The hit rate depends largely on how well the implementation of the Cache Management pattern matches the way that objects are requested. The policy that selects an object to remove from the cache to make room for another object is very important in this respect. If it is to always select the object that will be unneeded for the longest time, then the hit rate will be as high as the cache size permits it to be. On the other hand, if objects are always removed from the cache before they are reused, then the hit rate will be 0.

When objects are created with data from an external source, another consequence of using the Cache Management pattern is that the cache may become inconsistent with the original data source. The consistency problem breaks down into two separate problems that can be solved independently of each other. These problems are *read consistency* and *write consistency*.

Read consistency means that objects fetched from the cache always reflect updates to information in the original object source. Enforcing read consistency usually involves the data source notifying all object caches when an object that they have cached has been updated.

Write consistency means that the original object source always reflects updates to the cache.

Achieving absolute read or write consistency with the original object source for objects in a cache requires that you implement a mechanism that keeps them synchronized. Such mechanisms can be complicated to implement and can add considerable execution time. They generally involve techniques such as locking and optimistic concurrency, which are beyond the scope of this volume.

If it is not feasible to get the object source to send updates, you may be able to settle for *relative consistency*. Relative consistency does not guarantee that the contents of a cache will always appear to match the original object source. Instead, the guarantee is that if an update occurs in the cache or the original data source, the other will reflect the update within some specified amount of time.

For example, you may want to ensure that stock prices in a cache are not more than 15 minutes old. To accomplish this, you can simply remove an object from the cache after it has been there for 15 minutes.

IMPLEMENTATION

Implementing the Cache Management pattern involves making some potentially complex choices. Making optimal choices can involve much statistical analysis, queuing theory, and other sorts of mathematical analysis. However, it is usually possible to produce a reasonable implementation by being aware of what the choices are and experimenting with different solutions.

The most basic decision to make when implementing the Cache Management pattern is how to implement the cache itself. The considerations for picking a data structure for the cache are:

■ It must be able to quickly find objects when it is given their `ObjectKey`.

- Since search operations will be done more frequently than addition or removal, searching should be as fast or faster than those operations.
- Since we expect frequent additions and removals of objects, the data structure must not make those operations a lot more expensive than search operations.

A hash table satisfies these needs. When implementing in Java, a cache is usually implemented using an instance of the `java.util.Hashtable` class.

The remaining implementation issues relate to performance tuning. Performance tuning is not something to spend time on until after your program is functioning correctly. In the design and initial coding stages of your development effort, make some initial decisions about how to deal with these issues and then ignore them until you are ready to deal with performance-related issues.

There is always a maximum amount of memory that you can afford to devote to a cache. This means that you will have to set a limit on the objects that can be in the cache. If the potential set of objects that are available for collection in a cache is small, you don't have to impose an explicit limit. Most problems are not so conveniently self-limiting.

Specifying in advance a maximum amount of memory to devote to a cache is difficult since you may not know in advance how much memory will be available or how much memory the rest of your program will need. Enforcing a limit on the amount of memory a cache can use is especially difficult in Java because there is no definite relationship between an object and the amount of physical memory that it occupies.

An alternative to specifying and enforcing a limit that measures memory is to simply count objects. Object counting is a workable alternative to measuring actual memory usage if the average memory usage for each object is a reasonable approximation of the memory usage for each object. Counting objects is very straightforward, so you can simplify things by limiting the contents of a cache to a certain number of objects. Of course, the existence of a limit on the size of a cache raises the question of what should happen when the size of the cache reaches the maximum number of objects and another object is created. At this point, there is one more object than the cache is supposed to hold. The cache manager must now discard an object.

The selection of which object to discard is important because it directly affects the hit rate. If the discarded object is always the next one requested, then the hit rate will be 0%. On the other hand, if the object discarded will not be requested before any of the other objects in the cache, then discarding that object has the least negative impact on the hit rate.

Clearly, making a good choice of which object to discard requires a forecast of future object requests.

In some cases, it is possible to make an educated guess about which objects a program will need in the near future, based on knowledge of the application domain. In the most fortunate cases, it is possible to predict with high probability that a specific object will be the next one requested. In those cases, if the object is not already in the cache, it may be advantageous to asynchronously create it immediately rather than wait for the program to request it. This is called *prefetching* the object.

In most cases, the application domain will not provide enough clues to make such precise forecasts. However, there is a pattern that turns up in so many cases that it is the basis for a good default strategy for deciding which object to discard. This pattern is that the more recently a program has requested an object, the more likely it is to request the object again. The optimal strategy for that usage pattern is to always discard the least recently used (LRU) object.

Now let's take a look at setting a numeric limit on the number of objects in a cache. A mathematical analysis can give a precise value to use for the maximum number of objects that may be placed in a cache. It is unusual to do such an analysis for two reasons. The first is that the mathematical analysis involves probability and queuing theory that is beyond the knowledge of most programmers. The other reason is that such an analysis can be prohibitively time consuming. The number of details that need to be gathered about the program and its environment can be prohibitively large. However, you can usually arrive at a reasonable cache size empirically.

Begin by adding code to your CacheManager class to measure the hit rate as the number of object requests satisfied from the cache divided by the total number of object requests. You can then try running with different limits on the object size. As you do this, you will be looking for two things. The most important thing to look out for is that if the cache is too large it can cause the rest of your program to fail or slow down. The program can fail by running out of memory. If the program is garbage collected, as most Java programs are, it can slow down waiting for the garbage collector to finish scavenging memory for new objects. If the program is running in a virtual memory environment, a large cache can cause excessive paging.

Suppose that you want to tune a program that uses a cache. You run the program, under otherwise identical conditions, with different maximum cache sizes set. Let's say that you try values as large as 6000. At 6000 you find that the program takes three times as long to run as at 4000. This means that 6000 is too large. Look at the possible hit rates you could receive at the other values, as shown in Table 7.1.

TABLE 7.1 Cache Size and Hit Rates

Max Cache Size	Hit Rate, %
250	20
500	60
1000	80
2000	90
3000	98
4000	100
5000	100

Clearly, there is no need to allow the cache to be larger than 4000 objects, since that achieves a 100 percent hit rate. Under the conditions that you ran the program, the ideal cache size is 4000. If the program will be run only under those exact conditions, further tuning may be unnecessary. Many programs will be run under other conditions. If you are concerned that your program will be run under other conditions, you may want to use a smaller cache size to avoid problems under conditions where less memory is available. The number you pick will be a compromise between wanting a high hit rate and wanting a small cache size. Since lowering the cache size to 3000 only reduces the hit rate to 98 percent, then 3000 might be an acceptable cache size. If a 90 percent hit rate is good enough, then 2000 is an acceptable cache size.

If it is not possible to achieve a high hit rate with available memory and creating the objects is sufficiently expensive, then you should consider using a secondary cache. A secondary cache is typically a disk file that is used as a cache. The secondary cache takes longer to access than the primary cache that is in memory. However, if it takes sufficiently less time to fetch objects out of a local disk file than it would to create them again from their original source, then it can be advantageous to use a secondary cache.

The way that you use a secondary cache is to move objects from the primary cache to the secondary cache instead of discarding the objects when the primary cache is full.

CODE EXAMPLE

Suppose that you are involved in writing software for an employee timekeeping system. The system consists of timekeeping terminals and a timekeeping server. The terminals are small boxes mounted on the walls of a place of business. When an employee arrives at work or leaves work, he or she notifies the timekeeping system by running an ID card through a time-keeping terminal. The terminal reads the employee's ID and acknowledges the card by displaying the employee's name and options. The employee then presses a button to indicate that he or she is starting work, ending work, going on break, or other options. The timekeeping terminals transmit the comings and goings of each employee to the timekeeping server. At the end of each pay period, the business's payroll system gets the number of hours that each employee has worked from the timekeeping system and prepares paychecks.

The exact details of what an employee sees will depend on the employee profile that the terminal receives from the timekeeping server. The employee profile will include the employee's name, the language in which to display prompts for the employee, and what special options apply to the employee.

Most businesses assign their employees a fixed location in the business place to do their work. Employees with a fixed work location will normally use the timekeeping terminal nearest to their work location. To avoid long lines in front of timekeeping terminals, it is recommended that the terminals be positioned so that fewer than 70 employees with fixed work locations will use the same timekeeping terminal.

Because a substantial portion of the cost of the timekeeping system will be the cost of the terminals, the timekeeping terminals will have a minimal amount of memory to keep their cost down. On the other hand, to keep response time down, you want the terminals to cache employee profiles so that most of the time they will be able to respond immediately when presented with an ID card. This means that you will have to impose a maximum cache size that is rather modest. A reasonable basis for an initial maximum cache size is the recommendation that the terminals be positioned so that no more than 70 employees with fixed work locations will use the same terminal. Based on this we come up with an initial cache size of up to 80 employee profiles.

The reason for picking a number larger than 70 is that under some situations more than 70 employees may use the same timekeeping terminal. Sometimes one part of a business will borrow employees from another part of the business when it experiences a peak workload. Also, there will be employees, such as maintenance staff, that float from one location to another.

Figure 7.33 presents a class diagram that shows how the Cache Management pattern is applied to this problem.

Here is the code that implements the timekeeping terminal's cache management. First, here is the code for the `EmployeeProfileManager` class:

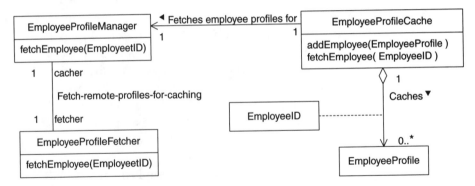

FIGURE 7.33 Timekeeping cache management.

```
class EmployeeProfileManager {
    private EmployeeCache cache = new EmployeeCache();
    private EmployeeProfileFetcher server
      = new EmployeeProfileFetcher();

    /**
     * Fetch an employee profile for the given employee id from the
     * internal cache or timekeeping server
     * @return employee's profile or null if profile not found.
     */
    EmployeeProfile fetchEmployee(EmployeeID id) {
        EmployeeProfile profile = cache.fetchEmployee(id);
        if (profile == null) {    // if profile not in cache try server
            profile = server.fetchEmployee(id);
            if (profile != null) { // Get the profile
                // put profile in the cache
                cache.addEmployee(profile);
            } // if != null
        } // if == null
        return profile;
    } // fetchEmployee(EmployeeID)
} // class EmployeeProfileManager
```

The logic in the `EmployeeProfileManager` class is rather straight-forward conditional logic. The logic of the `EmployeeCache` class is more intricate, since it has to manipulate a data structure to determine which employee profile to remove from the cache when adding an employee profile to a full cache.

```
class EmployeeCache {
    /**
     * We use a linked list to determine the least recently used
     * employee profile. The cache that itself is implemented by a
     * Hashtable object. The Hashtable values are linked list
```

```
 * objects that refer to the actual EmployeeProfile object.
 */
private Hashtable cache = new Hashtable();

/**
 * This is the head of the linked list that refers to the most
 * recently used EmployeeProfile.
 */
LinkedList mru = null;

/**
 * this is the end of the linked list that refers to the least
 * recently used EmployeeProfile.
 */
LinkedList lru = null;

/**
 * Maximum number of EmployeeProfile objects that may be in the
 * cache.
 */
private final int MAX_CACHE_SIZE = 80;

/**
 * The number of EmployeeProfile objects currently in the cache.
 */
private int currentCacheSize = 0;
/**
 * Objects are passed to this method for addition to the cache.
 * However, this method is not required to actually add an
 * object to the cache if that is contrary to its policy for
 * what object should be added. This method may also remove
 * objects already in the cache in order to make room for new objects.
 */
public void addEmployee(EmployeeProfile emp) {
    EmployeeID id = emp.getID();
    if (cache.get(id) == null) { // if profile not in cache
        // Add profile to cache, making it most recently used.
        if (currentCacheSize == 0) {
            // treat empty cache as a special case
            lru = mru = new LinkedList();
            mru.profile = emp;
        } else { // currentCacheSize > 0
            LinkedList newLink;
            if (currentCacheSize >= MAX_CACHE_SIZE) {
                // remove least recently used EmployeeProfile
                // from the cache
                newLink = lru;
                lru = newLink.previous;
                cache.remove(newLink);
                lru.next = null;
            } else {
                newLink = new LinkedList();
```

```
                } // if >= MAX_CACHE_SIZE
            newLink.profile = emp;
            newLink.next = mru;
            newLink.previous = null;
            mru = newLink;
        } // if 0
        // put the now most recently used profile in the cache
        cache.put(id, mru);
        currentCacheSize++;
    } else { // profile already in cache
        // addEmployee shouldn't be called when the object is
        // already in the cache. Since that has happened, do a
        // fetch so that the object becomes the most recently used.
        fetchEmployee(id);
    } // if cache.get(id)
} // addEmployee(EmployeeProfile)


/**
 * Return the EmployeeProfile associated with the given
 * EmployeeID or null if no EmployeeProfile is associated with
 * the given EmployeeID.
 */
public EmployeeProfile fetchEmployee(EmployeeID id) {
    LinkedList foundLink = (LinkedList)cache.get(id);
    if (foundLink == null)
      return null;
    if (mru != foundLink) {
        if (foundLink.previous != null)
          foundLink.previous.next = foundLink.next;
        if (foundLink.next != null)
          foundLink.next.previous = foundLink.previous;
        foundLink.previous = null;
        foundLink.next = mru;
        mru = foundLink;
    } // if currentCacheSize > 1
    return foundLink.profile;
} // fetchEmployee(EmployeeID)


/**
 * private doubly linked list class for managing list of most
 * recently used employee profiles.
 */
private class LinkedList {
    EmployeeProfile profile;
    LinkedList previous;
    LinkedList next;
} // class LinkedList
} // class EmployeeCache
```

Finally, here are the EmployeeProfile and EmployeeID classes:

```
class EmployeeProfile {
    private EmployeeID id;          // Employee Id
    private Locale locale;          // Language Preference
    private boolean supervisor;
    private String name;            // Employee name

    public EmployeeProfile(EmployeeID id,
                           Locale locale,
                           boolean supervisor,
                           String name) {
        this.id = id;
        this.locale = locale;
        this.supervisor = supervisor;
        this.name = name;
    } // Constructor(EmployeeID, Locale, boolean, String)

    public EmployeeID getID() { return id; }
    public Locale getLocale() { return locale; }
    public boolean isSupervisor() { return supervisor; }
} // class EmployeeProfile

class EmployeeID {
    private String id;

    /**
     * constructor
     * @param id A string containing the employee ID.
     */
    public EmployeeID(String id) {
        this.id = id;
    } // constructor(String)

    /**
     * Returns a hash code value for this object.
     */
    public int hashCode() { return id.hashCode(); }

    /**
     * Return true if the given object is an EmployeeId equal to
     * this one.
     */
    public boolean equals(Object obj) {
        return ( obj instanceof EmployeeID
                 && id.equals(((EmployeeID)obj).id) );
    } // equals(Object)

    /**
     * Return the string representation of this EmployeeID.
     */
    public String toString() { return id; }
} // class EmployeeID
```

RELATED PATTERNS

Façade   The Cache Management pattern uses the Façade pattern.

Publish-Subscribe   You can use the Publish-Subscribe pattern to ensure the read consistency of a cache.

Remote Proxy   The Remote Proxy provides an alternative to the Cache Management pattern by working with objects that exist in a remote environment rather than fetching them into the local environment.

Template Method   The Cache Management pattern uses the Template Method pattern to keep its Cache class reusable across application domains.

Virtual Proxy   The Cache Management pattern is often used with a variant of the Virtual Proxy pattern to make the cache transparent to objects that access objects in the cache.

Behavioral Patterns

The patterns in this chapter are used to organize, manage, and combine behavior.

Chain of Responsibility [GoF95]

SYNOPSIS

The Chain of Responsibility pattern allows an object to send a command without knowing what object or objects will receive it. It accomplishes that by passing the command to a chain of objects that is typically part of a larger structure. Each object in the chain may handle the command, pass the command on to the next object in the chain, or do both.

CONTEXT

Suppose that you are writing software to monitor a security system. Physically, the security system consists of sensing devices (motion detectors, smoke detectors, etc.) and a computer to which they transmit status information over a network. The computer's job is to log all status information, maintain a display showing current status information, and transmit alarms in the event of an emergency.

One of the goals for the monitoring software is that it should be highly scalable. It should be able to work for a small retail store, an office building, a warehouse or a multibuilding complex. That goal will have implications for the way that you design the monitoring software.

To keep things simple, your monitoring program should instantiate an object for every sensor it is to monitor. This provides a simple way to model each sensor's state. To ensure scalability, the objects responsible for individual sensors should not assume anything about their environment, except that they are at the bottom level of a hierarchical organization.

The organization will include objects corresponding to such real-world things as rooms, areas, floors, and buildings. Modeling the real world like that provides a straightforward way to display the status of different parts of buildings. It also allows the interpretation of a sensor's state to be based on its environment. For example, if the temperature of a closed room exceeds 180°F, then you may want the fire sprinklers in just that room to turn on. If the temperature in an open area of a warehouse exceeds 150°F, you may want to turn on the fire sprinklers over that area and the adjacent areas. On the other hand, if the temperature in a freezer exceeds 30°F, you may want to sound an alarm to let people know that that freezer is getting too warm.

In all of these cases, the object that models the sensor does not decide what to do with the state of the sensor. Instead, it delegates that decision to an object at a higher level of the hierarchy with more contextual knowledge. Such objects either decide what to do about a notification or pass it on to the object that is organizationally above it.

For example, in Figure 8.1, when a TemperatureSensor object contained in an area of a warehouse receives a notification of the current temperature from the physical sensor, it passes that notification to the Area object that contains it. Rather than decide the significance of the temperature, it passes the notification to the Warehouse object that contains the Area object. The Warehouse object determines the meaning of the temperature. If the temperature is above 150°F, the Warehouse object decides there is a fire. It turns on the sprinklers in the area that notified it and the surrounding areas. The Warehouse object does not pass on the temperature notification.

FORCES

- You want an object to be able to send a command to another object without specifying the receiver. The sending object does not care

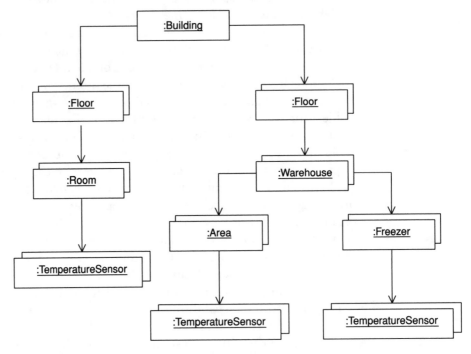

FIGURE 8.1 Physical security object organization.

which object handles the command, only that an object will receive the command and handle it.

- More than one object may be able to receive and handle a command, so you need a way to prioritize among the receivers without the sending object knowing anything about them.

SOLUTION

Figure 8.2 presents a class diagram that shows the organization of the Chain of Responsibility pattern. Following are explanations of the roles these classes play in the Chain of Responsibility pattern:

CommandSender   Instances of a `CommandSender` class send commands to the first object in a chain of objects that may handle the command. It sends a command by calling the first `CommandHandler` object's `postCommand` method.

CommandHandler   The `CommandHandler` class is the superclass of all of the objects in the chain of objects that may handle a command. It defines two methods:

1. Each subclass of `CommandHander` overrides the abstract `handleCommand` method to handle whatever commands instances of that class will handle. The `handleCommand` method is expected to return true if it handled a command or false if it did not.
2. Subclasses of `CommandHander` do not usually override the `postCommand` method. The `postCommand` method calls the

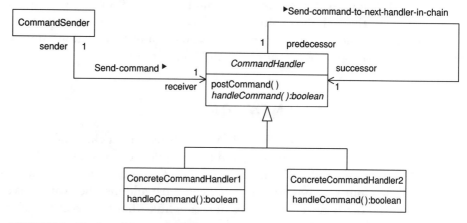

FIGURE 8.2 Chain of Responsibility pattern.

handleCommand method. If the handleCommand method returns false and there is a next object in the chain, it calls that object's postCommand method. If the handleCommand method returns true, that means there is no need to pass the command on to the next object in the chain.

ConcreteCommandHandler1, ConcreteCommandHandler2 Instances of classes in this role are objects in a chain of objects that can handle commands. It is common for a chain of CommandHandler objects to be part of a larger structure. This is the case in the example shown under the "Context" heading.

CONSEQUENCES

The Chain of Responsibility pattern reduces coupling between the object that sends a command and the object that handles the command. The sender of a command does not need to know what object will actually handle the command. It merely needs to be able to send the command to the object that is at the head of the chain of responsibility.

The Chain of Responsibility pattern also allows greater flexibility in deciding how to handle commands. Decisions about which object will handle a command can be varied by changing which objects are in the chain of responsibility or changing the order of the objects in the chain of responsibility.

The Chain of Responsibility pattern does not guarantee that every command will be handled. Commands that are not handled are ignored.

If the number of objects in a chain gets large, there can be efficiency concerns about the amount of time that it takes a command to propagate through the chain. A high percentage of commands that are not handled exacerbates the problem because commands that are not handled are propagated through the full length of the chain.

IMPLEMENTATION

In many cases, the objects that constitute a chain of responsibility are part of a larger structure, and the chain of responsibility is formed through some links of that larger structure. When links to form a chain of responsibility do not already exist, you must add instance variables and access methods to the classes to create links that form a chain of responsibility.

A decision to make, whenever implementing the Chain of Responsibility pattern, is how you will pass commands to and through the chain of objects. There are two basic ways to do it. One way is to encapsulate each kind of command in a single object that can be passed to a single `postCommand` method. The other way is to have as many different types of `postCommand` and `handleCommand` methods as there are different types of information associated with commands.

Passing commands in a single object is often the better choice. It incurs the cost of object creation, but minimizes the cost of passing parameters to the methods of the next object in the chain. That minimizes the cost of propagating a command through a chain of objects.

On the other hand, passing the information that comprises a command through separate parameters saves the cost of object creation at the cost of additional parameter passing. If you know that the chain of objects will be short, passing a command as multiple parameters can be the better choice.

JAVA API USAGE

The first version of Java, version 1.0, used the Chain of Responsibility pattern to handle user-interface events. That event-handling scheme used a user interface's container hierarchy as a chain of responsibility. When an event was posted to a button or other GUI component, it would either handle the event or post it to its container. Though it was usable, there were enough problems that the creators of Java took the drastic step of changing Java's event model. The two most serious problems related to efficiency and flexibility:

1. Some platforms generate many events that most GUIs do not handle or have any interest in. One such event is MOUSE_MOVE. It may be generated every time a mouse moves just one pixel. Some programs that were built using the original event model visibly slowed down whenever there was rapid mouse movement because they spent so much time passing MOUSE_MOVE events that were never handled through the container hierarchy.
2. The Chain of Responsibility pattern assumes that all the objects that can handle a command are instances of a common superclass or implement a common interface. That limits a program to posting commands to instances of that common superclass or interface. Java's original event model required that every object that could handle an event was an instance of the common superclass Component.

That meant it was impossible to deliver events directly to non-GUI objects, because only GUI objects are instances of Component.

CODE EXAMPLE

Continuing the physical security example, Figure 8.3 shows the classes used in the physical security example. Following is some of the code for these classes. First, here is code for the TemperatureSensor class, which begins the collaboration shown under the "Context" heading. Notice that the TemperatureSensor class does nothing with a reading from a temperature sensor but pass it on.

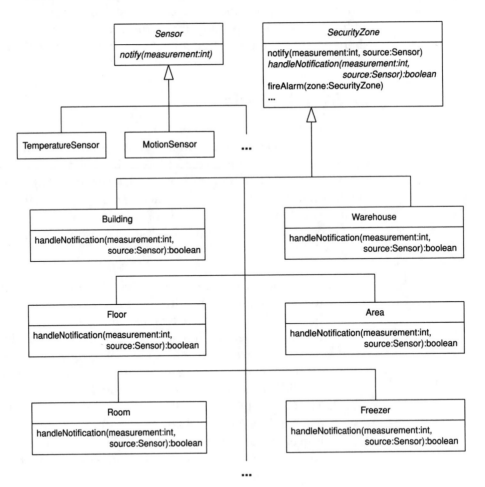

FIGURE 8.3 Physical security classes.

```
class TemperatureSensor extends Sensor {
    private SecurityZone zone;
...
    /**
     * When the temperature sensor associated with this object
     * observes a different temperature this method is called.
     */
    void notify(int measurement) {
        zone.notify(measurement, this);
    } // notify(int)
} // class TemperatureSensor
```

Here is the code for the SecurityZone class, which is the superclass of all of the classes that form the chains of responsibility in this example:

```
abstract class SecurityZone {
    private SecurityZone parent;
...
    /**
     * Return this object's parent zone.
     */
    SecurityZone getParent() {
        return parent;
    } // getParent()

    /**
     * Notify this zone of a new sensor measurement.
     */
    void notify(int measurement, Sensor sensor) {
        if ( ! handleNotification(measurement, sensor)
            && parent != null) {
            parent.notify(measurement, sensor);
        } // if
    } // notify(int, Sensor)

    /**
     * This method is called by the notify method so that this
     * object can have a chance to handle measurements.
     */
    abstract boolean handleNotification(int measurement,
                        Sensor sensor);

    /**
     * This method is called by a child zone to report a fire. It
     * is expected that the child zone has turned on sprinklers or
     * taken other measures to control the fire within the child
     * zone. The purpose of this method is to be overridden by
     * subclasses so it can take any necessary actions outside of
     * the child zone.
     */
```

```
      void fireAlarm(SecurityZone zone) {
         // Turn on sprinklers
...

         if (parent != null)
           parent.fireAlarm(zone);
      } // fireAlarm(SecurityZone)
} // class SecurityZone
```

Here are the subclasses of SecurityZone that were discussed under the "Context" heading:

```
class Area extends SecurityZone {
...
   /**
    * This method is called by the notify method so that this
    * object can have a chance to handle measurements.
    */
   boolean handleNotification(int measurement, Sensor sensor) {
      if (sensor instanceof TemperatureSensor) {
         if (measurement > 150) {
            fireAlarm(this);
            return true;
         } // if
      } // if
...
      return false;
   } // handleNotification(int, Sensor)
} // class Area
class Warehouse extends SecurityZone {
   ...
   /**
    * This method is called by the notify method so that this
    * object can have a chance to handle measurements.
    */
   boolean handleNotification(int measurement, Sensor sensor) {
...
      return false;
   } // handleNotification(int, Sensor)

   void fireAlarm(SecurityZone zone) {
      if (zone instanceof Area) {
         // Turn on sprinklers in surrounding areas
         ...
         // Don't call super.fireAlarm because that will turn on
         // the sprinkler for the whole warehouse.
         if (getParent() != null)
           getParent().fireAlarm(zone);
         return;
      } // if
...
```

```
        super.fireAlarm(zone);
    } // fireAlarm(SecurityZone)
} // class Warehouse
```

RELATED PATTERNS

Composite　When the chain of objects used by the Chain of Responsibility pattern is part of a larger structure, that larger structure is usually built using the Composite pattern.

Command　The Chain of Responsibility pattern makes the particular object that executes a command indefinite. The Command pattern makes the object that executes a command explicit and specific.

Template Method　When the objects that make up a chain of responsibility are part of a larger organization built using the Composite pattern, the Template Method pattern is often used to organize the behavior of individual objects.

Command [GoF95]

SYNOPSIS

Encapsulate commands in objects so that you can control their selection and sequencing, queue them, undo them, and otherwise manipulate them.

CONTEXT

Suppose that you want to design a word processing program so that it can undo and redo commands. A way to accomplish that is to materialize each command as an object with do and undo methods. The class diagram for this could look like the diagram in Figure 8.4.

When you tell the word processor to do something, instead of directly performing the command it creates an instance of the subclass of AbstractCommand corresponding to the command. It passes all necessary information to the instance's constructor. For example, when commanded to insert one or more characters, it creates an InsertStringCommand object. It passes, to the object's constructor, the position in the document to make the insertion and the string to insert at that position.

Once the word processor has materialized a command as an object, it calls the object's doIt method to execute the command. The word proces-

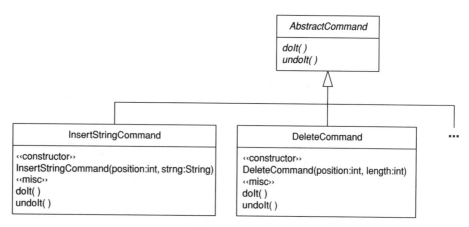

FIGURE 8.4 Do and undo class diagram.

sor also puts the command object in a data structure that allows the word processor to maintain a history of what commands have been executed. Maintaining a command history allows the word processor to undo commands in the reverse order that they were issued by calling their undo methods.

FORCES

- You need to control the sequencing, selection, or timing of command execution.
- One particular type of command manipulation that motivates the use of the Command pattern is undo and redo management.
- You need to maintain a persistent log of commands executed. You can generate such a log by enhancing command objects so that their doIt and undoIt methods generate log entries. Since you can use a persistent log to back out the effects of previously executed commands, a persistent log can be incorporated into a transaction management mechanism to allow commands to be undone if a transaction is aborted.

SOLUTION

Figure 8.5 presents a class diagram that shows classes that participate in the Command pattern. Explanations for the roles that these classes play in the Command pattern are:

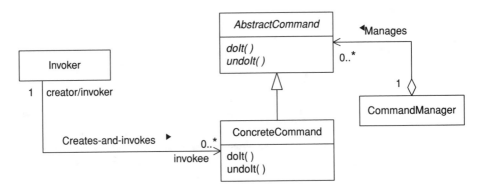

FIGURE 8.5 Command pattern.

AbstractCommand A class in this role is the superclass of classes that encapsulate commands. It minimally defines an abstract `doIt` method that other classes call to execute the command encapsulated by its subclasses. If undo support is required, an `AbstractCommand` class also defines an `undoIt` method that undoes the effects of the last call to the `doIt` method.

ConcreteCommand Classes in this role are concrete classes that encapsulate a specific command. Other classes invoke the command through a call to the class's `doIt` method. The undo logic for the command is invoked through a call to the class's `undoIt` method.

   The object's constructor normally supplies any parameters that the command requires. Most commands require at least one parameter, which is the object that the command acts on. For example, a command to save an object to disk normally requires that the object to be saved be passed to the command object's constructor.

Invoker A class in this role creates concrete command objects if it needs to invoke a command. It may call those objects' `doIt` method or leave that for the `CommandManager` object to do.

CommandManager A `CommandManager` class is responsible for managing a collection of command objects created by an `Invoker` object. The specific responsibilities of a `CommandManager` class can include managing the undo and redo of commands, sequencing commands, and scheduling commands.

   `CommandManager` classes are usually independent of the applications in which they are used and can be very reusable.

CONSEQUENCES

■ The object that invokes a command is not the same object that executes a command. That separation provides flexibility in the timing and sequencing of commands. Materializing commands as objects means that they can be collected, delegated to, and otherwise manipulated like any other kind of object.

■ Being able to collect and control the sequencing of commands means that you can use the Command pattern as the basis of a mechanism that supports keyboard macros. That is a mechanism that records a sequence of commands and allows them to be replayed later. The Command pattern can also be used to create other kinds of composite patterns.

- Adding new commands is usually easy because it does not break any dependencies.

IMPLEMENTATION

There are a few issues to consider when implementing the Command pattern. The first and possibly most important is to decide what the commands will be. If the commands are issued by a user interface that provides user-level commands, then a very natural way to identify concrete command classes is to have a concrete command class for each user-level command. If you stick with that strategy and there are any particularly complex user commands, then there will be equally complex command classes. To avoid putting too much complexity in one class, you may want to implement more complex user-level commands with multiple command classes.

If the number of external or user-level commands is very large, then you might follow the strategy of implementing them with combinations of command objects. That strategy may allow you to implement a large number of external commands with a smaller number of command classes.

Another implementation issue to consider is the capture of state information necessary to undo commands. In order to be able to undo the effects of a command, it is necessary to save enough of the state of the objects on which it operates to be able to restore that state.

There may be commands that cannot be undone because they involve saving an excessive amount of state information. For example, a global search-and-replace command may sometimes involve changing so much information that keeping all of the original information would take up a prohibitive amount of storage. There may be commands that can never be undone because it is not possible to restore the state that those commands change. Commands that involve the deletion of files often fall into that category.

The CommandManager object should be aware when a command is executed that is not undoable. There are a number of reasons for this:

- Suppose that a CommandManager object is responsible for the initial execution of commands. If it is aware that a command will not be undoable before it is executed, then it can provide a common mechanism for warning a user that a command that cannot be undone is about to be executed. When it warns a user, it can also offer the user the option of not executing the command.

■ Keeping a command history for undo purposes consumes memory and sometimes other resources. After executing a command that cannot be undone, any command history that is available can be disposed of. Keeping the command history after executing a command that is not undoable is a waste of resources.

■ Most user interfaces for programs that have an undo command have a menu item that users can use to issue an undo command. Good user interfaces avoid surprising users. Responding to an undo command, with a notification that the last command could not be undone surprises a user who expected an undo command to be carried out. A way to avoid that surprise is for the command manager object to enable or disable the undo menu item if the last executed command was undoable or not undoable.

You can simplify the pattern if you do not need to support undo operations. If no undo support is required, then the `AbstractCommand` class does not need to define an `undoIt` method.

There is a common extension to the Command pattern used when commands are issued by a user interface. The purpose of the extension is to avoid tying user-interface components to a specific command object or even requiring user-interface components to know about any concrete command classes. The extension consists of embedding the name of a command in the user-interface components and then using a factory method object to create the command objects, as shown in Figure 8.6.

In Figure 8.6, GUI component classes refer to the name of the command that they invoke, rather than the command class that implements that command or an instance of it. They invoke commands indirectly by passing the name of the command to a factory object that creates an instance of the appropriate concrete command class.

Invoking commands through a command factory provides a layer of indirection that can be very useful. The indirection allows multiple command issuing objects to transparently share the same command object. More important, the indirection makes it easier to have user-customizable menus and toolbars.

JAVA API USAGE

Java's core API does not have any good examples of the Command pattern. However, it does contain some support for the GUI extension to the Command pattern. Its button and menu item classes have methods called

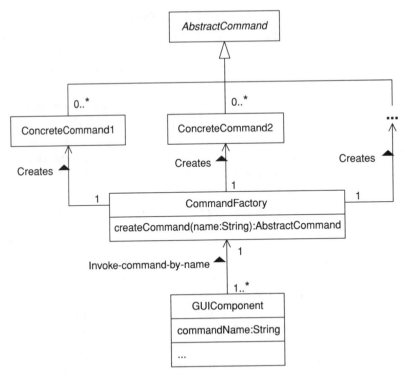

FIGURE 8.6 Command factory.

getActionCommand and setActionCommand that you can use to get and set the name of a command associated with the button or menu item.

CODE EXAMPLE

The example of commands in a word processor that can be undone and redone presented under the "Context" heading continues here. Figure 8.7 is a collaboration diagram that shows the normal collaboration that creates and executes commands.

Figure 8.7 shows an object creating an instance of the InsertStringCommand class, passing to its constructor the document into which to insert a string, the string to insert, and the position in which to insert the string. After initializing the InsertStringCommand object, the constructor calls the CommandManager object's invokeCommand method. The invokeCommand method calls the InsertStringCommand object's doIt method, which does the actual string insertion. If the doIt method returns

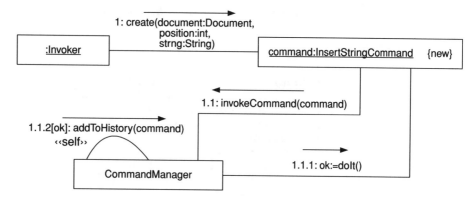

FIGURE 8.7 Word processor command collaboration.

true, indicating the command was successful and can be undone, then the `CommandManager` object adds the `InsertStringCommand` object to its command history.

Following is some code that implements this. First is the source for the `AbstractCommand` class, which is the superclass of all of the concrete command classes in this example:

```
public abstract class AbstractCommand {
    public final static CommandManager manager
      = new CommandManager();

    /**
     * Perform the command encapsulated by this object.
     * @return true if sucessful and can be undone.
     */
    public abstract boolean doIt();

    /**
     * Undo the last invocation of doIt.
     * @return true if the undo was successful
     */
    public abstract boolean undoIt();
} // class AbstractCommand
```

The `AbstractCommand` class creates the instance of `CommandManager` used to manage all of instances of `AbstractCommand`. Concrete subclasses of `AbstractCommand` are able to access the `CommandManager` object through the `AbstractCommand` class's `manager` variable.

Here is the source for a concrete subclass of the `AbstractCommand` class:

```
class InsertStringCommand extends AbstractCommand {
...
    /**
     * Constructor
     */
    InsertStringCommand(Document document,
                        int position, String strng) {
        this.document = document;
        this.position = position;
        this.strng = strng;
        manager.invokeCommand(this);
    } // Constructor(Document, int, String)

    /**
     * Perform the command encapsulated by this object.
     * @return true if this call to doCommand was successful
     *              and can be undone
     */
    public boolean doIt() {
        try {
            document.insertStringCommand(position, strng);
        } catch (Exception e) {
            return false;
        } // try
        return true;
    } // doIt()

    /**
     * Undo the command encapsulated by this object.
     * @return true if undo was successful
     */
    public boolean undoIt() {
        try {
            document.deleteCommand(position, strng.length());
        } catch (Exception e) {
            return false;
        } // try
        return true;
    } // undoIt()
} // class InsertStringCommand
```

The basic structure of most other subclasses of the `AbstractCommand` class is similar. Notable exceptions are the classes for undo and redo commands. They are shown later in this section.

Following is the source for the `CommandManager` class, which is responsible for managing the execution of commands. More specifically, for the purposes of the word processing program, instances of this class are responsible for maintaining a command history for undo and redo. Notice the special handling for undo and redo.

```
class CommandManager {
    // The maximum number of commands to keep in the history
    private int maxHistoryLength = 100;

    private LinkedList history = new LinkedList();
    private LinkedList redoList = new LinkedList();

    /**
     * Invoke a command and add it to the history,
     */
    public void invokeCommand(AbstractCommand command) {
        if (command instanceof Undo) {
            undo();
            return;
        } // if undo
        if (command instanceof Redo) {
            redo();
            return;
        } // if redo
        if (command.doIt()) {
            // doIt returned true, which means it can be undone
            addToHistory(command);
        } else { // cannot be undone, so clear command history
            history.clear();
        } // if
        // After command that isn't undo/redo, ensure redo list is empty.
        if (redoList.size() > 0)
            redoList.clear();
    } // invokeCommand(AbstractCommand)

    private void undo() {
        if (history.size() > 0) { // If the history is not empty
            AbstractCommand undoCommand;
            undoCommand = (AbstractCommand)history.removeFirst();
            undoCommand.undoIt();
            redoList.addFirst(undoCommand);
        } // if
    } // undo()

    private void redo() {
        if (redoList.size() > 0) { // If the redo list is not empty
            AbstractCommand redoCommand;
            redoCommand = (AbstractCommand)redoList.removeFirst();
            redoCommand.doIt();
            history.addFirst(redoCommand);
        } // if
    } // redo()

    /**
     * Add a command to the command history.
     */
```

```
        private void addToHistory(AbstractCommand command) {
            history.addFirst(command);
            // If size of history has exceded maxHistoryLength, remove
            // the oldest command from the history
            if (history.size() > maxHistoryLength)
              history.removeLast();
        } // addToHistory(AbstractCommand)
} // class CommandManager
```

You will notice that the CommandManager class does not actually call the methods of classes that represent the undo and redo commands. It just looks to see if their instances implement the Undo or Redo interfaces. Those interfaces are purely marker interfaces; they do not declare any members. Here is the source for the Undo interface:

```
interface Undo {
} // interface Undo
```

The source for the Redo interface is similar.

The reason for using these marker interfaces is to keep the CommandManager class independent of specific subclasses of the AbstractCommand class. Because the CommandManager class is responsible for managing undo and redo, all that classes representing undo and redo need to do is let a CommandManager object know that it should undo or redo the last command. It is preferable for it to do that in a way that does not require the CommandManager class to expose any of its special logic. This implies a mechanism that allows a CommandManager object to ask if it needs to perform an undo or redo, rather than being told. Being able to determine if an object implements the Undo or Redo interface allows a CommandManager object to ask if it should perform an undo or redo without having to know anything about the class that implements the interface.

Finally, here is source for the UndoCommand class. The RedoCommand class is very similar.

```
class UndoCommand implements Undo {
    /**
     * This implementation of doIt does not actually do anything.
     * The logic for undo is in the CommandManager class.
     */
    public boolean doIt() {
        // This method should never be called
        throw new NoSuchMethodError();
    } // doIt()
    /**
     * This implementation of undoIt does not actually do anything.
     * Undo commands are not undone. Instead a redo command is issued.
```

```
    */
    public boolean undoIt() {
        // This method should never be called
        throw new NoSuchMethodError();
    } // undoIt()
} // class UndoCommand
```

Because there should never be a reason to call the methods of this class, the methods always throw an exception.

RELATED PATTERNS

Factory Method   The Factory Method pattern is sometimes used to provide a layer of indirection between a user interface and command classes.

Little Language   You can use the Command pattern to help implement the Little Language pattern.

Marker Interface   You can use the Marker Interface pattern with the Command pattern to implement undo/redo processing.

Snapshot   If you want to provide a coarse-grained undo mechanism that saves the entire state of an object rather than a command-by-command account of how to reconstruct previous states, you can use the Snapshot pattern.

Template Method   The Template Method pattern can be used to implement the top-level undo logic of the Command pattern.

Little Language [Grand98]

The Little Language pattern is based on the Interpreter pattern documented in [GoF95] and the notional of little languages popularized by Jon Bentley[Bentley]. You can find more sophisticated techniques for designing and implementing languages in [ASU86].

SYNOPSIS

Suppose that you need to solve many similar problems and you notice that the solutions to these problems can be expressed as different combinations of a small number of elements or operations. The simplest way to express solutions to these problems may be to define a little language. Common types of problems that you can solve with little languages are searches of common data structures, creation of complex data structures, and formatting of data.

CONTEXT

Suppose that you need to write a program that searches a collection of files to find files that contain a given combination or combinations of words. You don't want to have to write a separate program for each search. Instead, you can define a little language that allows users to describe combinations of words and then write one program that finds files that contain a combination of words specified in the little language.

The definition of a language usually consists of two parts. The *syntax* of a language defines what words and symbols make up the language and how they may be combined. The *semantics* of a language defines the meaning of the words, the symbols, and their combinations that make up the language.

You usually define the syntax of a language by writing a grammar. A *grammar* is a set of rules that defines the sequences of characters that make up the words and symbols of the language. A grammar also contains rules that define how you can combine the words and symbols of the language to form larger constructs.

The precise definition of the semantics of a large language can be very complicated and lengthy. However, for a little language a few simple paragraphs of explanation may be good enough.

Returning to the idea of defining a little language to define combinations of words, one way to define a little language is to first create a few examples of what the language should look like. Then you can generalize from the examples to a complete definition.

Following that plan, consider some things that will be useful to say in a little language for specifying combinations of words. The most basic thing is to be able to specify a combination that consists of only a single word. The most obvious way to specify that is by just writing the word, like this:

```
bottle
```

You will also want to be able to specify combinations of words that don't contain a word. A simple way of doing that is to precede the word you don't want in combinations by the word "not," like this:

```
not box
```

That specifies all combinations of words that do not contain the word "box".

Using words such as "not" to mean something other than a word that can be part of a combination makes those words special. Such words are called *reserved words,* because they are reserved for a special purpose and cannot be used the way that other words can be used. If you treat the word "not" as a reserved word, then this means that you cannot specify a combination of words that contains the word "not" by just writing the word "not." As you read further in this discussion, you will see that there are reasons to treat other words as reserved words. This suggests that it will be useful to have a way of indicating a combination of words that contains any arbitrary word, sequence of words, or punctuation. A reasonable way of indicating a combination of words that includes an arbitrary sequence of words and punctuation is to enclose the sequence of words in quotes, like this:

```
"Yes, not the"
```

The next level of complexity would be to specify combinations of two words. Obviously, the syntax for a combination of two words must allow you to specify which words are in the combination. Since there are different ways to combine words, the syntax for specifying combinations of two words must also provide for specifying how the words are combined. One way to do that is to write one word of the combination, followed by a special word that indicates how the words are combined, followed by the second word of the combination. For example, you could write to indicate combinations of words that contain at least one of the words "bottle" or "jar":

```
bottle or jar
```

You will need additional words to indicate other ways to combine two words:

- Use the word "and" to indicate combinations of words that contain both words.
- Use the word "near" to indicate combinations that include the two words occurring within 25 words of each other.

If you wanted to combine the reserved word "and" with the reserved word "not" to indicate a combination of words that contains "garlic" but not "onions," it would be reasonable to write

```
garlic and not onions
```

These examples cover most of the things you will need to describe combinations involving two words. When you go beyond two words, you will need to deal with additional issues. It seems clear that

```
red and "pickup truck" and broken
```

means combinations of words that contain all three of the word "red," the phrase "pickup truck," and the word "broken."

When you mix different ways of combining words, the meaning becomes ambiguous. Does

```
turkey or chicken and soup
```

mean combinations of words that contain the word "turkey" or both of the words "chicken" and "soup"? Does it mean combinations of words that contain the word "soup" and at least one of the words "chicken" or "turkey"? One way to resolve this ambiguity is to require the use of parentheses to specify the order in which the logical connectors in a combination are used. To specify the first interpretation you could write

```
turkey or (chicken and soup)
```

To specify the second interpretation, you could write

```
(turkey or chicken) and soup
```

Most people don't like being forced to write parentheses, so a rule that resolves the ambiguity without parentheses is desirable. A common type of rule used in language definitions to resolve this sort of ambiguity is called a *precedence rule*.

A precedence rule is a rule that assigns a different precedence to the different operations that occur in a language. Its use is to provide a way of deciding the order of operations. Operations with a higher precedence are done before operations with a lower precedence. Suppose that you assign the following precedence values:

```
--------
near 3
--------
and 2
--------
or 1
--------
```

Given those precedence values, the meaning of

```
mansion or big near house and rich
```

would be combinations of words that include the word "mansion" or both the words "rich" and "big," with the word "big" occurring within 25 words of the word "house." In other words, it would be equivalent to

```
mansion or ((big near house) and rich)
```

Before you try to design any classes to make sense out of this little language, it is important to write a grammar that defines the syntax of the grammar. That will provide a clear specification from which to code. There are a few different strategies for organizing a grammar. The strategy used in this example is a top-down strategy. That means starting with the top-level construct in the language, a combination, and deciding all of the lower-level constructs that can comprise it until the grammar is complete.

Above the level of individual characters, the constructs that make up a grammar are called *tokens*. The tokens in a grammar are classified as either terminal tokens or nonterminal tokens. Terminal tokens correspond to a contiguous sequence of characters. The word in a combination, such as

```
fence
```

is a terminal token, as are parentheses and quoted strings. Higher-level constructs that are defined in terms of terminal tokens are called *nonterminal tokens*. A combination is a nonterminal token.

In most little languages, including this word combination language, terminal tokens may be separated by white-space characters that do not contribute to the meaning of the language.

The rules that determine how to recognize sequences of characters as terminal tokens are called *lexical analysis rules*. The rules that determine how to recognize nonterminal tokens as sequences of terminal and nonterminal tokens are called *productions*.

The notation used here for writing productions is called *Backus-Naur Form* or, more commonly, BNF. In BNF, terminal tokens and nonterminal tokens are written using different fonts to distinguish them. This book indicates terminal tokens like this:

quoted_string

This book indicates nonterminal tokens like this:

combination

A production consists of a nonterminal token and a sequence of terminal and nonterminal tokens that can be recognized as that first nonterminal. Here is an example of a production:

combination -> **word**

The preceding production says that a combination nonterminal token can consist of just a word terminal token.

If there are multiple sequences of tokens that can be recognized as nonterminal, then there will be multiple productions for this nonterminal sequence. There will be one production for each sequence that can be recognized as this nonterminal. For example, the following set of productions specifies the syntax for combinations that contain a particular word or don't contain a particular word:

combination -> **word**
combination -> **not word**

The technique that you use to specify that a nonterminal token should be recognized from an indefinitely long sequence of tokens is *recursion*. Here is a set of productions that captures most of the syntax of the preceding examples:

```
combination -> ( combination )
combination -> simpleCombination
combination -> simpleCombination or combination
combination -> simpleCombination and combination
combination -> simpleCombination near combination
simpleCombination -> word
simpleCombination -> not word
```

Notice that four of the productions for *combination* are recursive. Three of those four productions could have been written with *combination* as the first nonterminal token and *simpleCombination* as the second nonterminal token. Either way they would match the same sequences of tokens. However, for the implementation technique shown later in this section for turning productions into code, it makes a difference. For the technique we will discuss, it is always best to write productions as shown, in a right recursive way. *Right recursive* means that, where there is a choice about where to put a recursion in a production, we choose to put the recursion as far to the right as possible.

Though the preceding set of productions does not capture all the details of this word combination language, it captures enough that we can work through an example. We will examine how to use these productions to recognize this string as a combination:

```
fox and not brown
```

Looking at the productions for *combination*, we see that *combination* can begin with a left parenthesis or a *simpleCombination*. The string begins with a **word** token. Since the string we are trying to recognize as a *combination* does not begin with a left parenthesis, we try to recognize the beginning of the string as a *simpleCombination*. This matches the production

```
simpleCombination -> word
```

This leaves us having recognized this much of the string:

```
---
fox and not brown
```

The line over the string shows how much of the string has been recognized. This is what we have recognized:

```
simpleCombination
        |
     word
```

```
    |
    |
fox
```

In other words, what we have recognized is `simpleCombination` token that consists of a word token that is the word "fox." What we want to recognize is `combination`. Four productions for `combination` begin with `simpleCombination`. One of those productions is

```
combination -> simpleCombination
```

This gives us a choice of matching this production with what we have already recognized or trying to match a longer production for `combination`. When faced with this type of choice, we always try to match a longer production. If we are unable to match a longer production, then we back up and match the shorter production.

The next token in the string is an **and** token. There is one production for `combination` that begins with `simpleCombination` followed by **and**:

```
combination -> simpleCombination and combination
```

In order to finish matching the string this production, we will need to recognize the rest of the string as a `combination`.

The next token in the string is a **not** token. Looking at the productions for `combination`, we see that `combination` can begin with a left parenthesis or a `simpleCombination`. Since the string we are trying to recognize as a `combination` does not begin with a left parenthesis, we try to recognize the beginning of the string as a `simpleCombination`. There is a production for `simpleCombination` that begins with a **not** token. Now we are trying to finish matching the production

```
simpleCombination -> not word
```

so that we can finish matching

```
combination -> simpleCombination and combination
```

Because the production for the `simpleCombination` that we are trying to match, we expect the next token in the string to be a **word** token. We have recognized this much of the string:

```
--------
fox and not brown
```

The next token is a **word** token. This means that we have successfully matched the productions that we were trying to match. Because that also exhausts the content of the string, we have recognized the entire string as a combination with this internal structure:

This tree structure that was constructed while parsing the string is called a *parse tree*. For most languages, the implementation is simpler and faster if it first builds a parse tree data structure and then uses the parse tree to drive subsequent actions.

As mentioned before, the set of productions that we used to work through the preceding example do not capture all the details of the word combination language. The main thing missing is that they don't allow a combination to include quoted strings. They also don't capture precedence rules for **and**, **near**, or **or**.

There is another nuance that will be helpful to add to the productions. The previous set of productions uses the same nonterminal token to match the token sequences **word** and **not word**. This means that after we have built the parse tree, the same type of object will represent both kinds of sequences. It will simplify the interpretation of the parse tree and make it faster if it is possible to determine which type of sequence an object represents just by looking at its type. You can accomplish that by having productions that recognize those sequences as two different nonterminals.

Here is the final set of productions with those improvements added:

```
combination -> orCombination
orCombination -> andCombination or orCombination
orCombination -> andCombination
andCombination -> nearCombination and andCombination
andCombination -> nearCombination
nearCombination -> simpleCombination near nearCombination
nearCombination -> simpleCombination
simpleCombination -> ( orCombination )
simpleCombination -> wordCombination
simpleCombination -> notWordCombination
wordCombination -> word
wordCombination -> quoted_string
notWordCombination -> not word
notWordCombination -> not quoted_string
```

You may notice that if you use these productions to parse a string, creating a parse tree node object for each nonterminal, you will have more parse tree node objects than were produced by the previous set of productions. Here is the parse tree that would be produced by parsing the same string as in the previous example,

```
fox and not brown
```

and using the preceding productions to create a parse tree node object for each nonterminal:

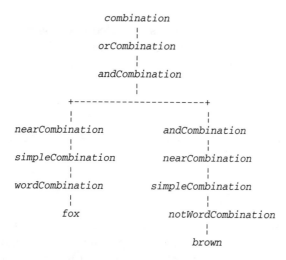

Notice that the preceding parse tree contains many nodes that do not add anything useful to the tree. Without losing any information, this parse tree could be simplified to the following:

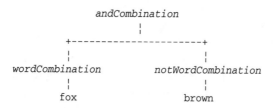

Before you write any code, you should decide which productions are purely organizational in nature and which productions provide useful information. A parser should only produce parse tree nodes that provide information.

The preceding discussion covers the basics of writing productions to recognize tokens. Now consider how to define lexical rules that determine how to recognize terminal tokens from sequences of characters.

In many little languages, the lexical rules are sometimes simple enough that you can adequately define them by a natural language set of descriptions, like this:

- White space consists of one or more consecutive space, tab, new-line, or carriage-return characters. White space can be used to separate terminal tokens. It has no other significance and is discarded.
- An **and** token consists of this sequence of three letters: **a, n, d**.
- ...

Where this approach does not seem adequate, you may prefer a more precise approach based on regular expressions. Regular expressions are a way of specifying how to match a sequence of characters. For example, the regular expression

```
[0-9]+
```

matches a sequence of one or more digits. There are a variety of regular expression notations you can use. The regular expression notation used in this section to define the lexical rules for the word combination language is explained in Table 8.1. It should be sufficiently expressive for most little languages.

Table 8.2 shows a set of lexical rules for the word combination language. In the first column is a regular expression. The second column contains the name of the terminal token, if any, that is recognized when the regular expression is matched. When a parser needs to find the next terminal token in its input, it will try the regular expressions in the order in which they appear until it finds one that matches the input. If no regular expression matches the input, then the parser knows that something is wrong with the input.

When a regular expression matches the input, if there is a terminal token in the second column then the parser recognizes that token and processes it according to whatever production it is trying to match. If there is no terminal token in the second column, then the input that the regular expression matches is discarded and the parser begins again with the first regular expression.

Now we have specified the syntax of the word combination language. In the process of specifying the syntax, we have also discussed the semantics of the language sufficiently. The next thing to do is to design the classes. Figure 8.8 shows the classes necessary to implement the word combination language.

TABLE 8.1 Word Combination Language

Regular Expression	What It Matches
c	Matches the character c if c is not one of the special characters described below.
\	If a \ is followed by one of the escape sequences that Java allows in strings, then it means the same thing as that escape. If a \ is followed by any of the characters that are considered special in regular expressions, then the pair of characters is treated as the second character without it being special. For example, \\ matches a backslash character.
.	Matches any character.
^	Matches the beginning of a line or a string.
$	Matches the end of a line or a string.
[s]	Matches a character that is in a set of characters and character ranges. For example, [aeiou] matches a lowercase vowel. [A-Za-z_] matches an uppercase or lowercase letter or an underscore.
[^s]	Matches a character that is *not* in a set of characters and character ranges. For example, [^0-9] matches a character that is not a digit. The ^ is treated specially only right after the [. For example, [+^] matches a plus sign or a circumflex.
r*	Matches zero or more occurrences of the regular expression r.
r+	Matches one or more occurrences of the regular expression r.
r?	Matches zero or one occurrences of the regular expression r.
rx	Matches what the regular expression r matches followed by what the regular expression x matches.
(r)	Matches what the regular expression r matches. For example, (xyz)* matches zero or more occurrences of the sequence xyz.
r|x	Matches any string that matches the regular expression r or the regular expression x. For example, (abc) | (xyz) matches the sequence abc or the sequence xyz.
r{m,n}	Matches at least m occurrences but no more than n occurrences of regular expression r.

The preceding class diagram shows an InputStream class. Instances of the LexicalAnalyzer class read characters of a word combination from an instance of the InputStream class. An instance of the Parser class reads tokens from an instance of the LexicalAnalyzer class by calling its nextToken method. The diagram indicates that the nextToken method returns a TerminalToken object. However, the diagram does not include any TerminalToken class. If it did, the TerminalToken class would be an abstract class that defines no methods or variables. The subclasses of the TerminalToken class would each correspond to a different

TABLE 8.2 Lexical Rules for the Word Combination Language

`[\u0000-\u0020]+`		
`[Oo] [Rr]`		`or`
`[Aa] [Nn] [Dd]`		`and`
`[Nn] [Ee] [Aa] [Rr]`		`near`
`[Nn] [Oo] [Tt]`		`not`
`[a-zA-Z0-9]+`		`word`
`\(`		`(`
`\)`		`)`
`"([^"]*(\\")*)*"`		`quoted_string`

terminal token. The subclasses of the `TerminalToken` class would define no methods and either no variables or one variable containing the string recognized as that terminal token. These would be very lightweight objects, encapsulating only the type of terminal token that the object represents and in some cases a string. Implementations of the Little Language pattern do not usually bother to encapsulate these pieces of information. Implementations of the `LexicalAnalyzer` class usually provide these pieces of information as unencapsulated pieces of information.

As a `Parser` object gets tokens from a `LexicalAnalyzer` object, it creates instances of subclasses of the `Combination` class, organizing them into a parse tree.

The `Combination` class is the abstract superclass of all the classes that are instantiated to create parse tree nodes. The `Combination` class defines an abstract method called `contains`. The `contains` method takes a string as its argument and returns an array of int. Subclasses of `Combination` override the `contains` method to determine if it meets the requirements of the particular subclass for containing the desired combination of words. If the string does contain the required combination of words, it passes back an array of int values that are the offsets in the string of the words that satisfied the combination. If the string does not contain the required combination of words, then the `contains` method returns null.

FORCES

- You need to identify, create, or format similar kinds of data using many different combinations of a moderate number of operations.
- A straightforward representation of combinations of operations can provide adequate performance.

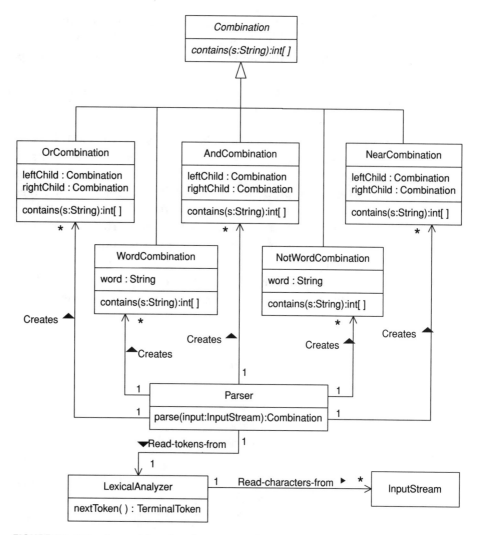

FIGURE 8.8 Word combination language classes.

SOLUTION

The Little Language pattern begins with the design of a little language that can specify combinations of operations needed to solve a specific type of problem. The design of a little language specifies its syntax using productions and lexical rules, as described under the "Context" heading. The semantics of a little language are usually specified informally by describing what the constructs of the language do using English or another natural language.

Once you have defined a little language, the next step is to design the classes that you will use to implement the language. Figure 8.9 presents a class diagram that shows the organization of classes that participate in the Little Language pattern.

Explanations of the roles that these classes play in the Little Language pattern are as follows:

Client An instance of a class in this role runs a little language program, feeding it whatever data it needs and using the results that the program produces. It creates an instance of the `Parser` class to parse programs that it supplies through `InputStream` objects. The `Parser` object's `parse` method returns an instance of the `AbstractNonterminal` class to the `Client` object. That object is the root of a parse tree. The `Client` object calls the `AbstractNonterminal` object's `execute` method to run the program.

Lexical Analyzer When a `Parser` object's `parse` method is called, it creates a `LexicalAnalyzer` object to read characters from the same

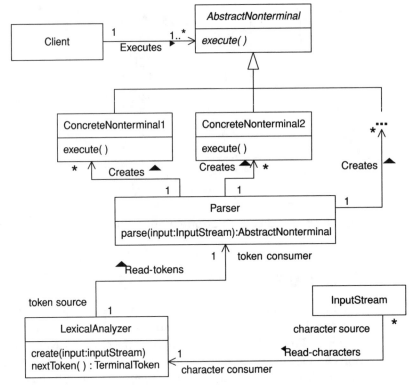

FIGURE 8.9 Little Language pattern classes.

InputStream object that was passed to it. The LexicalAnalyzer object reads characters from the InputStream object, recognizes terminal tokens it finds using the lexical rules, and returns those tokens to the Parser class when it calls the LexicalAnalyzer object's nextToken method. The nextToken method returns the next terminal token that it finds in the input.

Parser   A Client object creates an instance of the Parser class and then calls the Parser object's parse method to parse input from InputStream objects by matching the tokens in the input against the productions of the grammar. The parse method builds a parse tree as it matches the productions and returns a reference to the parse tree's root to the Client object.

AbstractNonterminal   A class in this role is the abstract superclass of all of the classes whose instances can be parse tree nodes. A Client object calls its abstract execute method to execute the program.

ConcreteNonterminal1, ConcreteNonterminal2   Instances of classes in these roles are used as parse tree nodes.

TerminalToken   This abstract class defines no variables or methods. Its subclasses correspond to the terminal tokens that the LexicalAnalyzer class recognizes.

InputStream   An instance of the InputStream class can be used to read a stream of characters. The InputStream class is part of the standard Java API.

CONSEQUENCES

- The Little Language pattern allows users to specify different combinations of operations. It is almost always easier to design and implement a little language than it is to design and implement a graphical user interface that provides as much flexibility and expressiveness as a little language. On the other hand, most users find the graphical user interface easier to use.
- A language is a form of user interface. Like any user interface, you learn what it makes easy and not so easy to use by using it and watching other people use it.
- A Parser class for a little language is usually implemented by writing private methods that mostly correspond to nonterminal tokens. That organization is easy to understand and grammar changes are easy to implement so long as the grammar remains relatively small. If the language gets too large, this organization becomes unmanageable.

For larger and full-service languages, there are different and more sophisticated design and implementation techniques. Tools exist that can automatically generate `Parser` and `LexicalAnalyzer` classes from productions and lexical rules. There are other tools that assist in the building and simplification of parse trees.

IMPLEMENTATION

Some people believe that it is better to implement a parser by spreading most of its logic through multiple classes that correspond to nonterminal tokens or even productions. A common reason given to explain this organization is that it is somehow more object oriented. However, that is a less maintainable organization for parsers than the one described previously. There are two reasons for that:

1. Spreading the parsing logic over a number of classes results in less-cohesive classes that are difficult to understand. The parser for little languages is usually small enough that people can understand it in its entirety. Spreading the parsing logic over multiple classes makes it much more difficult to understand in its entirety.

2. If a parser is too big to understand in its entirety, then it is big enough that its implementation would be worth changing so that it uses a tool that automatically generates the parser from productions. All available tools that are known to the author of this book generate a parser as a single class or as one main class with some helper classes. If there are other tools that generate a parser as multiple classes, it is very likely that the organization of these classes will be different than any manually generated organization. That means that if a parser is manually organized as many classes, switching to an automatically generated parser will involve fixing any classes that break because they refer to a defunct class of the manually generated parser. Manually generating a parser as multiple classes can make it more difficult to migrate to an automatically generated parser.

Most subclasses of `TerminalToken` do not contain any methods or variables. Those subclasses of `TerminalToken` that do contain variables usually contain just one variable whose value is the substring of the input that the class's instances match. Because subclasses of `TerminalToken` contain so little information, most implementations of the Little Language pattern do not bother using `TerminalToken` or its subclasses. Instead, they pass the type of token that the lexical analyzer recognized and the corresponding string from the lexical analyzer to the parser without encapsulating them in an object.

Parsers build parse trees from the bottom up. The root of a parse tree corresponds to at least as much of the program source as all of its children put together. As a parser parses its input, its creates small parse trees. It joins the small parse trees into larger parse trees with a common root as it recognizes larger and larger constructs. When the parser is done, there is just one big parse tree.

Many optimizations and design subtleties that are important to full-service languages are not important to little languages. The point is that the techniques described in this pattern are not sufficient for designing or implementing larger languages like Java.

JAVA API USAGE

Subclasses of `java.text.Format` use the Little Language pattern. The constructors of these classes are passed, explicitly or implicitly, a string that contains a description of a format in a little language. Each subclass has its own little language for such things as substituting text in messages (`MessageFormat`), formatting date and time information (`DateFormat`), and formatting decimal numbers (`DecimalFormat`).

Because of the flat structure of these little languages, their parsers do not generate a parse tree, but rather an array of objects.

CODE EXAMPLE

The first code example is the lexical analyzer. Because the word combination language's lexical rules are sufficiently similar to Java's lexical rules, the `java.io.StreamTokenizer` class can do much of the work. That is the same class that Sun's Java compiler uses for its lexical analysis.

```
class LexicalAnalyzer {
    private StreamTokenizer input;
    private int lastToken;

    // constants to identify the type of the last recognized token.
    static final int INVALID_CHAR = -1;// unexpected character.
    static final int NO_TOKEN = 0;// No tokens recognized yet.
```

```
        static final int OR = 1;
        static final int AND = 2;
        static final int NEAR = 3;
        static final int NOT = 4;
        static final int WORD = 5;
        static final int LEFT_PAREN = 6;
        static final int RIGHT_PAREN = 7;
        static final int QUOTED_STRING = 8;
        static final int EOF = 9;

        /**
         * Constructor
         * @param input The input stream that contains input to be lexed.
         */
        LexicalAnalyzer(InputStream in) {
            input = new StreamTokenizer(in);
            input.resetSyntax();
            input.eolIsSignificant(false);
            input.wordChars('a', 'z');
            input.wordChars('A', 'Z');
            input.wordChars('0', '9');
            input.wordChars('\u0000',' ');
            input.ordinaryChar('(');
            input.ordinaryChar(')');
            input.quotechar('"');
        } // constructor(InputStream)

        /**
         * Return the string recognized as word token or the body of a
         * quoted string.
         */
        String getString() {
            return input.sval;
        } // getString()

        /**
         * Return the type of the next token. For word and quoted string
         * tokens, the string that the token represents can be fetched by
         * callling the getString method.
         */
        int nextToken() {
            int token;
            try {
                switch (input.nextToken()) {
                  case StreamTokenizer.TT_EOF:
                      token = EOF;
                      break;
                  case StreamTokenizer.TT_WORD:
                      if (input.sval.equalsIgnoreCase("or"))
                        token = OR;
                      else if (input.sval.equalsIgnoreCase("and"))
```

```
                                token = AND;
                    else if (input.sval.equalsIgnoreCase("near"))
                        token = NEAR;
                    else if (input.sval.equalsIgnoreCase("not"))
                        token = NOT;
                    else
                        token = WORD;
                    break;
                case '"':
                    token = QUOTED_STRING;
                    break;
                case '(':
                    token = LEFT_PAREN;
                    break;
                case ')':
                    token = RIGHT_PAREN;
                    break;
                default:
                    token = INVALID_CHAR;
                    break;
            } // switch
        } catch (IOException e) {
            // Treat an IOException as an end of file
            token = EOF;
        } // try
        return token;
    } // nextToken()
} // class LexicalAnalyzer
```

Although the `LexicalAnalyzer` class uses the `StringTokenizer` class to do much of the lexical analysis, it provides its own codes to indicate the type of token that it recognized. That allows the implementation of the `LexicalAnalyzer` class to change without any impact on classes that use the `LexicalAnalyzer` class.

The parser implementation uses a technique called *recursive decent*. A recursive decent parser has methods that correspond to nonterminal tokens defined by grammar productions. The methods call each other using roughly the same pattern by which the corresponding grammar productions refer to each other. Where there is recursion in the grammar productions, there is generally recursion in the methods. One important exception to this is when the recursion is a self-recursion through the rightmost token in a production, like this:

orCombination -> *andCombination* **or** *orCombination*

Translating this in the obvious way into a self-recursive method produces a method that performs a self-recursion as the last thing it does before it returns. This type of recursion is a special case called *tail recursion*. Tail recursion is special because you can always change a tail recursion into a loop. In the following code for the `Parser` class, you will see that methods corresponding to nonterminals defined in a self-recursive way implement the self-recursion using a loop.

```java
public class Parser {
    private LexicalAnalyzer lexer; // lexical analyzer parser uses
    private int token;

    /**
     * Parse a word combination read from the given input stream.
     * @param input Read word combination source from this InputStream.
     * @return A combination object that is the root of the parse tree.
     */
    public Combination parse(InputStream input)
            throws SyntaxException{
        lexer = new LexicalAnalyzer(input);
        Combination c = orCombination();
        expect(LexicalAnalyzer.EOF);
        return c;
    } // parse(InputStream)

    private Combination orCombination() throws SyntaxException {
        Combination c = andCombination();
        while (token == LexicalAnalyzer.OR) {
            c = new OrCombination(c, andCombination());
        } // while
        return c;
    } // orCombination()

    private Combination andCombination() throws SyntaxException {
        Combination c = nearCombination();
        while (token == LexicalAnalyzer.AND) {
            c = new AndCombination(c, nearCombination());
        } // while
        return c;
    } // andCombination

    private Combination nearCombination() throws SyntaxException {
        Combination c = simpleCombination();
        while (token == LexicalAnalyzer.NEAR) {
            c = new NearCombination(c, simpleCombination());
        } // while
        return c;
    } // nearCombination()

    private Combination simpleCombination() throws SyntaxException {
        if (token == LexicalAnalyzer.LEFT_PAREN) {
```

```
        nextToken();
        Combination c = orCombination();
        expect(LexicalAnalyzer.RIGHT_PAREN);
        return c;
    } // if '('
    if (token == LexicalAnalyzer.NOT)
      return notWordCombination();
    else
      return wordCombination();
} // simpleCombination()


private Combination wordCombination() throws SyntaxException {
    if (token != LexicalAnalyzer.WORD
        && token != LexicalAnalyzer.QUOTED_STRING) {
        // print error message and throw SyntaxException
        expect(LexicalAnalzyer.WORD);
    } // if
    Combination c = new WordCombination(lexer.getString());
    nextToken();
    return c;
} // wordCombination()


private Combination notWordCombination()
                    throws SyntaxException {
    expect(LexicalAnalyzer.NOT);
    if (token != LexicalAnalyzer.WORD
        && token != LexicalAnalyzer.QUOTED_STRING) {
        // print error message and throw SyntaxException
        expect(LexicalAnalyzer.WORD);
    } // if
    Combination c = new NotWordCombination(lexer.getString());
    nextToken();
    return c;
    } // notWordCombination()


    // Get the next token from the lexer.
    private void nextToken() {
        token = lexer.nextToken();
    } // nextToken()
```

The remainder of the Parser class is a method called expect and a helper method for expect called tokenName. The expect method issues an error message if the current terminal token is not the type of token specified as an argument to the expect method. If the token is the expected kind of token, then the expect method reads the next token from the lexical analyzer.

Most recursive decent parsers have a method similar to expect and it is often called expect.

```
private void expect(int t) throws SyntaxException {
    if (token != t) {
        String msg = "found " + tokenName(token)
            + " when expecting " + tokenName(t);
        System.err.println("Syntax error: "+msg);
    } // if
    nextToken();
} // expect(int)

private String tokenName(int t) {
    String tname;
    switch (t) {
        case LexicalAnalyzer.OR:
            tname = "OR";
            break;
        case LexicalAnalyzer.AND:
            tname = "AND";
            break;
        case LexicalAnalyzer.NEAR:
            tname = "NEAR";
            break;
        case LexicalAnalyzer.NOT:
            tname = "NOT";
            break;
        case LexicalAnalyzer.WORD:
            tname = "WORD";
            break;
        case LexicalAnalyzer.LEFT_PAREN:
            tname = "(";
            break;
        case LexicalAnalyzer.RIGHT_PAREN:
            tname = ")";
            break;
        case LexicalAnalyzer.QUOTED_STRING:
            tname = "quoted string";
            break;
        case LexicalAnalyzer.EOF:
            tname = "end of file";
            break;
        default:
            tname = "???";
            break;
    } // switch
    return tname;
} // tokenName(int)
} // class Parser
```

There is an obvious relationship between the productions of the formal grammar and the preceding code for the Parser class. Because the relationship between the two is so obvious, you may feel tempted to skip writing the formal grammar and just define your little language with code. Skipping the formal grammar is usually a bad idea for the following reasons:

- Without a formal grammar there is no precise way to communicate the definition of your language to other people without having them read you source code.
- As the syntax for a language becomes larger or more complex, so does the parser for the language. As the parser becomes more complex, the code becomes cluttered with necessary details and the relationship between the code and the grammar it implements becomes less obvious.
- Over time, languages often evolve, gaining new features. When trying to make changes to a language that has no formal grammar, you may find it difficult to distinguish between changes to the language's grammar and changes to its implementation.

The next piece of code in this example is the `Combination` class, which is the abstract superclass of all parse tree objects:

```
abstract class Combination {
    /**
     * If the given string contains the words that this Combination
     * object requires, this method returns an array of ints. In most
     * cases, the array contains the offsets of the words in the string
     * that are required by this combination. However, if the array is
     * empty, then all the words in the string satisfy the combination
     * If the given string does not contain the words that this
     * Combination object requires, then this method returns null.
     * /
    abstract int[] contains (String s) ;
// class Combination
```

You will notice that the methods of `Combination` and its subclasses relate almost exclusively to the execution of combinations. There is almost no code related to the manipulation of the objects in the parse tree. Some larger languages require additional analysis of a program, after it is parsed, in order to turn it into an executable form. For such languages, a parse tree is an intermediate form for a program, distinct from its executable form. The Little Language pattern assumes that a language is simple enough that you can use a parse tree for both purposes.

Here is the source for `NotWordCombination`, which is the simplest subclass of `Combination`:

```
class NotWordCombination extends Combination {
    private String word;

    /**
     * constructor
     * @param word The word that this combination requires in a string
     * /
    NotWordCombination(String word) {
        this.word = word;
    } // constructor (String)

    /**
     * If the given string contains the word that this NotWordCombination
     * object requires, this method returns an array of the offsets where
     * the word occurs in the string. Otherwise this method returns null.
     */
    int[] contains (String s) {
        if (s.indexOf(word) >= 0)
          return null;
        return new int[0];
    } // contains(String)
} // class NotWordCombination
```

The WordCombination class is similar. The main difference is that it contains logic to return a vector of the offsets of all of the occurrences in a given string of the word associated with a WordCombination object.

The subclasses of Combination that represent logical operators, OrCombination, AndCombination, and NearCombination, are more complex. They are responsible for combining the results of two child Combination objects. Here is source code for AndCombination:

```
class AndCombination extends Combination {
    private Combination leftChild, rightChild;
    AndCombination(Combination leftChild, Combination rightChild) {
        this.leftChild = leftChild;
        this.rightChild = rightChild;
    } // constructor(Combination, Combination)

int[] contains(String s) {
        int[] leftResult = leftChild.contains(s);
        int[] rightResult = rightChild.contains(s);
        if (leftResult == null ||rightResult == null)
          return null;
        if (leftResult.length == 0)
          return rightResult;
        if (rightResult.length == 0)
          return leftResult;
```

```
    // Sort the results so that they can be compared and merged
    Sorter.sort(leftResult);
    Sorter.sort(rightResult);

    // Count common offsets to find out if there are common offsets
    // and how many there will be.
    int commonCount = 0;
    for int 1=0,r=0;
        1<leftResult.length && r<rightResult.length;){
        if (leftResult[1] < rightResult[r]) {
            1++;
        } else if (leftResult[1] > rightResult[r]) {
            r++;
        } else {
            commonCount++;
            1++;
            r++;
        } // if
    } // for
    if (commonCount == 0)
      return null; // There are no common results
    // merge common results
    int[] myResult = new int[commonCount];
    commonCount = 0;
    for ( int 1=0,r=0;
        1<leftResult.length && r<rightResult.length;) {
        if (leftResult[1] < rightResult[r]) {
            1++;
        } else if (leftResult[1] > rightResult[r]) {
            r++;
        } else {
            myResult[commonCount] = leftResult[1];
            commonCount++;
            1++;
            r++;
        } // if
    } // for
    return myResult;
  } // contains(String)
} // class AndCombination
```

RELATED PATTERNS

Composite   A parse tree is organized with the Composite pattern.

Visitor   The Visitor pattern allows you to encapsulate the logic for simple manipulations of a parse tree in a single class.

Mediator [GoF95]

SYNOPSIS

The Mediator pattern uses one object to coordinate state changes between other objects. Putting the logic in one object to manage state changes of other objects, instead of distributing the logic over the other objects, results in a more cohesive implementation of the logic and decreased coupling between the other objects.

CONTEXT

The Mediator pattern addresses a problem that commonly occurs in dialog boxes. Suppose that you have to implement a dialog box that looks like the one depicted in Figure 8.10, in order to specify information to select a banquet room in a hotel. The purpose of this dialog is to provide information needed to reserve a banquet room in a hotel. The requirements of the dialog give rise to a number of dependencies between the dialog's objects.

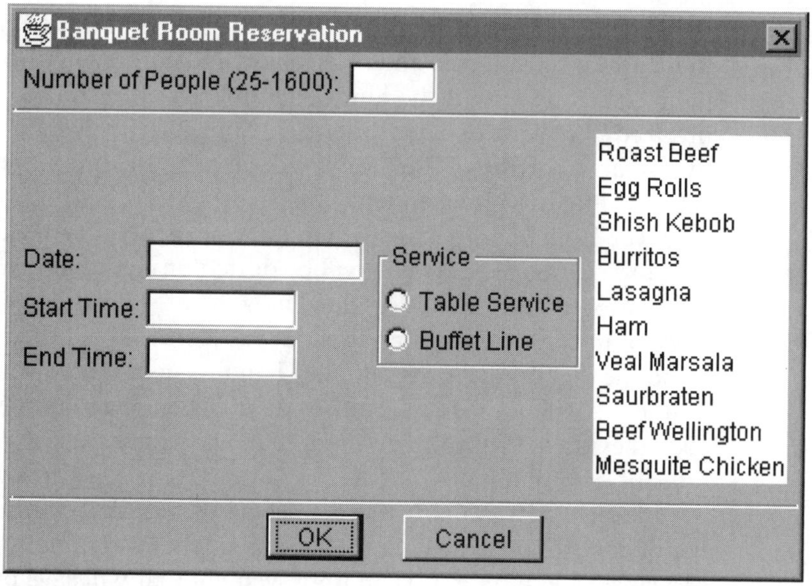

FIGURE 8.10 Banquet room dialog.

- When the dialog first comes up, only the fields labeled "Number of People" and the Cancel button are enabled. The rest of dialog is disabled until a number in the range of 25 to 1000 is entered into that field. At that point, the fields labeled "Date," "Start Time," and "End Time" become enabled, but they only allow times that a room of an appropriate size is available. The radio buttons are also enabled. Subsequent changes to the "Number of People" field clears the other fields and radio buttons.
- The start time must be earlier than the end time.
- When a user fills in the time and date fields and selects a radio button, then the list of foods becomes enabled. The date, time, and type of service requested determine the foods that appear in the list. Some foods are seasonal and the hotel offers them only between certain dates. Breakfast foods are on the list only for morning banquets. Some foods are not suitable for buffets and are suitable only for table service.
- When at least one food is selected and the text fields contain valid data, the OK button is enabled.

If each object in the dialog takes responsibility for the dependencies with which it is associated, the result is a highly coupled set of objects with low cohesion. The diagram in Figure 8.11 shows the relationships between the objects.

In the interest of simplifying this diagram in Figure 8.11, the association names, role names, and multiplicity indicators have been left out. The point of the diagram is the number of links. As you can see, each object is involved in at least two dependencies. Some are involved in as many as five. A large portion of the time it will take to implement the dialog will be spent coding the 15 dependency links.

The logic for dependency handling is spread out over eight objects. Because of this, the dialogue will be difficult to maintain. When a maintenance programmer works on the dialog, he or she will see only a small piece of the dependency handling. Because it will be difficult to understand the details of the dependency handling as a whole, maintenance programmers will not take the time to do it. When programmers maintain code they do not fully understand, the maintenance takes more time and is often of poor quality.

Clearly, reorganizing these objects in a way that minimizes the number of connections and gathers the dependency handling into one cohesive object is a good thing. It is an improvement that will save programmer time and produce more robust code. This is what the Mediator pattern is about. Instead of each object individually managing the dependencies it

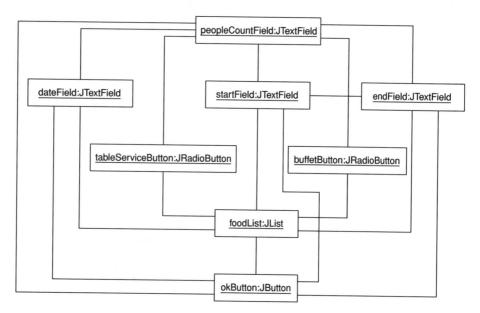

FIGURE 8.11 Decentralized dependency management.

has with other objects, you use another object that consolidates all of the dependency handling. In this arrangement, each of the other objects has only one dependency connection.

Figure 8.12 shows the dialog's objects organized with an additional object to centrally manage dependencies. In addition to making the implementation easier to code and maintain, the design shown in Figure 8.12 is easier to understand.

FORCES

- You have a set of related objects and most of the objects are involved in multiple dependency relationships.
- You find yourself defining subclasses so that individual objects can participate in dependency relationships.
- Classes are difficult to reuse because their basic function is entwined with dependency relationships.

SOLUTION

The collaboration diagram shown in Figure 8.13 demonstrates how classes and interfaces participate in the Mediator pattern in the general case.

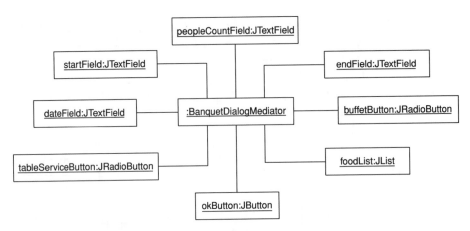

FIGURE 8.12 Centralized dependency management.

Explanations of the roles that these classes and interfaces play in the Mediator pattern are as follows:

Colleague1, Colleague2 Instances of classes in these roles have state related dependencies. There are two types of dependencies:

- One type of dependency requires an object to get approval from other objects before making specific types of state changes.
- The other type of dependency requires an object to notify other objects after it has made specific types of state changes.

Both types of dependencies are handled in a similar way. Instances of Colleague1, Colleague2... are associated with a Mediator object. When they want to get prior approval for a state change, they call a method of the Mediator object. When they need to notify other objects about a state change, they call a method of the Mediator object. The Mediator object's method takes care of the rest.

EventListener1, EventListener2 Interfaces in this role allow the Colleague1, Colleague2... classes to achieve a higher level of reuse. They do that by allowing these classes to be unaware that they are working with a Mediator object. Each of these interfaces defines methods related to a particular kind of event. To provide state notifications, Colleague objects call the appropriate method of the appropriate interface without knowing the class of the Mediator object that implements the method.

Mediator Instances of classes in the Mediator role have logic to process state notifications from Colleague1, Colleague2... objects. Mediator

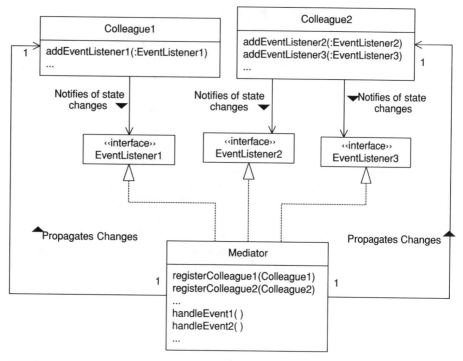

FIGURE 8.13 Mediator pattern classes.

classes implement one or more EventListener interfaces. Colleague1, Colleague2... objects call methods declared by EventListener interfaces to inform a Mediator object of state changes. The Mediator object then performs whatever logic is appropriate. For notifications of proposed state changes, this will typically include indicating approval or disapproval of the change. For notification of completed state changes, this will typically include propagating the notification to other objects.

Mediator classes have methods that can be called to associate them with Colleague1, Colleague2... objects. These methods are indicated in the diagram as registerColleague1, registerColleague2, ... They are passed an appropriate Colleague object and generally call one or more of its add...Listener methods to inform the Colleague object that it should inform the Mediator object of state changes.

The facilities that Colleague1, Colleague2... objects provide to allow other objects to express their interest in state change and the mechanism for providing notifications of these state changes normally conform to Java's delegation event model.

CONSEQUENCES

- Most of the complexity involved in managing dependencies is shifted from other objects to the `Mediator` object. This makes the other objects easier to implement and maintain.
- Putting all the dependency logic for a set of related objects in one place can make understanding the dependency logic easier, up to a point. If a `Mediator` class gets to be too large, then breaking it into smaller pieces can make it more understandable.
- Using a `Mediator` object usually means that there is no need to subclass `Colleague` classes just to implement their dependency handling.
- `Colleague` classes are more reusable because their core functionality is not entwined with dependency-handling code. Dependency-handling code tends to be specific to an application.
- Because dependency-handling code is usually application specific, `Mediator` classes are not usually reusable.

IMPLEMENTATION

In many cases, one object is responsible for creating all of the `Colleague` objects and their `Mediator` object. That object typically represents a frame or dialog and is a container for the objects that it creates. When there is a single object responsible for creating all of the `Colleague` objects and their `Mediator` object, the `Mediator` class is usually declared as a private member of that class. Limiting the visibility of a `Mediator` class increases the robustness of the program.

There are some decisions that you will have to make when you implement the `Mediator` pattern. One of those decisions is whether a `Mediator` object will maintain its own internal model of the state of `Colleague` objects or fetch the state of each object when it needs to know the object's state.

If you take the first approach, then the `Mediator` object begins by assuming the initial state of all of the `Colleague` objects for which it is responsible. It will have an instance variable for each `Colleague` object. A `Mediator` object sets the initial value of each of those instance variables to be what it expects the initial state of the corresponding `Colleague` object to be. When a `Colleague` object notifies the `Mediator` object that its state has changed, the `Mediator` object changes the values of its instance variables to match the new state. After the `Mediator` object updates its instance variable, it uses the values of its instance variables to make whatever decisions it needs to make.

If you take the second approach, the `Mediator` object does not try to model the state of `Colleague` objects with its instance variables. Instead, when a `Colleague` object notifies it of a state change, the `Mediator` object makes whatever decisions it needs to make by fetching the state of each `Colleague` object on which it must base its decisions.

When most people first try to implement the Mediator pattern, they think of the first approach. However, in most cases, the second approach is the better choice. The disadvantage of the first approach is that it is possible for the `Mediator` object to be wrong about the state of a `Colleague` object. To get a `Mediator` object to correctly model the state of `Colleague` objects may require it to have additional code to mimic the logic of the `Colleague` objects. If a maintenance programmer later modifies one of the `Colleague` classes, the modification may mysteriously break the `Mediator` class.

The advantage of the second approach is its simplicity. The `Mediator` object can never be wrong about the state of a `Colleague` object. This makes it easier to implement and maintain. However, if fetching the complete state of `Colleague` objects is too time consuming, then the approach of having the `Mediator` object model the state of `Colleague` objects may be more practical.

JAVA API USAGE

The examples of the Mediator pattern that occur in the Java API are a little different from the mediator classes you are likely to code. That is because mediator classes usually contain application-specific code, and the classes of the Java API are application independent.

Java-based graphical user interfaces can be built mostly from objects that are instances of subclasses of `java.awt.swing.Jcomponent`. `Jcomponent` objects use an instance of a subclass of `java.awt.swing.FocusManager` as a mediator. If `Jcomponent` objects are associated with a `FocusManager` object (they usually are), then they call its `processKeyEvent` method when they receive a `KeyEvent`. The purpose of a `FocusManager` object is to recognize keystrokes that should cause a different `Jcomponent` object to receive the focus and make it so.

The way that `Jcomponent` objects use a `FocusManager` object differs from the Mediator pattern described in this chapter in two ways:

1. `Jcomponent` objects only pass `KeyEvents` to `FocusManager` objects. Most mediator classes that you write will have to handle more than one kind of event.

2. Jcomponent objects do not access FocusManager objects through an interface. They directly refer to the FocusManager class. Having Jcomponent objects refer to FocusManager objects through an interface would provide a more flexible organization. Apparently, the designers of the Java API believed that, because the interaction between Jcomponent objects and FocusManager objects is at a low level, there is no need for that flexibility.

CODE EXAMPLE

The code example for the Mediator pattern is the code for a Mediator object for the dialog discussed under the "Context" heading. One thing you may notice about this example is that it is more complex than most of the other examples. This reflects the nature of the Mediator pattern, which is to make all the complexity of event handling the responsibility of Mediator classes.

The mediator class is implemented as a private inner class of the dialog's class called BanquetMediator:

```
private class BanquetMediator {
        private JButton okButton;
        private JTextComponent dateField;
        private JTextComponent startField;
...
```

As shown above, the BanquetMediator class has private instance variables that it uses to refer to the GUI objects that the dialog registers with it. The BanquetMediator class does not implement any EventListener interfaces to allow it to receive events from its registered GUI objects. Instead, it uses adapter objects to receive those events. There are two main reasons for the BanquetMediator class to use adapters to receive events:

1. The BanquetMediator class is able to ensure that only the GUI objects that are supposed to be sending events to a BanquetMediator object are able to do so. This makes the BanquetMediator class more robust. BanquetMediator objects achieve this by making their event-handling methods accessible only to the registered GUI objects. All of the BanquetMediator class's event-handling methods are private. The adapter objects are instances of private or anonymous inner classes that are able to call the BanquetMediator class's inner methods. Because the

adapter classes are private or anonymous, only the BanquetMediator class can create instances of them. Instances of the adapter classes are provided only to registered GUI objects.

2. Using a different adapter object to process events from each GUI object relieves the BanquetMediator class of the burden of having to determine which GUI object an event came from. The BanquetMediator class declares private or anonymous adapter classes that it uses to receive events only from objects in a specific role. By declaring additional classes, the BanquetMediator class relieves its adapter classes of the burden of selecting a behavior based on the source of an event.

You will see examples of these adapter classes later in the code listing. Anonymous adapter classes are used for processing types of events that must be processed differently for each event source. Private adapter classes are used to process types of events that do not require different behavior for different event sources. The BanquetMediator class declares instance variables to refer to the single instance that it creates of its private adapter classes.

```
private ItemAdapter itemAdapter = new ItemAdapter();
```

The BanquetMediator class's constructor declares and instantiates an anonymous adapter class that processes events that the enclosing dialog object sends when it is opened. The adapter calls the BanquetMediator method responsible for setting the registered GUI components to their initial state.

```
BanquetMediator() {
    WindowAdapter windowAdapter = new WindowAdapter() {
        public void windowOpened(WindowEvent e) {
            initialState();
        } // windowOpened(WindowEvent)
    };
    addWindowListener(windowAdapter);
} // Constructor()
```

The ItemAdapter class is a private adapter class defined and used by the BanquetMediator class to process events from both of the radio buttons in the dialog. When an ItemAdapter object receives an ItemEvent, it calls the BanquetMediator class's enforceInvariants method. This method is central to the purpose of the BanquetMediator class. The enforceInvariants method enforces all of the invariant relationships between the components of the dialog. It is called in response to events from all of the dialog's GUI components.

```
private class ItemAdapter implements ItemListener {
    public void itemStateChanged(ItemEvent e) {
        enforceInvariants();
    } // itemStateChanged(ItemEvent)
} // class ItemAdapter
```

The method responsible for registering a button object in the OK role is very simple because the BanquetMediator class is not responsible for processing events from that button. It is responsible only for determining whether or not the OK button should be enabled or disabled.

```
public void registerOkButton(JButton ok) {
    okButton = ok;
} // registerOkButton(JButton)
```

The registration methods for other GUI objects are more complex because they are concerned with custom event handling for objects registered in a particular role. The motivation for the custom event handling will be to verify the contents of individual GUI objects. The following registration method is more typical. It registers the field for entering the number of people that will be attending a banquet.

```
public
void registerPeopleCountField(final JTextComponent field) {
    peopleCountField = field;
    DocumentAdapter documentAdapter;
    documentAdapter = new DocumentAdapter() {
        protected void parseDocument() {
            int count = PEOPLE_COUNT_DEFAULT;
            try {
                count = Integer.parseInt(field.getText());
            } catch (NumberFormatException e) {
            }
            if (MIN_PEOPLE<=count && count<=MAX_PEOPLE )
              peopleCount = count;
            else
              peopleCount = PEOPLE_COUNT_DEFAULT;
        } // parseDocument()
    };
    field.getDocument() .addDocumentListener(documentAdapter);
} // registerPeopleCountField(JTextComponent)
```

This registration method provides an anonymous adapter object that goes beyond just calling the enforceInvariants method. The anonymous adapter's superclass takes care of that. Before the superclass's code calls the BanquetMediator object's enforceInvariants method, it calls its own parseDocument method. The anonymous adapter class overrides that so that it sets the `BanquetMediator` object's `peopleCount` instance variable. If the field contains a valid value for the number of people who will attend the banquet, then it sets `peopleCount` to be that value. Otherwise, it sets `peopleCount` to a special value that will tell the `enforceInvariants` method that there is no valid value that has been entered for the number of people who will be attending the banquet.

The registration methods for the other text fields are similar. They provide an adapter object that validates the value in the field, sets an instance variable, and then calls the `enforceInvariants` method.

The `enforceInvariants` method may change the state of some GUI components in order to force them to comply with some of the invariant relationships. When it changes the state of some of those GUI components, they produce events. The `BanquetMediator` object, through its adapters, is listening for some of these events. When a GUI component responds to one of the `enforceInvariants` method's state changes by delivering an event to one of the `BanquetMediator` object's adapters, it recursively calls the `enforceInvariants` method. To avoid an infinite recursion, the `BanquetMediator` class uses a flag to recognize recursive calls to the `enforceInvariants` method.

```
    private boolean busy = false;
...
    private void enforceInvariants() {
        if (busy)
          return;
        busy = true;
        protectedEnforceInvariants();
        busy = false;
    } // enforceInvariants()
```

As you can see from the preceding piece of code, the `enforceInvariants` method does not directly do the work of enforcing invariant relationships. What it does do is to immediately return if it is called recursively; otherwise, it calls the `protectedEnforceInvariants` method.

The preceding code detects recursive calls by first testing and then setting the value of the `busy` variable. Because the Java event model guarantees synchronous delivery of events, the `enforceInvariants` method is not written to deal with being called to handle one event while it is still processing another. In a situation like this, the method would have to be synchronized in a manner appropriate for the semantics of the events it has to process.

Here are the invariant relationships that the `protectedEnforce-Invariants` method enforces:

- The "Date," "Start Time," and "End Time" fields are enabled if and only if the "Number of People" field contains a valid value.
- If the Radio buttons are disabled, then they are in an unselected state.
- The food list is enabled if and only if the "Date," "Start Time," and "End Time" fields are enabled, and the Buffet button or Table button is selected. To be considered valid, end time must be at least one hour later than start time.
- The OK button is enabled if and only if the food list is enabled and one or more foods on the list has been selected.

```
private void protectedEnforceInvariants() {
    // set enable to true if number of people has been set.
    boolean enable = (peopleCount != PEOPLE_COUNT_DEFAULT);

    // Date, start, end, buffet button and table button are
    // enabled if, and only if, a valid value is in the number
    // of people field.
    dateField.setEnabled(enable);
    startField.setEnabled(enable);
    endField.setEnabled(enable);
    buffetButton.setEnabled(enable);
    tableServiceButton.setEnabled(enable);
    if (enable) {
        // Food list is enabled if and only if date or time
        // fields or radio buttons are enabled and end time is
        // at least one hour later than start time and the
        // buffet button or table button is selected.
        enable = (buffetButton.isSelected()
                    || tableServiceButton.isSelected());
        foodList.setEnabled(endAtLeastOneHourAfterStart());
    } else {
        // if date or time fields or radio buttons are disabled
        // then food list must also be disabled.
        foodList.setEnabled(false);
        // radio buttons not enabled so they must be deselected.
        buffetButton.setSelected(false);
        tableServiceButton.setSelected(false);
    } // if enable
    okButton.setEnabled(foodList.isEnabled()
                    && foodList.getMinSelectionIndex()>-1);
} // protectedEnforceInvariants()
```

Mediator classes often have internal auxiliary methods that supplement the logic of the primary invariant enforcing method. Putting some of the logic in an auxiliary method helps keep the primary invariant enforcing method to a manageable size. The following method returns true if the

"Date," "Start," and "End" fields contain valid values and the time in the "End" field is at least one hour after the "Start" field.

```
private boolean endAtLeastOneHourAfterStart() {
        Calendar startCalendar = getStartCalendar();
        if (startCalendar == null)
          return false;
        Calendar endCalendar = getEndCalendar();
        if (endCalendar == null)
          return false;
        startCalendar.add(Calendar.MINUTE, 59);
        return getEndCalendar().after(startCalendar);
    } // endAtLeastOneHourAfterStart()
```

RELATED PATTERNS

Adapter   `Mediator` classes often use adapter objects to receive notifications of state changes.

Interface   The Mediator pattern uses the Interface pattern to keep the `Colleague` classes independent of the `Mediator` class.

Observer   The Observer pattern is a large portion of Java's delegation event model. If you want to use the Mediator pattern in a context for which you think Java's event model is inappropriate, you can substitute the Observer pattern.

Low Coupling/High Cohesion   The Mediator pattern is an good example of an exception to the advice of the Low Coupling/High Cohesion pattern (described in Volume 2).

Snapshot [Grand98]

There is a simpler form of the Snapshot pattern that is known as the Memento pattern, documented in [GoF95]. It includes only the portion of the Snapshot pattern that uses `Memento` objects.

SYNOPSIS

Capture a snapshot of an object's state so that the object's state can be restored later. The object that initiates the capture or restoration of the state does not need to know anything about the state information. It needs to know only that the object whose state it is restoring or capturing implements a particular interface.

CONTEXT

Suppose that you are writing a program to play a role-playing game. For the purposes of this discussion, the details of the game are not important. What is important is that it is a single-player game. To play the game, a player directs a character to interact with various computer-controlled characters and computer-simulated objects. One way that a game can end is for the character under the player's control to die. Players of the game will not consider that a desirable outcome.

Among the many features planned for the game are two that involve saving and restoring the state of the game. The program needs these features because playing one of these games to its conclusion can take a few days of nonstop play.

- To allow a player to play the game over multiple short intervals, it must be possible to save the state of the game to a file so that it can be continued later.
- To arrive at the game's conclusion, a player must successfully guide his or her character through many adventures. If the player's character dies before the game is over, the player will have the option of starting the game over from the very beginning. That may be an unattractive option because the player may be well into the game and have played

through the earlier portions of the game a number of times. The program will also offer the player the option of resuming the game at an earlier point than when the character died.

It will do this by saving part of the game's state, including credit for the character's previous experiences and a record of some of the character's possessions. It will perform a partial state change when the player's character has accomplished a major task. As the game proceeds, these checkpoints become part of the game's overall state, needing to be saved when the rest of the state is saved to disk.

Though the game will involve many classes, there are only a few that will share the responsibility for creating these snapshots of the game's state. (See Figure 8.14.)

The classes in Figure 8.14 participate in two distinct state-saving mechanisms: a mechanism for saving part of a game's state when the play-

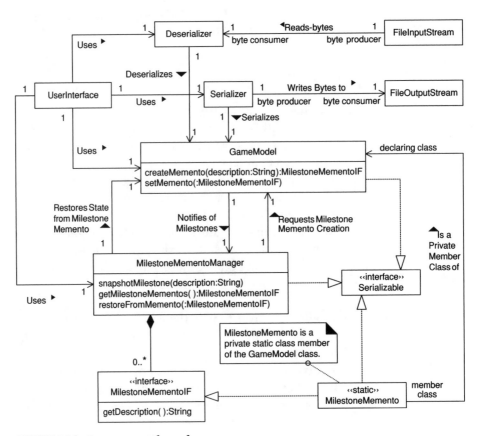

FIGURE 8.14 Game snapshot classes.

er's character achieves a milestone and a mechanism for saving and restoring an entire game. There are two classes in Figure 8.14 that participate in both mechanisms:

UserInterface   All player-initiated actions come through the UserInterface class. A UserInterface object delivers most of the actions that a player initiates to a GameModel object. However, player-initiated snapshots of the game follow different routes, which are discussed below.

GameModel   The GameModel class is responsible for maintaining the state of the game during play. A UserInterface object notifies a GameModel object when the player does something related to the game. The GameModel object determines the consequences of this action, modifies the state of the game accordingly, and notifies the user interface. A GameModel object may also initiate actions. It always reports the consequences of any action it initiates to the user interface but will not always report the action itself.

The UserInterface class's involvement in making snapshots is to initiate one kind of snapshot and both kinds of restores. Because the GameModel class is the top-level class responsible for the state of the game, it must be involved in any operation that manipulates the game's state.

These are the other classes and interfaces involved in performing partial state saves and restores:

MilestoneMemento   The MilestoneMemento class is a private class defined by the GameModel class. A GameModel object creates instances of MilestoneMemento that contain copies of the values that make up the partial state to be saved. Given a MilestoneMemento object, a GameModel object can restore itself to the previous state contained in the MilestoneMemento object.

MilestoneMementoIF   The MilestoneMemento class implements this interface. This interface is public. Outside the GameModel class, instances of the MilestoneMemento class can be accessed only as instances of the Object class or through the MilestoneMementoIF interface. Neither mode of access allows an object to access the state information encapsulated in MilestoneMemento objects.

MilestoneMementoManager   The MilestoneMementoManager class contributes to the decision to create MilestoneMemento objects. It also manages their use after they are created.

Here is how the capture of a game's partial state happens after the player's character has achieved a milestone.

A GameModel object enters a state indicating that the player's character has achieved one of the game's major milestones.

There is a MilestoneMementoManager object associated with each GameModel object. When the GameModel object enters a milestone state, it calls the associated MilestoneMementoManager object's snapshotMilestone method. It passes a string to the method that is a description of the milestone. The player's character may previously have achieved that milestone, died, and then returned to an earlier milestone. If a MilestoneMemento object already exists for a milestone, then another MilestoneMemento object should not be created for that milestone.

A MilestoneMementoManager object determines if a MilestoneMemento object already exists for a milestone by comparing the description string passed to its snapshotMilestone method to the descriptions of the MilestoneMemento objects that already exist. If a MilestoneMemento object already exists with the given description, then the snapshotMilestone method takes no additional action.

If the MilestoneMementoManager object determines that there is no MilestoneMemento object that already exists for the milestone, then the MilestoneMementoManager object initiates the creation of a MilestoneMemento object to capture the game's partial state. It does that by calling the GameModel object's createMemento method, passing it the same description that was passed to the MilestoneMementoManager object.

The createMemento method returns a freshly created MilestoneMemento object that the MilestoneMementoManager object adds to its collection of MilestoneMementoIF objects.

When a player's character dies, the UserInterface object offers the player the option for the character to start from a previously achieved milestone, rather from the very beginning. It is able to offer the player a list of milestones to choose from by calling the MilestoneMementoManager object's getMilestoneMementos method. This method returns an array of MilestoneMementoIf objects that the MilestoneMementoManager object has collected.

If the player indicates that he or she wants his or her character to start over from one of the previously achieved milestones, the UserInterface object passes the corresponding MilestoneMemento object to the MilestoneMementoManager object's restoreFromMemento method. The method, in turn, calls the GameModel object's setMemento method, passing it the chosen MilestoneMemento object. Using the information in that object, the GameModel object restores its state.

The other snapshot mechanism is the one that saves the complete state of the game to disk, including the `MilestoneMementoManager` object and its collection of `MilestoneMemento` objects. This mechanism is based on Java's serialization facility. If you are unfamiliar with Java's serialization facility, it is a way to copy the state of an object to a stream of bytes and then create a copy of the original object from the contents of the byte stream. There is a somewhat more detailed description of serialization under the "Implementation" heading for this pattern.

The classes that are involved in saving and restoring a complete snapshot of the game's state to and from a file are as follows:

Serializer   The `Serializer` class is responsible for serializing a `GameModel` object. It copies the state information of the `GameModel` object and the other objects to which it refers that are part of the game's state as a byte stream to a file.

FileOutputStream   This is the standard Java class `java.io.FileOutputStream`. It writes a stream of bytes to a file.

Deserializer   The `Deserializer` class is responsible for a serialized byte stream and creating a copy of the `GameModel` object and other objects that were serialized to create the byte stream.

FileInputStream   This is the standard Java class `java.io.FileInputStream`. It reads a stream of bytes from a file.

Here is the sequence of events that occurs when the user requests that the game be saved to a file or restored from a file:

- The player tells the user interface that he or she wants to save the game to a file. The `UserInterface` object then creates a `Serializer` object, passing the name of the file and a reference to the `GameModel` object to its constructor. The `Serializer` object creates an `ObjectOutputStream` object and a `FileOutputStream` object. It uses the `ObjectOutputStream` object to serialize the `GameModel` object and all of the other game-related objects to which it refers into a byte stream. It uses the `FileOutputStream` object to write that byte stream to a file.
- When the player wants to restore the game from a file, he or she tells the user interface. The `UserInterface` object then creates a `Deserializer` object, passing the name of the file and a reference to the `GameModel` object to its constructor. The `Deserializer` object creates an `ObjectInputStream` object and a `FileInputStream` object. It

uses the `FileInputStream` object to read a serialized byte stream from a file. It uses the `ObjectInputStream` object to deserialize the `GameModel` object and all of the other game-related objects to which it refers from the byte stream.

Most of the patterns in this book describe only one way to solve a problem. The Snapshot pattern is different from most of the other patterns described in this book because it describes two ways of solving the problem of making a snapshot of an object's state.

FORCES

- You need to create a snapshot of an object's state and also be able to restore the state of the object.
- You want a mechanism that saves and restores an object's state to be independent of the object's internal structure, so that the internal structure can change without having to modify the save/restore mechanism.

SOLUTION

Following are two general solutions to the problem of saving a snapshot of an object's state and restoring its state from the snapshot. First is a description of using `Memento` objects to create a nonpersistent copy to an object's partial state. Then there is a description of how to use serialization to restore an object's state, followed by a comparison of the two techniques.

Figure 8.15 shows the general organization for objects that use `Memento` objects to save and restore an object's state.

Here are descriptions of the roles the classes shown in Figure 8.15 play in the variation of the Snapshot pattern that uses `Memento` objects:

Originator   A class in this role is a class whose instance's state information is to be saved and restored. When its `createMemento` method is called, it creates a `Memento` object that contains a copy of the `Originator` object's state information. Later, you can restore the `Originator` object's state by passing a `Memento` object to its `setMemento` method.

Memento   A class in this role is a private static class of the `Originator` class that implements the `MementoIF` interface. Its purpose is to encap-

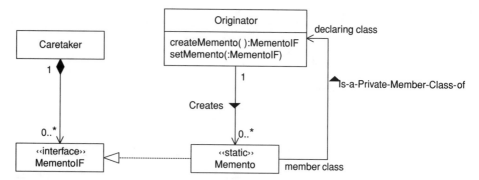

FIGURE 8.15 Snapshot using memento objects.

sulate snapshots of an `Originator` object's state. Because it is a private member of the `Originator` class, only the `Originator` class is able to access it. Other classes must access instances of the `Memento` class either as instances of `Object` or through the `MementoIF` interface.

MementoIF   Classes other than the `Originator` class access `Memento` objects through this interface. Interfaces in this role usually declare no methods. If they do declare any methods, the methods should not allow the encapsulated state to be changed. This ensures the consistency and integrity of the state information.

Caretaker   Instances of the `Caretaker` class maintain a collection of `Memento` objects. After a `Memento` object is created, it is usually added to a `Caretaker` object's collection. When an undo operation is to be performed, a `Caretaker` object typically collaborates with another object to select a `Memento` object. After the `Memento` object is selected, it is typically the `Caretaker` object that calls the `Originator` object's `setMemento` method to restore its state.

The other mechanism for creating a snapshot of an object's state is serialization. Serialization is different from most other object-oriented techniques in that it works by violating the encapsulation of the object being serialized. Most, but not necessarily all, of the violation is through Java's reflection mechanism, which will be discussed in more detail in the explanation of the roles that classes play in Figure 8.16.

Here are descriptions of the roles the classes shown in Figure 8.16 play in the form of the Snapshot pattern that uses serialization:

Target   An `ObjectOutputStream` object converts the state of instances of classes in this role to a byte stream. An `ObjectInputStream` object

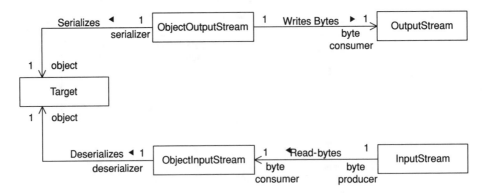

FIGURE 8.16 Snapshot using serialization.

restores the state of instances of classes in this role from a byte stream. The role of the `Target` object in these activities is purely passive. The `ObjectOutputStream` object or `ObjectInputStream` object do all of the work.

ObjectOutputStream   The class in this role is usually the standard Java class `java.io.ObjectOutputStream`. It discovers and accesses a `Target` object's state information and writes it to a byte stream with additional information that allows an `ObjectInputStream` object to restore the state information.

OutputStream   An object in this role is an instance of a subclass of the standard Java class `java.io.OutputStream`. If the state information needs to be saved indefinitely, then the `OutputStream` object may be a `FileOutputStream`. If the state information needs to be saved no longer than the duration of a program run, then the `OutputStream` object may be a `ByteArrayOutputStream`.

ObjectInputStream   The class in this role is the standard Java class `java.io.ObjectInputStream` or a subclass of it. Instances of these classes read serialized state information from a byte stream and restore it.

If you do not override the default behavior, an `ObjectInputStream` object puts the original `Target` object's state information in a new instance of the `Target` object's class. Using techniques described under the "Implementation" heading, you can arrange for `ObjectInputStream` objects to restore the saved state to an existing instance of the `Target` class.

Table 8.3 shows some key differences between the two techniques for creating and managing snapshots of an object's state.

TABLE 8.3 Comparison of State Saving by Serialization and Memento Objects

	Serialization	*Memento*
Persistence	You can use serialization to save state in a persistent form by serializing it to a file.	Using `Memento` objects does not provide persistence.
Complexity of implementation	Serialization can be the simpler technique for saving the entire state of an object. That is especially true for objects whose state includes references to other objects whose state must also be saved.	Using `Memento` objects is often a simpler way to capture part of an object's state.
Object Identity	Absolute object identity is lost unless you supply additional code to preserve it. The default way that serialization restores an object's state is by creating a copy of the object. If the original object contains other objects and there are multiple references to the same object, then the duplicate object will contain references to an identical but distinct object. Among the objects referred to by the restored object, serialization preserves relative object identity.	Object identity is preserved. Using `Memento` objects is a simpler way to restore the state of an object so that it refers to the same object that it referred to before.
Overhead	Using serialization adds considerable overhead to the process of creating a snapshot to be saved in memory. The bulk of the overhead comes from the fact that serialization works through Java's reflection mechanism and creates new objects when restoring state.	There is no particular overhead associated with using `Memento` objects.
Expertise Required	In cases where you need to make a snapshot of an object's complete state, all of the objects involved implement the `Serializable` interface, and preserving object identity is not important, serialization requires minimal expertise. As situations vary from those constraints, the required level of expertise quickly increases. Some situations may require an in-depth knowledge of serialization internals, reflection, and other arcane aspects of Java.	Using `Memento` objects requires no specialized knowledge.

CONSEQUENCES

Both forms of the Snapshot pattern keep a lot of the complexity of saving and restoring an object's state out of its class.

The Snapshot pattern is not very suitable for undoing a fine-grained sequence of commands. Making many snapshots of an object can consume a prohibitive amount of storage. Capturing the changes to an object's state (the Command pattern) may be more efficient.

IMPLEMENTATION

Using `Memento` objects to make snapshots of an object's state is very straightforward to implement. Using serialization requires additional expertise and sometimes additional complexity. A complete description of serialization is beyond the scope of this book.* Following is a description of some of the features of serialization relevant to the Snapshot pattern.

To serialize an object, you first create an `ObjectOutputStream` object. You can do that by passing an `OutputStream` object to its constructor, like this:

```
FileOutputStream fout = new FileOutputStream("filename.ser");
ObjectOutputStream obOut = new ObjectOutputStream(fout);
```

The `ObjectOutputStream` object will write the byte stream it produces to the `OutputStream` object passed to its constructor.

Once you have created an `ObjectOutputStream` object, you can serialize an object by passing it to the `ObjectOutputStream` object's `writeObject` method, like this:

```
ObOut.writeObject(foo);
```

The `writeObject` method uses Java's reflection facility to discover the instance variables of the object that `foo` references and access them. It writes values of instance variables that are declared with a primitive type such as `int` or `double` directly to the byte stream. If the value of an instance variable is an object reference, then the `writeObject` method also serializes that object.

---

* You can find a complete description of serialization on Sun's Java web page: java.sun.com. At the time of this writing, the URL for the serialization specification is http://java.sun.com/products/jdk/1.2/docs/guide/serialization/.

Turning a serialized byte stream into an object is called *deserialization*. To deserialize a byte stream, you first create an `ObjectInputStream` object. You can do that by passing an `InputStream` object to its constructor, like this:

```
FileInputStream fin = new FileInputStream("filename.ser");
ObjectInputStream obIn = new ObjectInputStream(fin);
```

The `ObjectInputStream` object will read from the byte stream passed to its constructor.

Once you have created an `ObjectInputStream` object, you can deserialize its associated byte stream by calling its `readObject` method, like this:

```
GameModel g = (GameModel)obIn.readObject();
```

The `readObject` method is declared to return a reference to an `Object`. Since you will usually want to treat the object it returns as an instance of a more specialized class, you will usually typecast the result of `readObject` method to a more specialized class.

There is one other thing that you must do in order to serialize an object. You can serialize an instance of a class only if the class gives its permission to be serialized. A class permits the serialization of its instances if the class implements the `java.io.Serializable` interface, like this:

```
import java.io.serializable;
...
class foo extends bar implements Serializable {
```

The `Serializable` interface is a marker interface. It does not declare any members. Declaring that a class implements the `Serializable` interface is simply a way to indicate that its instances may be serialized. If you pass an object to an `ObjectOutputStream` object's `writeObject` method that does not implement the `Serializable` interface, then at runtime the `writeObject` method will throw an exception.

So far, serialization seems simple. Though there are many situations in which the preceding details are all that you need to know, there are also many situations that are more complex.

The default behavior, when serializing an object, is to also serialize all of the objects that it refers to and all of the objects that they refer to until the complete set has been serialized. Though an object may be an instance of a class that implements the `Serializable` interface, if it refers to any objects that are not `Serializable`, then any attempt to serialize the object will fail. It will fail when the `ObjectOutputStream` object's `writeObject` method calls itself recursively to serialize the object that cannot be serialized and throws an exception. There is a way to avoid that problem: You can specify that the serialization mechanism should ignore some of an object's instance variables. The simplest way to do this is to declare the variable with the transient modifier, like this:

```
transient ObjectOutputStream obOut;
```

Because the serialization mechanism ignores transient variables, it does not matter to the serialization mechanism if a transient variable refers to an object that cannot be serialized. Instances of some classes refer to other objects that refer to many objects that do not need to be saved. Serializing those objects would just add overhead to serialization and deserialization.

Declaring instance variables transient solves a few problems during serialization. It also creates a problem during deserialization. The serialized byte stream does not contain values for transient variables. If you make no other arrangements, after deserialization an object's transient variables will contain the default value for their declared type. For example, transient variables declared with a numeric type will have the value 0. Transient variables that are declared as an object type will have the value null. Serialization ignores initializers and constructors. Unless it is acceptable for an object to suddenly find its transient variables unexpectedly set to null or zero, this is a problem.

The `ObjectInputStream` class provides mechanisms that allow you to modify the default way that deserialization handles transient variables. It allows you to provide code that is executed after deserialization has performed its default actions. Often, that code requires information to reconstruct the values of transient variables that are not provided by the default actions of serialization. The `ObjectOutputStream` class provides mechanisms that allow you to add additional information to the information provided by the default actions of serialization. If you can add enough information to a serialized byte stream to be able to reconstruct the values of an object's transient variables, then you have solved most of the problem.

To add information to what the `ObjectOutputStream` class's `writeObject` method normally provides, you can add a method called `writeObject` to a serializable class. If an object is an instance of a class that defines a `writeObject` method in the required way, then instead of deciding how to handle the object's instance variables internally, an

`ObjectOutputStream` object calls that object's `writeObject` method. This allows a class to determine how its own instances variables will be serialized.

To take responsibility for the serialization of its instance variables, a class must have a method like this

```
private void writeObject(ObjectOutputStream stream)
            throws IOException {
    stream.defaultWriteObject();
    ...
} // writeObject(ObjectOutputStream)
```

Notice that the method is private. It must be private to be recognized by an `ObjectOutputStream` object. These private `writeObject` methods are only responsible for writing the instance variables that their own classes declare. They are not responsible for variables declared by superclasses.

The first thing that most private `writeObject` methods do is to call the `ObjectOutputStream` object's `defaultWriteObject` method. Calling that method causes the `ObjectOutputStream` object to perform its default serialization actions for the class that called it. After doing this, a private `writeObject` method calls other methods of the `ObjectOutputStream` object to write whatever additional information will be needed to reconstruct the values of transient variables. The `ObjectOutputStream` class is a subclass of `DataOutputStream`, so in addition to its `writeObject` method it inherits methods to write strings and all of the primitive data types.

To make use of the additional information during deserialization, a class must also define a `readObject` method, like this:

```
private void readObject(ObjectInputStream stream)
            throws IOException {
    try {
        stream.defaultReadObject();
    } catch (ClassNotFoundException e) {
        ...
    } // try
    ...
```

```
} // readObject(ObjectInputStream)
```

Just as the `writeObject` method must be private, the `readObject` method must also be private for it to be recognized. It begins by calling the `ObjectInputStream` object's `defaultReadObject` method. Calling that method causes the `ObjectInputStream` object to perform its default deserialization actions for the class that called it. After doing this, a private readObject method will call other methods of the ObjectInputStream object to read whatever additional information was supplied to reconstruct the values of transient variables. The ObjectInputStream class is a subclass of DataInputStream, so, in addition to its readObject method, it inherits methods to read strings and all of the primitive data types.

To show how these private methods can fit together, here is an example:

```
public class TextFileReader implements Serializable {
    private transient RandomAccessFile file;
    private String browseFileName;
    ...
    private
    void writeObject(ObjectOutputStream stream) throws IOException{
        stream.defaultWriteObject();
        stream.writeLong(file.getFilePointer());
    } // writeObject(ObjectOutputStream)

    private
    void readObject(ObjectInputStream stream) throws IOException {
        try {
            stream.defaultReadObject();
        } catch (ClassNotFoundException e) {
            String msg = "Unable to find class";
            if (e.getMessage() != null)
              msg += ": " + e.getMessage();
            throw new IOException(msg);
        } // try
        file = new RandomAccessFile(browseFileName, "r");
        file.seek(stream.readLong());
    } // readObject(ObjectInputStream)
} // class TextFileReader
```

This class is called TextFileReader. It has an instance variable named file that refers to a RandomAccessFile object. The RandomAccessFile class does not implement the Serializable interface. In order for instances of TextFileReader to be successfully serialized and deserialized, it is not sufficient that the TextFileReader class implement the Serializable interface. It must also

- Prevent its reference to a RandomAccessFile object from being serialized.
- Add additional information to the serialized byte stream so that it is possible to reconstruct the RandomAccessFile object.

- Provide logic to allow the `RandomAccessFile` object to be reconstructed during deserialization.

To prevent its reference to a `RandomAccessFile` object from being serialized, the `TextFileReader` class declares its `file` variable to be transient.

The `TextFileReader` class has an instance variable that refers to a string that is the name of the file that the `RandomAccessFile` object accesses. This is sufficient information to create another `RandomAccessFile` object that accesses this file. However, to make the state of the new `RandomAccessFile` object match the state of the original, it is necessary to add the `RandomAccessFile` object's current position in the file to the byte stream. The `TextFileReader` class's private `writeObject` method accomplished this.

To reconstruct the original object's `RandomAccessFile` object, the `TextFileReader` class defines a private `readObject` method. This method reads the file position that was written to the serialized byte stream and passes it to the new `RandomAccessFile` object's `seek` method.

Another issue you may need to deal with is the fact that the `ObjectInputStream` class's `readObject` method normally returns a newly created object. In situations like the role-playing game described under the "Context" heading, this can be inconvenient because other objects already refer to the existing object. To modify their references to refer to the new object would be to involve those objects in the details of another object's deserialization. The `ObjectInputStream` class allows you to resolve the situation without involving any class other than the one it is deserializing.

If the class being deserialized implements the `Resolvable` interface, then, instead of setting the instance values of an object it creates, an `ObjectInputStream` object calls that class's `readResolve` method. Its `readResolve` method returns an instance of that class and the `ObjectInputStream` object sets that object's instance variables. If the `readResolve` method returns the existing object, then the `ObjectInputStream` object will set its instance variables. You can see this technique used in the example that follows.

CODE EXAMPLE

Following is some of the code to implement the design discussed under the "Context" heading. First is the code for the `GameModel` class, which is central to any state-saving operation:

```
public class GameModel implements Serializable, Resolvable {
    private static GameModel theInstance = new GameModel();
    private MilestoneMementoManager mementoManager;
...
    /**
     * This constructor is private to force other classes to call
     * this class's getGameModel methods to get an instance of it.
     */
    private GameModel() {
        mementoManager = new MilestoneMementoManager(this);

        ...
    } // constructor()

    /**
     * Return the single instance of this class.
     */
    public static GameModel getGameModel() { return theInstance; }
```

The point of the preceding portion of the GameModel class is to make the GameModel class a singleton class. By making its constructor private, other classes are unable to use its constructor. That forces them to get an instance of the GameModel class by calling its getGameModel method.

When an ObjectInputStream object is deserializing a byte stream, it creates objects without calling constructors. Because of this, the GameModel class uses a different mechanism to get an ObjectInputStream object to call its getGameModel method during deserialization.

When an ObjectInputStream object is deserializing a byte stream, it normally uses a special mechanism that creates objects without calling constructors or evaluating variables' initializers. After it has an instance of a class, it sets the object's instance variables to the values that it finds in the serialized byte stream. If a class implements the Resolvable interface, then, instead of using its special mechanism to get an instance of the class, it calls that class's readResolve method.

The GameModel class implements the Resolvable interface. Following is its implementation of the readResolve method, which simply calls the getGameModel method.

```
public Object readResolve() {
    return getGameModel();
// readResolve()
```

The remaining portions of the GameModel class related to the Snapshot pattern are involved in the management of Memento objects.

There are a few noteworthy things about the implementation of the MilestoneMemento class. It is a private class of the GameModel class. This prevents any other class, except the GameModel class from directly accessing its members. The MilestoneMemento class is declared static. This is a minor optimization that saves the expense of having MilestoneMemento objects maintain a reference to their enclosing GameModel object.

One other noteworthy aspect of the implementation of the MilestoneMemento class is its lack of access methods. Normally, it is good practice to allow other classes to access an object's instance variables only through accessor (get and set) methods. This practice results in well-encapsulated objects. Because of the close relationship between the MilestoneMemento class and the GameModel class, GameModel objects directly access the instance variables of MilestoneMemento objects. Because other classes can access the MilestoneMemento class only through the MilestoneMementoIF interface, a MilestoneMemento object's instance variables are hidden from all other classes.

```
      private static class MilestoneMemento
                       implements MilestoneMementoIF {
          private String description;
...
          /**
           * constructor
           * @param description The reason this object was created.
           */
          MiletoneMemento(String description) {
              this.description = description;
          } // constructor(String)

          /**
           * Return a description of why this memento was created.
           */
          public String getDescription() { return description; }

          // The following variables are set by a GameModel object
          MilestoneMementoManager mementoManager;
          ...
      } // class MilestoneMemento
```

Following are the methods that the GameModel class provides for creating Memento objects and for restoring state from a Memento object:

```
/**
 * Create a memento object to encapsulate this object's state.
 */
MilestoneMementoIF createMemento(String description) {
    // Create a memento object and set its instance variables
    MilestoneMemento memento;
    Memento = new MilestoneMemento(description);
    memento.mementoManager = mementoManager;
```

```
    ...
    return memento;
} // CreateMemento(String)

/**
 * Restore this object's state from the given memento object.
 */
void setMemento(MilestoneMementoIF memento) {
    MilestoneMemento m = (MilestoneMemento)memento;
    mementoManager = m.mementoManager;
    ...
} // setMemento(MilestoneMemento)
```

RELATED PATTERNS

Command   The Command pattern allows state changes to be undone on a command-by-command basis without having to make a snapshot of an object's entire state after every command.

Observer [GoF95]

The Observer pattern is very well known and widely used. Since it was originally documented, patterns have evolved. It is important to know about the Observer pattern when working with existing designs that use it.

The Delegation Event Model is usually a superior choice for new designs. It produces designs that are more reusable. Use of the Delegation Event Model complies with the Java Bean specification. A number of CASE and programming tools provide assistance for the construction and use of classes designed to work with the Delegation Event Model.

SYNOPSIS

Allows objects to dynamically register dependencies between objects, so that an object will notify those objects that are dependent on it when its state changes.

CONTEXT

Suppose that you are working for a company that manufactures smoke detectors, motion sensors, and other security devices. In order to take advantage of new market opportunities, your company plans to introduce a new line of devices. These devices will be able to send a signal to a security card that can be installed in most computers. The hope is that companies that make security monitoring systems will integrate these devices and cards into their systems. To make it easy to integrate the cards into monitoring systems, you have been given the task of creating an easy-to-use API.

The API must allow objects in the programs that your future customers will integrate it into to receive notifications from the security card. It must work without forcing the customers to alter the architecture of their existing software. All it is allowed to assume about the customer's software is that at least one and possibly more than one object will have a method that should be called when a notification is received from a security device. Figure 8.17 shows a design for the API.

Instances of the `SecurityNotifier` class receive notifications from the security card. They, in turn, notify objects that previously requested to receive notifications. Only objects that implement the `SecurityObserver`

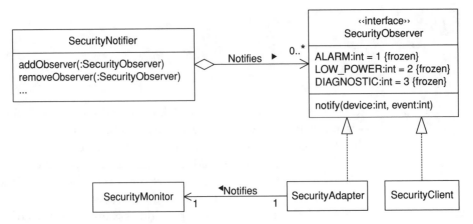

FIGURE 8.17 Security notification API.

interface can be registered with a `SecurityNotifier` object to receive notifications from it. A `SecurityObserver` object becomes registered to receive notifications from a `SecurityNotifier` object when it is passed to the `SecurityNotifier` object's `addObserver` method. Passing it to the `SecurityNotifier` object's `removeObserver` method ends the `SecurityObserver` object's registration to receive notifications.

A `SecurityNotifier` object passes a notification to a `SecurityObserver` object by calling its `notify` method. The parameters it passes to its `notify` method are a number that uniquely identifies the security device that the original notification came from and a number that specifies the type of notification.

The remaining classes in the diagram are not part of the API. They are classes that would already exist or would be added to potential customers' monitoring software. The class indicated in the diagram as `SecurityClient` corresponds to any class a customer adds to its monitoring software that implements the `SecurityObserver` interface. Customers may add such classes to their monitoring software to process notifications from a `SecurityNotifier` object.

The class indicated in the diagram as `SecurityMonitor` corresponds to an existing class in a customer's monitoring software that does not implement the `SecurityObserver` interface, but does have a method that should be called to process notifications from security devices. The customer is able to have instances of such a class receive notifications without modifying the class. The customer is able to do that by writing an adapter class that implements the `SecurityObserver` interface so that its `notify` method calls the appropriate method of the `SecurityMonitor` class.

FORCES

- You are implementing two otherwise independent classes. An instance of one will need to be able to notify other objects when its state changes. An instance of the other will need to be notified when an object it has a dependency on changes state. However, the two classes are not specifically intended to work with each other and, to promote reuse, should not have direct knowledge of each other.
- You have a one-to-many dependency relationship that may require an object to notify multiple objects that are dependent on it when it changes its state.

SOLUTION

Figure 8.18 shows a class diagram that demonstrates the roles that classes and interfaces play in the Observer pattern. You will notice that this diagram is more complicated than the one that appears in Figure 8.17. The diagram in Figure 8.17 incorporates some simplifications that are described in the "Implementation" section.

Here are the descriptions of the roles that the classes and interfaces in the diagram in Figure 8.18 play in the Observer pattern:

ObserverIF   An interface in this role defines a method that is typically called `notify` or `update`. An `Observable` object calls this method to provide a notification that its state has changed, passing it whatever arguments are appropriate. In many cases, a reference to the `Observable` object is one of the arguments that allows the method to know what object provided the notification.

Observer   Instances of classes in this role implement the `ObserverIF` interface and receive state-change notifications from `Observable` objects.

ObservableIF   `Observable` objects implement an interface in this role. The interface defines two methods that allow `Observer` objects to register and unregister to receive notifications.

Observable   A class in this role implements the `ObservableIF` interface. Its instances are responsible for managing the registration of `ObserverIF` objects that want to receive notifications of state changes. Its instances are also responsible for delivering the notifications. The `Observable` class does not directly implement those responsibilities. Instead, it delegates those responsibilities to a `Multicaster` object.

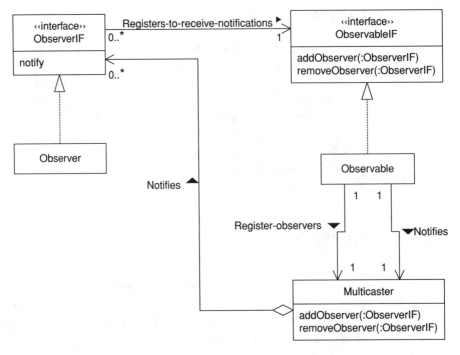

FIGURE 8.18 Observer pattern.

Multicaster   Instances of a class in this role manage registration of `ObserverIF` objects and deliver notifications to them on behalf of an `Observable` object. Delegating these responsibilities to a `Multicaster` class allows their implementation to be reused by all `Observable` classes that implement the same `ObservableIF` interface or deliver notifications to objects that implement the same `ObserverIF` interface.

Figure 8.19 summarizes the collaborations between the objects that participate in the Observer pattern.

Following is a more detailed description of the interactions shown in Figure 8.19.

   1. Objects that implement an `ObserverIF` interface are passed to the `addObserver` method of an `ObservableIF` object.

   1.1 The `ObservableIF` object delegates the `addObserver` call to its associated `Multicaster` object. It adds the `ObservableIF` object to the collection of `ObserverIF` objects that it maintains.

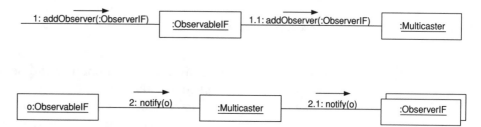

FIGURE 8.19 Observer collaboration.

2. The `ObservableIF` object labeled o needs to notify other objects that are dependent on it that its state has changed. It initiates the notification by calling the `notify` method of its associated `Multicaster` object.

2.1 The `Multicaster` object calls the `notify` method of each one of the `ObserverIF` objects in its collection.

CONSEQUENCES

The observer pattern allows an object to deliver notifications to other objects without the object sending or the objects receiving the notifications being aware of each other's class.

There are some situations in which the Observer pattern can have unforeseen and undesirable results:

- Delivering notifications can take a long time if an object has a large number of objects to deliver notifications to. This can happen because one object has many observers directly registered to receive its notifications. It can also happen because an object has many indirect observers because its notifications are cascaded by other objects.
- A more serious problem happens if there are cyclic dependencies. Objects call each other's `notify` methods until the stack fills up and a `StackOverflowError` is thrown. Though serious, this problem can be easily solved by adding an internal flag to one of the classes involved in the cycle that detects a recursive notification, like this:

```
private boolean inNotify = false;
public void notify(ObservableIF source) {
    if (inNotify)
      return;
    inNotify = true;
```

```
    ...
    inNotify = false;
} // notify(ObservableIF)
```

- If a notification can be delivered asynchronously of other threads, as is the case in the example under the "Context" heading, there are some additional consequences to consider. You need to ensure that the asynchronous delivery of notifications is done in a way that ensures the consistency of the objects that receive the notifications. It may also be important to ensure that notification does not block waiting for another thread for any length of time.

When an `Observer` object receives a notification, it knows which object has changed, but it does not know in what way it has changed. Avoid requiring an `Observer` object to determine which attributes of an `ObservableIF` object have changed. It is usually simpler for an observer to act on all of an `ObservableIF` object's attributes rather than going to the trouble of determining which have changed and then acting on just those.

IMPLEMENTATION

An `Observable` object will normally pass a self-reference as a parameter to an `Observer` object's `notify` method. In most cases, the `Observer` object needs access to the `Observable` object's attributes in order to act on the notification. Here are some ways to provide that access:

- Add methods to the `ObservableIF` interface for fetching attribute values. This is usually the best solution. However, it only works if all the classes that implement the `ObservableIF` interface have a common set of attributes sufficient for `Observer` objects to act on notifications.
- You can have multiple `ObservableIF` interfaces, with each providing access to enough attributes for an `Observer` object to act on notifications. To make this work, `ObserverIF` interfaces must declare a version of their `notify` method for each one of the `ObservableIF` interfaces. However, requiring observer objects to be aware of multiple interfaces removes much of the original motivation for having `ObservableIF` interfaces. Requiring a class to be aware of multiple interfaces is not much better than requiring it to be aware of multiple classes, so this is not a very good solution.
- You can pass attributes that `ObserverIF` objects need as parameters to their `notify` methods. The main disadvantage of this solution is

that it requires Observable objects to know enough about ObserverIF objects to provide them with the correct attribute values. If the set of attributes required by ObserverIF objects changes, then you must modify all of the Observable classes accordingly.

■ You can dispense with the ObservableIF interface and pass the Observable objects to ObserverIF objects as instances of their actual class. This implies overloading the ObserverIF interface's notify method, so that there is a notify method for each Observable class that will deliver notifications to ObserverIF objects. The main disadvantage of this approach is that Observer classes must be aware of the Observable classes that will be delivering notifications to its instances and know how to fetch the attributes it needs from them. On the other hand, if only one Observable class will be delivering notifications to Observer classes, then this is the best solution. It adds no complexity to any classes. It substitutes a dependency on a single interface for a dependency on a single class. Then it simplifies the design by eliminating the ObservableIF interface. The example under the "Context" heading uses this simplified solution.

Another simplification that is often made to the Observer pattern is to eliminate the Multicaster class. If an Observable class is the only class delivering notifications to objects that implement a particular interface, then there is no need for the reusability a Multicaster class provides. This is the reason why the example under the "Context" heading does not have a class in the Multicaster role. Another reason not to have a Multicaster class is that an Observable object will never have to deliver notifications to more than one object. In this case, the management and delivery of notifications to Observer objects is so simple that a Multicaster class adds more complexity than it saves.

It may not be necessary or useful to notify Observer objects of every change to an Observable object. If this is the case, you can avoid unnecessary notifications by batching state changes and waiting until an entire batch of state changes is complete before delivering notifications. If another object makes changes to an Observable object's state, then providing a single notification for a batch of changes is more complicated. You will have to add a method to the Observable object's class that other objects can call to indicate the beginning of a batch of state changes. When a state change is part of a batch, it should not cause the object to deliver any notifications to its registered observers. You will also have to add a method to the Observable object's class that other objects call to indicate the end of a batch of state changes. When this method is called, if any state changes have occurred since the beginning of the batch, the object should deliver notifications to its registered observers.

If multiple objects will initiate changes to an Observable object's state, then determining the end of a batch of changes may be more complicated. A good way to manage this complexity is to add an additional object that coordinates the state changes initiated by the other objects and understands their logic well enough to determine the end of a batch of changes. See the description of the Mediator pattern for a more detailed description of how to use one object to coordinate the actions of other objects.

The Observer pattern is usually used to notify other objects that an object's state has changed. A common variation on this is to define an alternate ObservableIF interface that allows objects to request that they receive a notification before an object's state changes. The usual reason for sending state-change notifications after a state change is to allow the change to propagate to other objects. The usual reason for sending a notification before a state change is so that other objects can veto a state change. The usual way to implement this is to have an object throw an exception to prevent a proposed state change.

JAVA API USAGE

Java's delegation event model is a specialized form of the Observer pattern. Classes whose instances can be event sources participate in the Observable role. Event listener interfaces participate in the ObserverIF role. Classes that implement event listener interfaces participate in the Observer role. Because there are a number of classes that deliver various subclasses of java.awt.AwtEvent to their listeners, there is a Multicaster class that they use called java.awt.AWTEventMulticaster.

CODE EXAMPLE

Following is the code that implements some of the security monitoring design presented under the "Context" heading. The first piece of code is the SecurityObserver interface. In order for the instances of a class to be able to receive notifications, it must implement the SecurityObserver interface.

```
public interface SecurityObserver {
    public final int ALARM = 1;
    public final int LOW_POWER = 2;
    public final int DIAGNOSTIC = 3;
```

```
/**
 * This method is called to deliver a security notification.
 * @param device Identifies the source of this notification.
 * @param event This should be one of the above constants.
 */
public void notify(int device, int event);
} // interface SecurityObserver
```

The following piece of code is the `SecurityNotifier` class that is responsible for delivering the notifications that a computer receives from security devices.

```
class SecurityNotifier {
    private ArraySet observers = new ArraySet();
...
    public void addObserver(SecurityObserver observer) {
        observers.add(observer);
    } // addObserver(SecurityObserver)

    public void removeObserver(SecurityObserver observer) {
        observers.remove(observer);
    } // removeObserver(SecurityObserver)

    private void notify(int device, int event) {
        Iterator iterator = observers.iterator();
        while (iterator.hasNext()) {
            ((SecurityObserver)iterator.next()).notify (device,
                                                        event);
        } // while
    } // notify(int, int)
} // class SecurityNotifier
```

Finally, here is an adapter class that allows instances of the `SecurityMonitor` class to receive notifications, even though the `SecurityMonitor` class does not implement the `SecurityObserver` class.

```
class SecurityAdapter implements SecurityObserver {
    private SecurityMonitor sm;

    SecurityAdapter(SecurityMonitor sm) {
        this.sm = sm;
    } // Constructor(SecurityMonitor)

    /**
     * This method is called to deliver a security notification.
     * @param device Identifies the source of this notification.
     * @param event This should be one of the above constants.
     */
    public void notify(int device, int event) {
```

```
      switch (event) {
        case ALARM:
            sm.securityAlert(device);
            break;
        case LOW_POWER:
        case DIAGNOSTIC:
            sm.diagnosticAlert(device);
            break;
      } // switch
    } // notify(int, int)
} // class SecurityAdapter
```

RELATED PATTERNS

Adapter   The Adapter pattern can be used to allow objects that do not implement the required interface to participate in the Observer pattern by receiving notifications.

Delegation   The Observer pattern uses the Delegation pattern.

Mediator   The Mediator pattern is sometimes used to coordinate state changes initiated by multiple objects to an `Observable` object.

Publisher-Subscriber   The Publisher-Subscriber pattern is a specialized version of the Observer pattern for reliable delivery notifications to remote and distributed objects. It is described in [BMRSS96].

State [GoF95]

SYNOPSIS

Encapsulates the states of an object as discrete objects, each belonging to a separate subclass of an abstract state class.

CONTEXT

Many objects are required to have a dynamically changing set of attributes, called a *state*. Such objects are called *stateful objects*. An object's state will usually be one of a predetermined set of values. When a stateful object becomes aware of an external event, its state may change. The behavior of a stateful object is in some ways determined by its state.

For an example of a stateful object, suppose that you are writing a dialog for editing parameters of a program. The dialog will have buttons for specifying the disposition of changes you have made:

- The dialog will have an *OK* button that saves the parameter values in the dialog to both a file and the program's working values.
- The dialog will have a *Save* button that just saves the parameter values to a file.
- The dialog will have an *Apply* button that just saves the parameter values to the program's working values.
- The dialog will have a *Revert* button that restores the dialog values from the file.

It is possible to design such a dialog so that it is stateless. If a dialog is stateless, then it will always behave in the same way. The OK button will be enabled regardless of whether you have edited the values in the dialog. The Revert button will be enabled even if the user has just reverted the dialog values to the contents of the file. If there are no other considerations, then designing this dialog to be stateless is satisfactory.

In some cases, the dialog's stateless behavior may be a problem. Updating the values of the program's working values may be disruptive. Storing parameter values to a file might take an annoyingly long time if the file is on a remote shared file server. A way to avoid unnecessary saves to the file or unnecessary setting of the program's working parameter values is to make the dialog stateful so that it will not perform these operations when they are not useful. Instead, it will allow them only when updating the file or working values with values different than those already contained. Figure 8.20 shows a state diagram that demonstrates the four states needed to produce this behavior.

To implement Figure 8.20, you can design the four classes shown in Figure 8.21, which the diagram shows four classes corresponding to the four states in the state diagram and their common superclass. The superclass, DirtyState, has a public method called processEvent. The processEvent method takes an event identifier as its argument and returns the next state. Each subclass of DirtyState overrides the processEvent method in an appropriate way. The DirtyState class also has a static

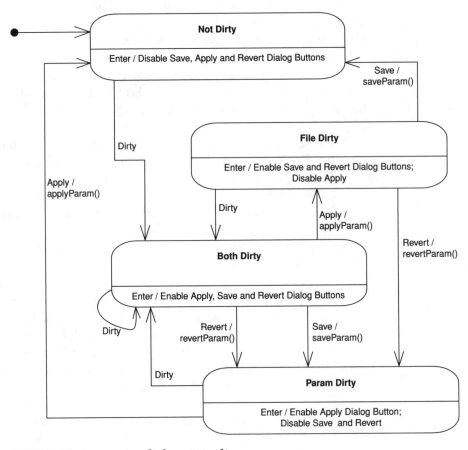

FIGURE 8.20 Parameter dialog state diagram.

method called `start`. The `start` method gets things going by creating an instance of each subclass of the `DirtyState` class and returning the initial state. The `start` method also creates an instance of the `DirtyState` class and assigns its variables `notDirty`, `fileDirty`, `paramDirty`, and `bothDirty` to the corresponding subclass instances that it creates.

The `DirtyState` class defines a protected method called `enter`. A `DirtyState` object's `enter` method is called when it becomes the current state. The `enter` method defined by the `DirtyState` class doesn't do anything. However, its subclasses override the `enter` method to implement their entry actions.

The `DirtyState` class defines some static constants. The constants identify event codes that are passed to the `processEvent` method.

FORCES

- An object's behavior is determined by an internal state that changes in response to events.
- The organization of logic that manages an object's state should be able to scale up to many states without becoming one unmanageably large piece of code.

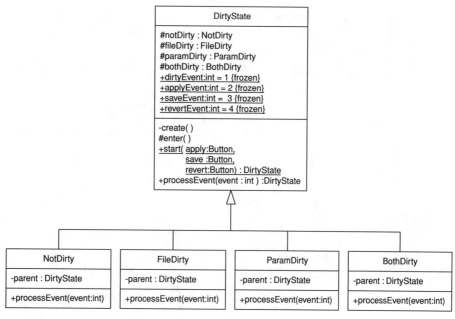

FIGURE 8.21 DirtyState class diagram.

SOLUTION

The diagram in Figure 8.22 shows the basic class organization for a State pattern. An explanation of the roles these classes play are listed here:

Context   Context is a class whose instances exhibit stateful behavior. Instances of Context determine their current state by keeping a reference to an instance of a concrete subclass of the ContextState class. The subclass of the ContextState class determines the state.

ContextState   The ContextState class is the superclass of all classes used to represent the state of Context objects. A ContextState class defines these methods:

- The start method performs any necessary initialization of state management objects and returns an object corresponding to the client object's initial state.
- The processEvent method is an abstract method that takes an argument that indicates the occurrence of an event and returns the

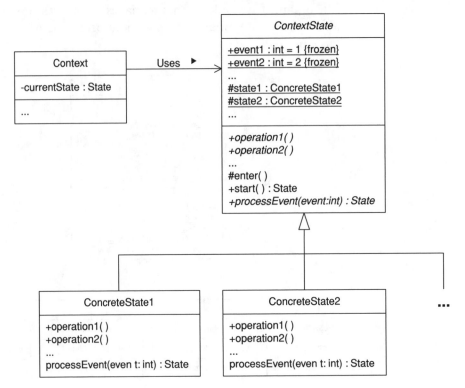

FIGURE 8.22 State class diagram.

new current state. Each concrete subclass of `ContextState` overrides the `processEvent` method in a manner appropriate for the state it represents. The `processEvent` method executes any exit actions associated with the previous state.

- Before returning an object that corresponds to the initial or next state, the `start` and `processEvent` methods call that `ContextState` object's `enter` method. The `enter` method is responsible for executing any entry actions associated with a state. The default `enter` method implementation provided by the `ContextState` class doesn't do anything. Concrete classes that represent states that have entry actions associated with them override the default implementation to perform their entry actions.
- The methods `operation1`, `operation2`... implement operations that behave differently for each state. For example, if an object has states associated with it called `On` and `Off`, the implementation for an operation for the `On` state might do something and the implementation for the `Off` state might do nothing.

The `ContextState` class defines constants that are symbolic names for the event codes passed to the `processEvent` method.

Unless a `ConcreteState` class has instance variables, there is no need to have more than one instance of it. If there is only one instance of a concrete subclass of `ContextState`, then the `ContextState` class will have a static variable that refers to that instance. Implementations of the `processEvent` method return the instances referred to by those variables rather than create additional instances.

ConcreteState1,ConcreteState2   These are concrete subclasses of `ContextState`. They must implement the `processEvent` method to provide an appropriate response to events for that method. `ConcreteState` classes that represent states that have associated entry actions override the `enter` method to implement those actions.

CONSEQUENCES

The code for each state is in its own class. This organization makes it easy to add new states without unintended consequences. For this reason, the State pattern works well for small and large numbers of states.

State transitions appear to be atomic to clients of state objects. A client calls the current state's `processEvent` method and it returns with the client's new state.

State objects that represent nonparametric states can be shared as singletons if there is no need to create a direct instance of the State class. In some cases, such as the example shown under the "Context" heading, there is a need to create an instance of the ContextState class to provide a set of state objects a way of sharing data. Even in those cases, for each subclass of the State class that represents a nonparametric state, there can be a single instance of that class associated with an instance of the ContextState class.

IMPLEMENTATION

No class other than the ContextState class needs to be aware of the subclasses of the ContextState class. You can ensure that no class other than the ContextState class is aware of its subclasses by declaring the subclasses of the ContextState class as private member classes of the ContextState class.

CODE EXAMPLE

Here is the code that implements the class diagram shown under the "Context" heading:

```
class DirtyState {
    // Symbolic constants for events
    public static final int DIRTY_EVENT = 1;
    public static final int APPLY_EVENT = 2;
    public static final int SAVE_EVENT = 3;
    public static final int REVERT_EVENT = 4;

    // Symbolic constants for states
    private final BothDirty bothDirty = new BothDirty();
    private final FileDirty fileDirty = new FileDirty();
    private final ParamDirty paramDirty = new ParamDirty();
    private final NotDirty notDirty = new NotDirty();

    private Parameters parameters;
    private Button apply, save, revert;

    /**
     * This constructor would be private to prevent other classes
     * from using it. It is not private because subclasses of this
     * class are implemented as inner classes and Java 1.2 does not
     * support access of a private constructor by inner classes.
     */
```

```
DirtyState() {
} // constructor()
```

The `DirtyState` class's start method initializes the state machine. Its arguments are the `Parameters` object that the state machine can use to update the programs working values and the buttons that the state machine will enable and disable. The start method returns the initial state.

```
public static DirtyState start(Parameters p,
                               Button apply,
                               Button save,
                               Button revert){
    DirtyState d = new DirtyState();
    d.parameters = p;
    d.apply = apply;
    d.save = save;
    d.revert = revert;
    return d.notDirty;
} // start(Button, Button, Button)

    /**
     * Respond to a given event.
     * All subclasses are expected to override this method.
     * @return the next state.
     */
    public DirtyState processEvent(int event) {
    // This non-overridden method should never be called.
    throw new IllegalAccessError();
} // processEvent(int)
```

This `processEvent` method is not abstract because the class is not abstract.

```
/**
 * This method is called when this object becomes the current state.
 */
protected void enter() { }
```

The four concrete subclasses of `DirtyState` are implemented in private classes. For the sake of brevity, only one of them is shown here.

```
/**
 * An instance of this class represents the state when fields of
 * the dialog do not match the file or working parameter values.
 */
private class BothDirty extends DirtyState {
    /**
     * Respond to a given event.
     * @return the next state.
```

```
        */
    public DirtyState processEvent(int event) {
        switch (event) {
          case DIRTY_EVENT:
              return this;
          case APPLY_EVENT:
              if (parameters.applyParam()) {
                  fileDirty.enter();
                  return fileDirty;
              } // if
          case SAVE_EVENT:
              if (parameters.saveParam()) {
                  paramDirty.enter();
                  return paramDirty;
              } // if
          case REVERT_EVENT:
              if (parameters.revertParam()) {
                  paramDirty.enter();
                  return paramDirty;
              } // if
          default:
              String msg = "unexpected event "+event;
              throw new IllegalArgumentException(msg);
        } // switch (event)
    } // processDirtyStateEvent(int)

    /**
     * This method is called when this object becomes
     * the current state.
     */
    protected void enter() {
        apply.setEnabled(true);
        revert.setEnabled(true);
        save.setEnabled(true);
    } // enter
  } // class BothDirty
} // class DirtyState
```

RELATED PATTERNS

Flyweight   You can use the Flyweight pattern to share state objects.

Mediator   You can often use the State pattern with the Mediator pattern when implementing user interfaces.

Singleton   You can implement nonparametric states using the Singleton pattern.

Null Object [Woolf97]

SYNOPSIS

The Null Object pattern provides an alternative to using `null` to indicate the absence of an object to delegate an operation to. Using `null` to indicate the absence of such an object requires a test for `null` before each call to the other object's methods. Instead of using `null`, the Null Object pattern uses a reference to an object that doesn't do anything.

CONTEXT

You have been given the task of writing some classes to encapsulate an enterprise's business rules. Because these classes will be used in a variety of environments, there is a requirement that these objects be able to route warning messages to a dialog box, a log file, other destinations, or nowhere at all. A simple way to arrange this is to define an interface called `WarningRouter` for routing warning messages and then have the classes you write delegate the routing of warnings to objects that implement that interface, as shown in Figure 8.23.

To handle the situation in which warning messages should not be routed anywhere, you could have the variable that would otherwise refer to a `WarningRouter` object contain `null`. Using this technique means that before a `BusinessRule` object can issue a warning message, it must first

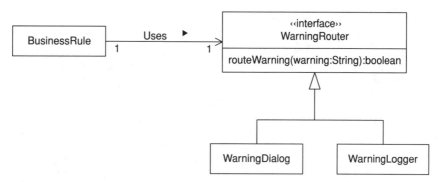

FIGURE 8.23 WarningRouter interface.

test to see if a variable is `null`. Depending on the specific business-rule class, there may be just one or many places that refer to a `WarningRouter` object. There are procedural techniques for limiting the amount of additional complexity implied by those tests for `null`. However, every call to a `WarningRouter` object's methods is an opportunity for someone to forget to put a test for `null` in the code.

An alternative to using `null` to indicate no action is to create a class that implements `WarningRouter` and does nothing with a warning message, as shown in Figure 8.24.

The advantage of having an `IgnoreWarning` class is that you can use it just like any other class that implements the `WarningRouter` interface. It does not require a test for `null` or any other special logic.

FORCES

- A class delegates an operation to another class. The delegating class does not usually care how the other class implements the operation. However, it sometimes does require that the operation be implemented by doing nothing.
- You want the class delegating the operation to delegate it in all cases, including the do-nothing case. You do not want the do-nothing case to require any special code in the delegating class.

SOLUTION

Figure 8.25 shows a class diagram that demonstrates the structure of the Null Object pattern. Here are the descriptions of the roles that the classes shown in Figure 8.25 play in the Null Object pattern.

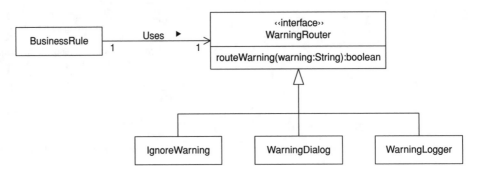

FIGURE 8.24 Ignore warning class.

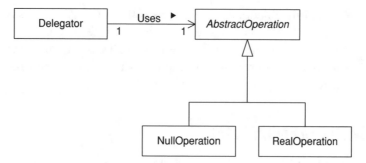

FIGURE 8.25 Null Object pattern.

Delegator   A class in this role participates in the Null Object pattern by delegating an operation to a possibly abstract class or to an interface. It performs this delegation without taking responsibility for the do-nothing case of an operation. It simply assumes that the object it delegates to will encapsulate the correct behavior, even if that is to do nothing.

In particular, an object in the `Delegator` role does not need to test for `null` before invoking methods of the object it is delegating to.

AbstractOperation   A class in the `Delegator` role delegates an operation to a class in the `AbstractOperation` role. Classes in this role are not necessarily abstract. An interface can also fill this role.

RealOperation   Classes in this role implement the operation the `Delegator` class delegates to the `AbstractOperation`.

NullOperation   Classes in this role provide a do-nothing implementation of the operation the `Delegator` class delegates to the `AbstractOperation`.

CONSEQUENCES

- The Null Object pattern relieves a class that delegates an operation to another class of the responsibility for implementing the do-nothing version of that operation. This results in simpler code that does not have to test for `null` before calling the method that implements the delegated operation. It results in more reliable code because the Null Object pattern eliminates some opportunities to create bugs by omitting the test for `null` from code.

- The do-nothing behavior encapsulated by a class in the `NullOperation` role is reusable, if there is one consistent do-nothing behavior that works for all `Delegator` classes.

- The Null Object pattern increases the number of classes in a program. If there is not already a class or interface in the `AbsractOperation` role, then the Null Object pattern may introduce more complexity through the introduction of additional classes than it removes by the simplification of code.

IMPLEMENTATION

It is often the case that instances of `NullOperation` classes contain no instance-specific information. When this is the case, you can save time and memory by implementing the `NullOperation` class as a singleton class.

CODE EXAMPLE

Following is the code that implements the classes presented under the "Context" heading. First is the `WarningRouter` interface that is implemented by classes that provide environment-appropriate handling for warning messages.

```
public interface WarningRouter {
    /**
     * This method sends a warning message to whatever destination it
     * considers appropriate.
     * @return true if caller should proceed with its current operation.
     */
    public boolean routeWarning(String msg) ;
} // interface WarningRouter
```

Next is some code from the `BusinessRule` class that delegates the handling of warning messages to objects that implement the `WarningRouter` interface.

```
class BusinessRule {
    private WarningRouter warning;
    private Date expirationDate = new Date(Long.MAX_VALUE);
    ...
    BusinessRule() {
        ...
        if (new Date().after(expirationDate)) {
            String msg = getClass().getName()+" has expired.";
            warning.routeWarning msg);
        } // if
        ...
    } // constructor()
} // class BusinessRule
```

Next is a class that implements the `WarningRouter` interface by popping up a dialog box that displays the warning message.

```
class WarningDialog implements WarningRouter {
    public boolean routeWarning(String warning) {
        int r;
        r = JOptionPane.showConfirmDialog(null,
                            warning,
                            "Warning",

                        JOptionPane..OK_CANCEL_OPTION,
                        JOptionPane.WARNING_MESSAGE) ;
        return r == 0;
    } // routeWarning(String)
} // class WarningDialog
```

The `WarningDialog` class's `routeWarning` method returns true if the user clicks the dialog box' OK button or false if the user clicks its Cancel button. The `IgnoreWarning` class is listed next. Because it encapsulates do-nothing behavior, its `routeWarning` method always returns true.

```
class IgnoreWarning implements WarningRouter {
    public boolean routeWarning(String warning) {
        return true;
    } // routeWarning(String)
} // class IgnoreWarning
```

RELATED PATTERNS

Singleton   If instances of a `NullOperation` class contain no instance-specific information, then you can save time and memory by implementing that `NullOperation` class as a singleton class.

Strategy   The Null Object pattern is often used with the Strategy pattern.

Strategy [GoF95]

SYNOPSIS

Encapsulates related algorithms in classes that are subclasses of a common superclass. This allows the selection of algorithm to vary by object and also allows it to vary over time.

CONTEXT

Suppose that you have to write a program that displays calendars. One of the requirements for the program is that it be able to display holidays celebrated by different nations and different religious groups. The user must be able to specify which sets of holidays to display.

You would like to satisfy the requirement by putting the logic for each set of holidays in a separate class, so that you have a set of small classes to which you could easily add additional sets of classes. You would also like the classes that use these holiday classes to be unaware of any specific holidays or of any specific set of holidays (see Figure 8.26).

Here is how classes in Figure 8.26 work with each other. If a CalendarDisplay object has a Holiday object to work with, it consults with that object about each day that it displays in order to find out if that day is a holiday. The object that a CalendarDisplay object works with is never a direct instance of the Holiday class. Instead, it is either an

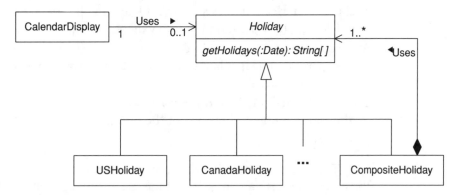

FIGURE 8.26 Holiday classes.

instance of a class like USHoliday that encapsulates the logic to identify a single set of dates or it is an instance of CompositeHoliday. The CompositeHoliday class is used when the user requests the display of multiple sets of holidays. It is instantiated by passing an array of Holiday objects to its constructor.

This arrangement allows a CalendarDisplay object to find out what holidays fall on particular dates without having do any more than call a Holiday object's getHolidays method.

FORCES

- A program has to provide multiple variations of an algorithm or behavior.
- You can encapsulate the behavioral variations in separate classes that provide a consistent way of accessing the behaviors.
- Putting these behaviors in separate classes means that classes that use these behaviors do not need to know anything about how these behaviors are implemented. Giving these classes a common super-class or interface allows classes that use them to be unaware how to select a behavior or which behavior is selected.

SOLUTION

Figure 8.27 shows a class diagram that demonstrates the roles that classes play in the Strategy pattern. Here are the descriptions of the roles that classes play in Figure 8.27:

Client A class in the Client role delegates an operation to an abstract class or interface. It does so without knowing the actual class of the object it delegates the operation to or how that class implements the operation.

AbstractStrategy A class in this role provides a common way to access the operation encapsulated by its subclasses. You can also use an interface in this role.

ConcreteStrategy1,ConcreteStrategy2 Classes in this role implement alternative implementations of the operation that the Client class delegates.

The Strategy pattern always occurs with a mechanism for determining the ConcreteStrategy object that the Client object will use. However, the

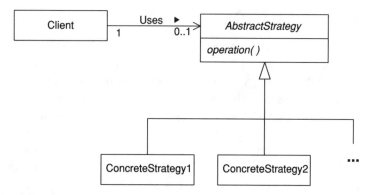

FIGURE 8.27 Strategy pattern.

actual mechanism varies so much that no particular mechanism is included in the pattern.

CONSEQUENCES

The Strategy pattern allows the behavior of Client objects to be dynamically determined on a per-object basis.

The Strategy pattern simplifies Client objects by relieving them of any responsibility for selecting behavior or implementing alternate behaviors. It simplifies the code for Client objects by eliminating if and switch statements. In some cases, it can also increase the speed of Client objects because they do not need to spend any time selecting a behavior.

IMPLEMENTATION

It is common for ConcreteStrategy classes to share some common behavior. You should factor the common behavior that they share into a common superclass.

There may be situations in which none of the behaviors encapsulated in ConcreteStrategy classes are appropriate. A common way to handle such a situation is for the Client object to have a null instead of a reference to a Strategy object. This means having to check for null before calling a Strategy object's method. If the structure of the Client object makes this inconvenient, consider using the Null Object pattern.

JAVA API USAGE

The java.util.zip package contains some classes that use the Strategy pattern. The CheckedInputStream and, CheckedOutputStream classes both use the Strategy pattern to compute checksums on byte streams. These two classes both participate as Client classes. The constructors for both classes take a Checksum argument. Checksum is an interface that participates in the AbstractStrategy role. Two classes implement the Checksum interface: Adler32 and CRC32. These classes participate in the ConcreteStrategy role. Figure 8.28 shows a diagram that presents the relationship between these classes.

CODE EXAMPLE

Following is the code that implements the design presented under the "Context" heading. The first listing is for the Holiday class. The Holiday class is an abstract class that defines a method that returns an array of the names of holidays that fall on a given date. It participates in the Strategy pattern in the AbstractStrategy role.

```
public abstract class Holiday {
    protected final static String[] noHoliday = new String[0];
    /**
     * Return array of strings describing holidays falling on a date.
     * If no holidays fall on the given date, returns a zero length array.
     */
    abstract public String[] getHolidays(Date dt) ;
} // class Holiday
```

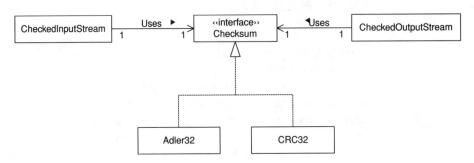

FIGURE 8.28 Checksum-related classes.

The `Holiday` class creates a zero-length array that its subclass's implementation of `getHolidays` may return to indicate that no holiday falls on a given date. Returning this array saves the expense of creating another zero-length array for every day that is not a holiday.

Next is a partial listing of the `CalendarDisplay` class, which participates in the Strategy pattern as a `Client` class.

```java
class CalendarDisplay {
    private Holiday holiday;
    private static final String[]noHoliday = new String[0];
...
    /**
     * Private class used to cache information about dates.
     */
    private class DateCache {
        private Date date;
        private String[] holidayStrings;

        DateCache(Date dt) {
            date = dt;
            ...
            if (holiday == null) {
                holidayStrings = noHoliday;
            } else {
                holidayStrings = holiday.getHolidays(date);
            } // if
            ...
        } // constructor(Date)
    } // class DateCache
...
} // class CalendarDisplay
```

Notice that aside from having to handle the possibility of not having any `Holiday` object to work with, the `CalendarDisplay` class is totally unburdened with any details of determining which holidays fall on a date.

The various subclasses of `Holiday` participate in the Strategy pattern in the `ConcreteStrategy` role. They are not particularly interesting with respect to the Strategy pattern and have this basic structure:

```java
public class USHoliday extends Holiday {
...
    public String[] getHolidays(Date dt) {
        String[] holidays = noHoliday;
        ...
        return holidays;
    } // getHolidays(Date)
```

```
...
} // class USHoliday
```

RELATED PATTERNS

Adapter   The Adapter pattern is structurally similar to the Strategy pattern. The difference is in the intent. The Adapter pattern allows a `Client` object to carry out its originally intended function in collaboration by calling method of objects that implement a particular interface. The Strategy pattern provides objects that implement a particular interface for the purpose of altering or determining the behavior of a `Client` object.

Flyweight   If there are many client objects, `ConcreteStrategy` objects may be best implemented as Flyweights.

Null Object   The Strategy pattern is often used with the Null Object pattern.

Template Method   The Template Method pattern manages alternate behaviors through subclassing rather than through delegation.

Template Method [GoF95]

SYNOPSIS

Write an abstract class that contains only part of the logic needed to accomplish its purpose. Organize the class so that its concrete methods call an abstract method where the missing logic would have appeared. Provide the missing logic in subclass methods that override the abstract methods.

CONTEXT

Suppose that you have the task of writing a reusable class for logging users into an application or applet. In addition to being reusable and easy to use, the tasks of the class will be to:

- Prompt the user for a user ID and password.
- Authenticate the user ID and password. The result of the authentication operation should be an object. If the authentication operation produces some information needed later as proof of authentication, then the object produced by the authentication operation should encapsulate that information.
- While the authentication operation is in progress, the user should see a changing and possibly animated display that tells the user that authentication is in progress and all is well.
- Notify the rest of the application or applet that login is complete and make the object produced by the authentication operation available to the rest of the application.

Two of these tasks, prompting the user and assuring the user that authentication is in progress, are application independent. Though the strings and images displayed to the user may vary with the application, the underlying logic will always be the same.

The other two tasks, authenticating the user and notifying the rest of the application, are application specific. Every application or applet will have to provide its own logic for these tasks.

The way in which you organize your Logon class will be a large factor in how easy it is for developers to use. Delegation is a very flexible mechanism. You could simply organize a Logon class so that it delegates the tasks of authenticating the user and notifying the rest of the application. Though this approach gives a programmer a lot of freedom, it does not help guide a programmer to a correct solution.

Programmers are unlikely to make frequent use of your Logon class. This means that when they do use it, they will probably not be very familiar with it. Just as it can be easier to fill in the blanks of a preprinted form than to write a document from scratch, giving your Logon class a fill-in-the-blanks organization can guide programmers to the correct use of the Logon class. You can achieve a fill-in-the-blanks organization by defining the Logon class as an abstract class that defines abstract methods corresponding to the application-dependent tasks that the programmer must supply code for. To use the Logon class, a programmer must define a subclass of the Logon class. Because the methods corresponding to the tasks that the programmer must code are abstract methods, a Java compiler will complain if the programmer does not fill in the blanks by overriding the abstract methods.

Figure 8.29 shows the organization of a Logon class organized in this way, with its subclass.

The AbstractLogon class has a method called logon that contains the top-level logic for the top-level task of logging a user onto a program. It calls the abstract methods authenticate and notifyAuthentication to perform the program-specific tasks of authenticating a user and notifying the rest of the program when the authentication is accomplished.

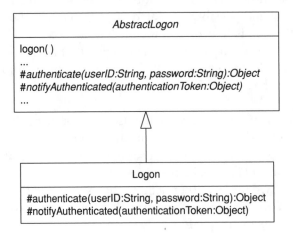

FIGURE 8.29 Logon class and subclass.

FORCES

- You have to design a class that will be used in multiple programs. Though the overall responsibility of the class will always be the same, portions of its behavior will be different in each program in which it is used. To ensure that programmers who use the class supply logic for all of the program-specific responsibilities, you implement the class as an abstract class and the program-specific responsibilities as abstract methods. To use the class, a programmer must define a concrete subclass. A compiler will insist that it override all of its superclass's abstract methods, thereby forcing the programmer to supply code for all of the application-specific responsibilities.

- You have an existing design that contains a number of classes that do similar things. To minimize code duplication, you factor those classes, identifying what they have in common and what is different. You organize the classes so that their differences are completely contained in discrete methods with common names. The remainder of the code in the classes should be common code that you can move into a new common superclass. You define methods to encapsulate specialized logic in the superclass as abstract methods. This causes the compiler to force any new subclasses of that class to conform to the same organization as the other subclasses.

SOLUTION

Figure 8.30 shows a class diagram that demonstrates the organization of the Template Method pattern.

Here are the descriptions of the roles played by classes in the Template Method pattern:

AbstractTemplate   A class in this role has a concrete method that contains the class's top-level logic. This method is indicated in the diagram as `templateMethod`. This method calls other methods, defined in the `AbstractTemplate` class as abstract methods, to invoke lower-level logic that varies with each subclass of the `AbstractTemplate` class.

ConcreteTemplate   A class in this role is a concrete subclass of an `AbstractTemplate` class. It overrides the abstract methods defined by its superclass to provide the logic needed to complete the logic of the `templateMethod` method.

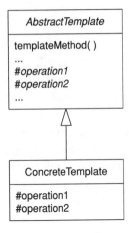

FIGURE 8.30 Template Method pattern.

CONSEQUENCES

A programmer writing a subclass of an `AbstractTemplate` class is forced to override those methods that must be overridden to complete the logic of the superclass. A well-designed template method class has a structure that provides a programmer with guidance in providing the basic structure of its subclasses.

IMPLEMENTATION

An `AbstractTemplate` class provides guidance by forcing the programmer to override abstract methods with the intention of providing logic to fill in the blanks of its template method's logic. You can provide additional structure by having additional methods in the `AbstractTemplate` class that subclasses can override to provide supplemental or optional logic. For example, consider a reusable class called `Paragraph` that represents paragraphs in a word processor document.

One of the `Paragraph` class's responsibilities is to determine how to wrap the words that it contains into lines so that they fit within specified margins. The `Paragraph` class has a template method that is responsible for wrapping the words in a paragraph. Because some word processors allow paragraphs to wrap around graphics, the `Paragraph` class defines an abstract method that the class's word-wrapping logic calls to determine the margins for a line of text. Concrete subclasses of the paragraph class are forced to provide an implementation of that method to determine the margins for each line.

Some word processors include a hyphenation engine that automatically determines where words can be hyphenated. This feature allows longer words to be split between lines to allow the lines of a paragraph to be of more even lengths. Since not every word processor will require the `Paragraph` class to support hyphenation, it does not make sense for the `Paragraph` class to define an abstract hyphenation method and force subclasses to override it. However, it is helpful for the `Paragraph` class to define a concrete hyphenation method that is called by the word-wrapping logic and that does nothing. The point of such a method is that a subclass of `Paragraph` can override the method in those cases where hyphenation needs to be supported.

Methods that can be optionally overridden to provide additional or customized functionality are called *hook methods*. To make it easier for a programmer to be aware of the hook methods that a class provides, you can apply a naming convention to hook methods. Two of the more common naming conventions for hook methods are to either begin the names of hook methods with the prefix `do-` or end the names of hook methods with the suffix `-Hook`. For example, following these naming conventions, the name of the `Paragraph` class's hyphenation method might be `doHyphenation` or `hyphenationHook`.

CODE EXAMPLE

Following is some code that implements the design presented under the "Context" heading. First is the `AbstractLogon` class. It participates in the Template Method pattern in the `AbstractTemplate` role. Its template method is called `logon`. The `logon` method puts up a dialog that prompts the user for a user ID and password. When the user has supplied a user ID and password, the `logon` method pops up a window telling the user that the authentication is in progress. This window stays up while the `logon` method calls the abstract method `authenticate` to authenticate the user ID and password. If the authentication is successful, then it takes down the dialog boxes and calls the abstract method `notifyAuthentication` to notify the rest of the program that the user has been authenticated.

```
public abstract class AbstractLogon {
    /**
     * This method authenticates a user.
     * @param frame The parentframe for this method's dialogs.
     * @param programName The name of the program
     */
```

```
public void logon(Frame frame, String programName) {
        Object authenticationToken;
        LogonDialog logonDialog;
        logonDialog = new LogonDialog(frame,
                                  Log on to "+programName);
        JDialog waitDialog = createWaitDialog(frame);
```

The `LogonDialog` class implements a dialog that prompts the user for logon information. The object referred to by the `waitDialog` variable is a window that contains a message to tell the user that authentication is in progress.

```
while(true) {
    waitDialog.setVisible(false);
    logonDialog.setVisible(true);
    waitDialog.setVisible(true);
    try {
        String userID = logonDialog.getUserID();
        String password = logonDialog.getPassword();
        authenticationToken = authenticate(userID,
                                             password);
        break;
    } catch (Exception e) {
        // Tell user that Authentication failed
        JOptionPane.showMessageDialog(frame,
                                  e.getMessage(),
                               "Authentication Failure",
                          JOptionPane.ERROR_MESSAGE);

    } // try
} // while
// Authentication successful
waitDialog.setVisible(false);
logonDialog.setVisible(false);
notifyAuthentication(authenticationToken);
} // logon()
...
```

The remainder of this listing simply shows the abstract methods that the `AbstractLogon` class defines and that the `logon` method calls.

```
/**
 * Authenticate the user's user id and password.
 * @param userID the supplied user id
 * @param password the supplied password
 * @return object encapsulating proof of authentication
 * @exception Exception If user id/password cannot be
 *                      authenticated.
 */
```

```
abstract protected Object authenticate(String userID,
                         String password)
            throws Exception;

    /**
     * Notify the rest of program that the user has been
     * authenticated.
     * @param authentication What authenticate returned.
     */
    abstract protected void notifyAuthentication(Object authentication) ;
} // class AbstractLogon
```

Subclasses of the `AbstractLogon` class must override its abstract methods like this:

```
public class Logon extends AbstractLogon {
    ...
    protected Object authenticate(String userID, String password)
                   throws Exception {
       if (userID.equals("abc") && password.equals("123"))
          return userID;
       throw new Exception("bad userID");
    } // authenticate

    protected void notifyAuthentication(Object authenticationToken) {
       ...
    } // notify(Object)
} // class Logon
```

RELATED PATTERNS

Strategy   The Strategy pattern modifies the logic of individual objects. The Template Method pattern modifies the logic of an entire class.

Visitor [GoF95]

SYNOPSIS

One way to implement an operation that involves the objects in a complex structure is to provide logic in each of their classes to support the operation. The Visitor pattern provides an alternate way to implement such operations that avoids complicating the classes of the objects in the structure by putting all of the necessary logic in a separate Visitor class. The Visitor pattern also allows the logic to be varied by using different Visitor classes.

CONTEXT

Suppose that you have the assignment of adding new features to a word processor that relate to its ability to produce a table of contents. From the viewpoint of a user, there will be a dialog that allows the user to specify information that guides the building of a table of contents. The word processor allows a style name to be associated with each paragraph. The dialog will allow the user to specify which paragraph styles correspond to headings that should appear in the table of contents.

The word processor uses information specified in the dialog to build an internal table that contains all the information it needs to build a multilevel table of contents. In the rest of this description, that table is referred to as the *internal ToC table*. The information in each row of the table will include a level number that can correspond to chapter, section, or any other hierarchical organization that the user wants it to represent. The rows of the table will also include a paragraph style and other information for formatting the table of contents. If a paragraph style appears in the table, it means that paragraphs with that style are headings whose first line will appear in that level of a table of contents.

In addition to adding the dialog and internal ToC table to the word processor, you will have to add these table-of-contents-related features:

- Generate and insert a table of contents for a single file document into that document.
- Reorganize a single file document into a multifile document, based on a heading level in the internal ToC table.

Because these operations involve manipulating a word processing document, any design for implementing the table of contents features will have to involve the classes that the word processor uses to represent documents. Figure 8.31 shows some of the classes that the word processor uses to represent documents.

The classes that will be of interest to a table of contents mechanism are Document, Paragraph, and LineOfText. A document contains paragraphs, which contain lines of text. Any design for generating a table of contents should recognize that Document objects may contain objects that are not Paragraph objects. It should also recognize that some kinds of objects other than Document objects may contain Paragraph objects. Finally, the design should not add complexity to the classes that represent documents.

There are two basic approaches that you could take towards implementing the table of contents features. One approach is to put the necessary logic in the various classes that represent a document. For the reasons discussed in the previous paragraph, this is not a good solution. The other approach is to put all of the logic in a separate class. When a table of contents operation is to be done, the object responsible for the operation exam-

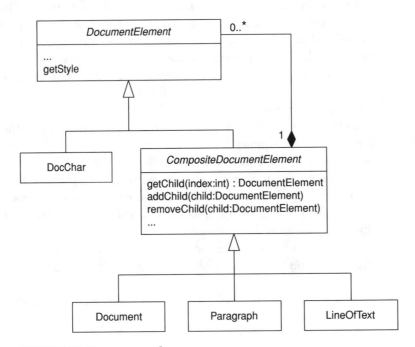

FIGURE 8.31 Document classes.

ines a Document object and objects that it contains. It looks for Paragraph objects that the Document object directly contains. When it finds Paragraph objects that have a style that is in the internal ToC table that drives the table of contents operation, it takes the appropriate action. This is the approach demonstrated in the class diagram shown in Figure 8.32.

Figure 8.32 includes the classes for representing word processing documents that were shown in Figure 8.31. It also includes the following classes:

WordProcessor The WordProcessor class is responsible for creating and editing the objects that represent a document. It uses the other classes in the diagram to edit a document.

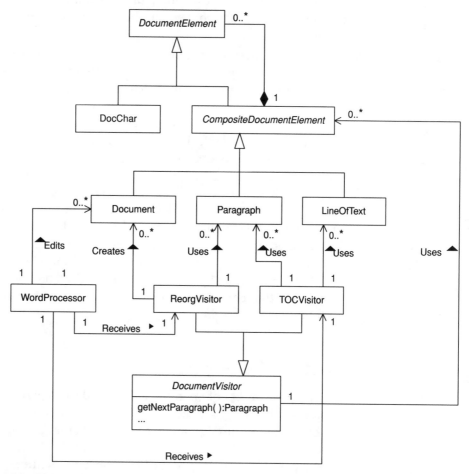

FIGURE 8.32 Table of contents classes.

DocumentVisitor   This is an abstract class. Its subclasses explore the objects that constitute a document in order to produce a table of contents or reorganize a document into multiple files. The `DocumentVisitor` class provides logic that its subclasses use to navigate among those objects.

The concept is that instances of subclasses of the `DocumentVisitor` class visit the objects that comprise a document, gather information from each object, and then act on the information.

TOCVisitor   This subclass of the `DocumentVisitor` class is responsible for generating a table of contents. It works by examining each `Paragraph` object that is directly owned by a `Document` object. When it finds a `Paragraph` object that has a style that is in the internal ToC table, it generates a corresponding table of contents entry. The table of contents entry uses the contents of the first `LineOfText` object that belongs to the `Paragraph` object.

ReorgVisitor   This subclass of the `DocumentVisitor` class is responsible for automatically separating a document into multiple files. It begins by being told to look for paragraphs that correspond to a certain level of organization in a document. It finds that level of organization in the internal ToC table. It fetches the style associated with that level of organization from the table. It then examines all of the `Paragraph` objects that directly belong to a `Document` object. It looks for `Paragraph` objects that have the style it fetched from the table. When it finds a `Paragraph` object with that style, it creates a new `Document` object. It moves the `Paragraph` object that it found, along with all of the `Paragraph` objects immediately following it that are at a lower level of organization, to the newly created `Document` object. It writes the new `Document` object and all of the paragraph objects now associated with it to a file. It replaces the `Paragraph` objects it moved from the original `Document` object with a new object that contains the name of the file that the moved paragraphs are now stored in.

FORCES

- There are a variety of operations that need to be performed on an object structure.
- The object structure is composed of objects that belong to different classes.
- The types of objects that occur in the object structure do not change often and the ways that they are connected are consistent and predictable.

SOLUTION

This section contains two forms of the Visitor pattern. The first is an ideal solution that produces a very clean result. Unfortunately there are many situations for which the ideal solution will not work or will be inefficient. The second form of the Visitor pattern works for a wider range of situations at the expense of introducing additional dependencies between classes.

Figure 8.33 shows a class diagram that demonstrates the roles that classes play in the ideal version of the Visitor pattern. Here is a description of the roles that classes play in Figure 8.33:

Client   An instance of a class in this role is responsible for manipulating an object structure and the objects that constitute it. It uses `ConcreteVisitor` objects to perform computations on the object structures for which it is responsible.

ObjectStructure   An instance of a class in this role serves as the root object of an object structure. When visiting objects in an object structure, a `Visitor` object begins with an instance of an `ObjectStructure` class and then moves on to other objects in the object structure.

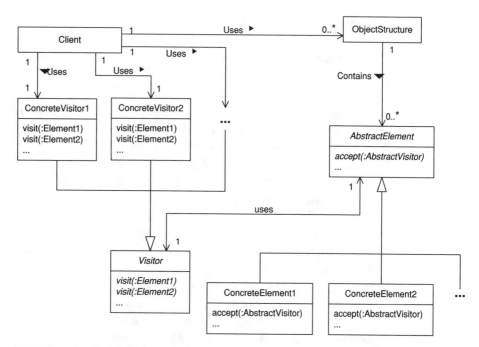

FIGURE 8.33 Ideal Visitor pattern.

It is possible for a class to participate in the Visitor pattern in the `ObjectStructure` role and also to participate in the `ConcreteElement` role as an element of the object structure.

AbstractElement   A class in this role is an abstract superclass of the objects that comprise an object structure. It defines an abstract method shown in Figure 8.33 as `accept`. It takes an `AbstractVisitor` object as its argument. Subclasses of an `AbstractElement` class provide an implementation of `accept` that calls a method of the `AbstractVisitor` object and then passes the `AbstractVisitor` object to the `accept` method of other `AbstractElement` objects.

ConcreteElement1,ConcreteElement2   An instance of a class in this role is an element of an object structure. Computations are done on the objects of an object structure by passing an `AbstractVisitor` object to the `ConcreteElement` object's `accept` method. The `accept` method passes the `ConcreteElement` object to one of the `AbstractVisitor` object's methods so that it can include the `ConcreteElement` object in its computation. When this is done, the `ConcreteElement` object passes the `AbstractVisitor` object to another `ConcreteElement` object's `accept` method.

Visitor   A class in this role is an abstract superclass of classes that perform computations on the elements of an object structure. It defines a method for each class that its subclasses will visit, so that their instances can pass themselves to `Visitor` objects to be included in their computations.

ConcreteVisitor1,ConcreteVisitor2   Instances of classes in this role comprise an object structure.

Figure 8.34 shows a collaboration diagram that demonstrates more clearly how `Visitor` objects collaborate with object structures. It shows the collaboration between a `Visitor` object and the elements of an object structure. After a `Visitor` object is presented to an `ObjectStructure` object, the `ObjectStructure` object passes the `Visitor` object to a `ConcreteElement` object's `accept` method. This `ConcreteElement` object passes itself to the `Visitor` object's `visit` method to allow that object to include the `Visitor` object in its computation. The `ConcreteElement` object then passes the `Visitor` object to another `ConcreteElement` object so that the `Visitor` object may visit it. The cycle continues on, with the `Visitor` object being passed on to other `ConcreteElement` objects. A `ConcreteElement` object may be associated with any number of other `ConcreteElement` objects. It may pass a `Visitor` object to some, all, or none of its associated `ConcreteElement` objects.

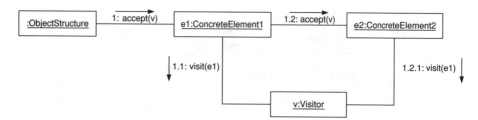

FIGURE 8.34 Ideal Visitor collaboration.

In this version of the Visitor pattern, the `AbstractElement` objects determine which elements of an object structure a `Visitor` object visits and the order in which it visits them. This works well in cases where it works for all `Visitor` objects to follow the same path in visiting elements of an object structure. It has the advantage of keeping `Visitor` classes independent of the structure of the object structure. However, there are situations where this does not work. These situations include:

- Visitors that modify an object structure. The example in the "Context" section of a `Visitor` object that splits a document into multiple files is such a situation.
- Object structures that are so large that it would add an unacceptable amount of execution time for a `Visitor` to visit every object when it only needs to visit a small subset of the objects in the structure.

Figure 8.35 shows another version of the Visitor pattern. In this version of the Visitor pattern, `Visitor` classes are responsible for navigating their own way through an object structure. Visitors organized in this way are able to modify an object structure or selectively navigate it. The drawback to this organization is that the `Visitor` classes are not as reusable because they have to make assumptions about the structure of an object structure in order to navigate through it.

In this version of the Visitor pattern, the `AbstractElement` class does not contain any methods specifically related to `Visitor` objects. Instead, the `Visitor` class defines methods that its subclasses use to navigate an object structure.

CONSEQUENCES

A direct consequence of the Visitor pattern is that `ConcreteElement` classes must provide access to enough of their state to allow `Visitor`

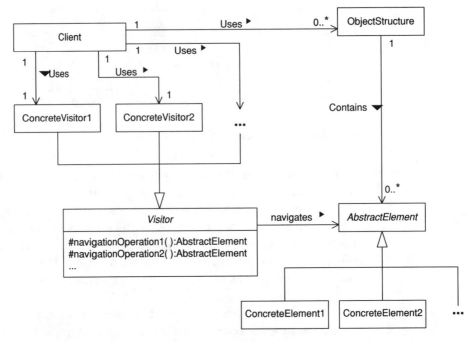

FIGURE 8.35 Visitor pattern.

objects to perform their computations. This may mean that you expose information that would otherwise be hidden by the class's encapsulation.

The Visitor pattern makes it easy to add new operations to an object structure. Because the ConcreteElement classes have no dependencies on Visitor classes, adding a new Visitor class does not require making any changes to an AbstractElement class or any of its subclasses.

The Visitor pattern allows the logic for an operation to be in one cohesive ConcreteVisitor class. This is easier to maintain than operations that are spread out over multiple ConcreteElement classes. A related consequence of the Visitor pattern is that a single Visitor object captures the state needed to perform an operation on an object structure. This is easier to maintain and more efficient than the way that state information has to be passed as discrete values from one object to another if the logic for operations is spread out over multiple classes.

One other consequence of the Visitor pattern is the additional work it takes to add new ConcreteElement classes. The ideal version of the Visitor pattern requires you to add a new visit method to each ConcreteVisitor class for each ConcreteElement class that you add. For the other version of the Visitor pattern, you may need to change the logic that Visitor classes use to navigate the object structure.

IMPLEMENTATION

When implementing the Visitor pattern, the first decision you will have to make is whether you can use the ideal version of the pattern. When it is possible, you should use the ideal version of the Visitor pattern because it requires less effort to implement and maintain. When you can't use the ideal version of the Visitor pattern, put as much of the logic as possible for navigating the object structure in the Visitor class rather than its subclasses. This will minimize the number of dependencies that ConcreteVisitor objects have on the object structure and will make maintenance easier.

CODE EXAMPLE

Following is the code for some of the classes presented in the table of contents design under the "Context" heading. First is code for the WordProcessor class that contains top level logic for a word processor. It is responsible for initiating operations that manipulate documents.

```
public class WordProcessor {
    // The document currently being edited
    private Document activeDocument;
...
    /**
     * Reorganize a document into subfiles.
     */
    private void reorg(int level) {
        new ReorgVisitor(activeDocument, level);
    } // reorg

    /**
     * Build a table of contents
     */
    private TOC buildTOC() {
        return new TOCVisitor(activeDocument).buildTOC();
    } // buildTOC()
} // class WordProcessor
```

The next listing is for the DocumentVisitor class. The DocumentVisitor class is an abstract superclass of classes that implement operations that have to visit many of the objects that constitute a document.

```
abstract class DocumentVisitor {
    private Document document;
```

```
            private int docIndex = 0;   // index used to navigate children
                                        // of document.
        DocumentVisitor(Document document) {
            this.document = document;
        } // constructor(Document)

        protected Document getDocument() { return document; }

        /**
         * Return next paragraph that is a direct part of the document
         */
        protected Paragraph getNextParagraph() {
            Document myDocument = document;
            while (docIndex < myDocument.getChildCount()) {
                DocumentElement docElement;
                docElement = myDocument.getChild(docIndex);
                docIndex += 1;
                if (docElement instanceof Paragraph)
                    return (Paragraph)docElement;
            } // while
            return null;
        } // getNextParagraph()
    ...
} // class DocumentVisitor
```

The next listing is for the `ReorgVisitor` class, which is responsible for visiting the paragraphs of a document and moving those that are at a specified level of organization in the table of contents to a separate document.

```
class ReorgVisitor extends DocumentVisitor {
    private TocLevel[] levels;

    ReorgVisitor(Document document, int level) {
        super(document);
        this.levels = document.getTocLevels();
        Paragraph p;
        while ((p = getNextParagraph()) != null) {
            ...
        } // while
    } // constructor(Document)
} // class ReorgVisitor
```

As you can see from the preceding listing, the `ReorgVisitor` class concerns itself with `Document` and `Paragraph` objects.

The final listing is for the `TOCVisitor` class. The `TOCVisitor` class is responsible for building a table of contents. It navigates more deeply into a document's object structure, concerning itself with `Document` objects, `Paragraph` objects, and `LineOfText` objects. Its interest in `LineOfText` objects is that a table of contents entry will contain the text of the first

`LineOfText` object in the paragraph that the table of contents entry corresponds to.

```
class TOCVisitor extends DocumentVisitor {
    private Hashtable tocStyles = new Hashtable();

    TOCVisitor(Document document) {
        super(document);
        TocLevel[] levels = document.getTocLevels();
        // put styles in a hashtable.
        for (int i=0; i < levels.length; i++) {
            tocStyles.put(levels[i].getStyle(), levels[i]);
        } // for
    } // constructor(Document)

    TOC buildTOC() {
        TOC toc = new TOC();
        Paragraph p;
        while ((p = getNextParagraph()) != null) {
            String styleName = p.getStyle();
            if (styleName != null) {
                TocLevel level = (TocLevel)tocStyles.get(styleName);
                if (level != null) {
                    LineOfText firstLine = null;
                    for (int i = 0; i < p.getChildCount(); i++) {
                        DocumentElement e = p.getChild(i);
                        if (e instanceof LineOfText) {
                            firstLine = (LineOfText)e;
                            break;
                        } // if
                        ...
                    } // for
                } // if
            } // if
        } // while
        return toc;
    } // buildTOC()
} // class TOCVisitor
```

RELATED PATTERNS

Iterator   The Iterator pattern is an alternative to the Visitor pattern when the object structure to be navigated has a linear structure.

Little Language   In the Little Language pattern, you can use the Visitor Pattern to implement the interpreter part of the pattern.

Composite   The Visitor pattern is often used with object structures that are organized according to the Composite pattern.

Concurrency Patterns

The patterns in this chapter involve coordinating concurrent operations. These patterns primarily address two different types of problems:

1. **Shared resources.**   When concurrent operations access the same data or other type of shared resource, there may be the possibility that the operations will interfere with each other if they access the resource at the same time. To ensure that such operations execute correctly, the operations must be constrained to access their

shared resource one at a time. However, if the operations are overly constrained, then they may deadlock and not be able to finish executing.

Deadlock is a situation in which one operation waits for another operation to do something before it proceeds. Because each operation is waiting for the other to do something, they both wait forever and never do anything.

2. **Sequence of operations.** If operations are constrained to access a shared resource one at a time, then it may be necessary to ensure that they access the shared resource in a particular order. For example, an object cannot be removed from a data structure before it is added to the data structure.

The Single Threaded Execution pattern is the most important pattern in this chapter to know. Most shared resource issues can be resolved with just the Single Threaded Execution pattern. Situations where the sequence of operations matters are less common.

Single Threaded Execution [Grand98]

The Single Threaded Execution pattern is also known as Critical Section.

SYNOPSIS

Some methods access data or other shared resources in a way that produces incorrect results if there are concurrent calls to a method and both calls access the data or other resource at the same time. The Single Threaded Execution pattern solves this problem by preventing concurrent calls to the method from resulting in concurrent executions of the method.

CONTEXT

Suppose you are writing software for a system that monitors the flow of traffic on a major highway. At strategic locations on the highway, sensors in the road monitor the number of cars passing per minute. The sensors send information to a central computer that controls electronic signs located near major interchanges. The signs display messages to drivers, advising them of traffic conditions so that they can select alternate routes.

At the places in the road where sensors measure the flow of cars, there is a sensor for each traffic lane. The sensor in each lane is wired to a controller that totals the number of cars that pass that place in the road each minute. The controller is attached to a transmitter that transmits each minute's total to the central computer. Figure 9.1 shows a class diagram that demonstrates these relationships.

Figure 9.1 contains the following classes:

TrafficSensor   Each instance of this class corresponds to a physical sensor device. Each time a vehicle passes a physical sensor device, the corresponding instance of the `TrafficSensor` class calls a `TrafficSensorController` object's `vehiclePassed` method. Each `TrafficSensor` object will have its own thread to allow it to handle inputs from its associated sensor asynchronously of other sensors.

TrafficTransmitter   Instances of this class are responsible for transmitting the number of vehicles that pass a place on the road each minute. A

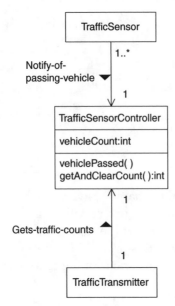

FIGURE 9.1 Traffic sensor classes.

`TrafficTransmitter` object gets the number of vehicles that have passed a place on the road by calling the `getAndClearCount` method of its corresponding `TrafficSensorController` object. The `TrafficSensorController` object's `getAndClearCount` method returns the number of vehicles that have passed the sensors since the previous call to the `getAndClearCount` method.

TrafficSensorController   Instances of the `TrafficSensor` class and the `TrafficTransmitter` class call the methods of the `TrafficSensorController` class to update, fetch, and clear the number of vehicles that have passed a place on the road.

It is possible for two `TrafficSensor` objects to call a `TrafficSensorController` object's `vehiclePassed` method at the same time. If both calls execute at the same time, they produce an incorrect result. Each call to the `vehiclePassed` method is supposed to increase the vehicle count by one. However, if two calls to the `vehiclePassed` method execute at the same time, the vehicle count is incremented by one instead of two. Here is the sequence of events that will occur if both calls execute at the same time:

- Both calls fetch the same value of `vehicleCount` at the same time.
- Both calls add one to the same value.
- Both calls store the same value in `vehicleCount`.

Clearly, allowing more than one call to the vehiclePassed method to execute at the same time will result in the undercounting of passing vehicles. Though a slight undercount of vehicles may not be a serious problem for this application, there is a similar problem that is more serious.

A TrafficTransmitter object periodically calls a TrafficSensorController object's getAndClearCount method. The getAndClearCount method fetches the value of the TrafficSensorController object's vehicleCount variable and then sets it to zero. If a TrafficSensorController object's vehiclePassed method and getAndClearCount method are called at the same time, this creates a situation called a *race condition*.

A race condition is a situation whose outcome depends on the order in which concurrent operations finish. If the getAndClearCount method finishes last, then it sets the value of the vehicleCount variable to zero, wiping out the result of the call to the vehiclePassed method. This is just another way for undercounts to happen. However, the problem is more serious if the vehiclePassed method finishes last.

If the vehiclePassed method finishes last, it replaces the zero set by the getAndClearCount method with a value equal to the value it fetched plus one. This means that the next call to the getAndClearCount method will return a value that includes vehicles counted before the previous call to the getAndClearCount method. An overcount like this could be large enough to convince the central computer that a traffic jam is starting and that it should display messages on the electronic signs suggesting that drivers follow alternate routes. An error like this could cause a traffic jam.

A simple way to avoid these problems is to require that no more than one thread at a time is executing a TrafficSensorController object's vehiclePassed method or getAndClearCount method. You can indicate this design decision by indicating that the concurrency of these methods is guarded: In a UML drawing, indicating that a method's concurrency is guarded is equivalent to declaring it synchronized in Java (see Figure 9.2).

Any number of threads may call the guarded methods of the same object at the same time. However, only one thread at a time is allowed to execute the object's guarded methods. While one thread is executing an object's guarded methods, other threads will wait until that thread is finished. This ensures single threaded execution of an object's guarded methods.

FORCES

- A class implements methods that update or set instance or class variables.

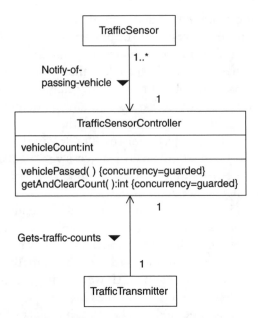

FIGURE 9.2 Synchronized traffic sensor classes.

- A class implements methods that manipulate external resources in a way that will work correctly only if the methods are executed by one thread at a time.
- The class's methods may be called concurrently by different threads.

SOLUTION

The Single Threaded Execution pattern ensures that operations that cannot be correctly performed concurrently are not performed concurrently. It accomplishes this by making methods that should not be executed concurrently guarded. Figure 9.3 shows the general case.

The class in Figure 9.3 has two kinds of methods. It has unguarded methods named safeOp1, safeOp2... that can safely be called concurrently by different threads. It has synchronized methods named unsafeOp1, unsafeOp2... that cannot safely be executed concurrently by different threads. When different threads call the guarded methods of a Resource object at the same time, only one tread at a time is allowed to execute the method. The rest of the threads wait for that thread to finish.

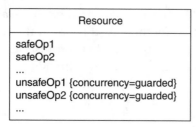

FIGURE 9.3 Single Threaded Execution pattern.

CONSEQUENCES

- If a class has methods that access variables or other resources in a way that is not thread-safe, making all of its methods guarded that perform thread-unsafe accesses to resources makes them thread-safe.
- It is often the case that it takes longer to call a guarded method than an unguarded method. Making methods guarded that do not need to be can reduce performance.
- Making methods guarded can introduce the opportunity for threads to become *deadlocked*. Deadlock occurs when two threads each have the exclusive use of a resource and each thread waits for the other to release the other's resource before continuing. Since each thread is waiting for a resource that the other thread already has exclusive access to, both threads will wait forever without gaining access to the resource. Consider the example collaboration diagram in Figure 9.4.

  In Figure 9.4, thread 1a calls object x's foo method and thread 1b calls object y's bar method at the same time. Thread 1a then calls object y's bar method and waits for thread 1b to finish its call to that

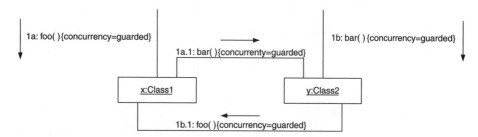

FIGURE 9.4 Deadlock.

method. Thread 1b calls object x's foo method and waits for thread 1a to finish its call to that method. At this point, the two threads are deadlocked. Each is waiting for the other to finish its call.

■ Deadlock can also involve more than two threads.

IMPLEMENTATION

Guarded methods are implemented in Java by declaring methods to be synchronized. It usually takes longer to call a synchronized method than an unsynchronized method. Consider the collaboration diagram in Figure 9.5.

Figure 9.5 shows that a synchronized method in class A calls class B's doIt method. The doIt method is synchronized. If the doIt method is called only from synchronized methods of class A, then as an optimization, it is possible to make the doIt method an unsynchronized method. It will still be executed by only one thread at a time because it is called only by methods that are executed only by one thread at a time.

This optimization is called *synchronization factoring*. Synchronization factoring is an unsafe optimization in the sense that if the program is modified so that concurrent calls can be made to the doIt method, it will stop working correctly. For this reason, if you decide that this optimization is worth doing, you should put comments in the design diagrams and code to warn and remind people that the optimization has been performed.

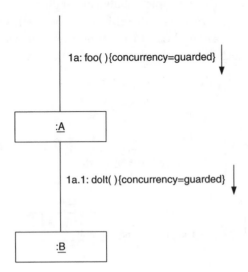

FIGURE 9.5 Synchronization factoring.

Some Java environments, such as Sun's hot spot, perform automatic synchronization factoring. When performed automatically by the run time environment, synchronization factoring is safe.

JAVA API USAGE

Many of the methods of the `java.util.Vector` class are synchronized to ensure single threaded access to the internal data structures of `Vector` objects.

CODE EXAMPLE

Following is some of the code that implements the traffic sensor design discussed under the "Context" heading. The first class shown is the `TrafficSensor` class. Instances of the `TrafficSensor` class are associated with a traffic sensor. A traffic sensor detects the passing of a vehicle over a place in a traffic lane. When the traffic sensor associated with an instance of the `TrafficSensor` class detects a passing vehicle, the instance's `detect` method is called. Its `detect` method is responsible for notifying other interested objects of the passing vehicle.

```java
public class TrafficSensor implements Runnable {
    private TrafficObserver observer;

    /**
     * Constructor
     * @param observer The object to notify when this object's
     *                 traffic sensor detects a passing vehicle.
     */
    public TrafficSensor(TrafficObserver observer) {
        this.observer = observer;
        new Thread(this).start();
    } // constructor(TrafficObserver)

    /**
     * Top level logic for this object's thread.
     */
    public void run() {
        monitorSensor();
    } // run()

    // This method calls this object's detect method when
    // its associated traffic sensor detects a passing vehicle.
    private native void monitorSensor() ;
```

```
// This method is called by the monitorSensor method to
// report the passing of a vehicle to this object's observer.
private void detect() {
    observer.vehiclePassed();
} // detect()
...
/**
 * Classes must implement this interface to be notified of
 * passing vehicles by a TrafficSensor object.
 */
public interface TrafficObserver {
    /**
     * called when a TrafficSensor detects a passing vehicle.
     */
    public void vehiclePassed();
} // interface TrafficObserver
} // class TrafficSensor
```

The next class shown is the `TrafficTransmitter` class. Instances of the `TrafficTransmitter` class are responsible for transmitting the number of vehicles that have passed a place in the road every minute.

```
public class TrafficTransmitter implements Runnable {
    private TrafficSensorController controller;
    private Thread myThread;

    /**
     * constructor.
     * @param controller The TrafficSensorController this object
     *                    will get vehicle counts from.
     */
    public TrafficTransmitter(TrafficSensorController controller) {
        this.controller = controller;
        ...
        myThread = new Thread(this);
        myThread.start();
    } // constructor(TrafficSensorController)

    /**
     * transmit a vehicle count every minute
     */
    public void run() {
        while (true) {
            try {
                myThread.sleep(60*1000);
                transmit(controller.getAndClearCount());
            } catch (InterruptedException e) {
            } // try
        } // while
    } // run()
```

```
    // Transmit a vehicle count.
    private native void transmit(int count);
} // class TrafficTransmitter
```

The final class shown here is the `TrafficSensorController` class. Instances of the `TrafficSensorController` class maintain a running total of the number of vehicles that have passed the traffic sensors associated with the instance. Notice that its methods are implemented as synchronized methods.

```
public class TrafficSensorController
            implements TrafficSensor.TrafficObserver {
    private int vehicleCount = 0;
...
    /**
     * This method is called when a traffic sensor detects a
     * passing vehicle. It increments the vehicle count by one.
     */
    public synchronized void vehiclePassed() {
        vehicleCount++;
    } // vehiclePassed()

    /**
     * Set the vehicle count to 0 and return the previous count.
     */
    public synchronized int getAndClearCount() {
        int count = vehicleCount;
        vehicleCount = 0;
        return count;
    } // getAndClearCount()
} // class TrafficSensorController
```

RELATED PATTERNS

Most other temporal patterns use the Single Threaded Execution pattern.

Guarded Suspension [Lea97]

SYNOPSIS

Suspends execution of a method call until a precondition is satisfied.

CONTEXT

Suppose that you have to create a class that implements a queue data structure. A queue is a first-in, first-out data structure. Objects are removed from a queue in the same order as they are added. Figure 9.6 shows a Queue class.

The class in Figure 9.6 has two methods. The push method adds objects to a queue and the pull method removes objects from the queue. When the queue is empty, you want the get method to wait until a call to add an object to the queue for it to return. The methods are synchronized to allow concurrent access to a Queue object. Simply making both methods synchronized creates a problem when there is a call to a Queue object's pull method and the queue is empty. The pull method waits for a call to the push method to provide it with an object to return. However, because they are both synchronized, calls to the push method cannot execute until the pull method returns, and the pull method will never return until a call to the push method executes.

A solution to this problem is to add a precondition to the pull method so that it does not execute when the queue is empty. Consider the collaboration diagram in Figure 9.7.

Figure 9.7 shows concurrent calls to a Queue object's push and pull methods. If the pull method is called when the Queue object's isEmpty method returns true, then the thread waits until isEmpty returns false

Queue
isEmpty( ):boolean push(:Object) {concurrency=guarded} pull( ):Object {concurrency=guarded}

FIGURE 9.6 Queue class.

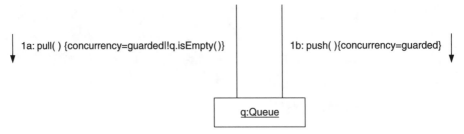

FIGURE 9.7 Queue collaboration.

before executing the `pull` method. Because it does not actually execute the `pull` method while the queue is empty, there is no problem with a call to the `push` method being able to add objects to an empty queue.

FORCES

- A class's methods must be synchronized to allow safe concurrent calls to them.
- An object may be in a state that makes it impossible for one of its synchronized methods to execute to completion. In order for the object to leave that state, a call to one of the object's other synchronized methods must execute. If a call to the first method is allowed to proceed while the object is in that state, it will deadlock and will never complete. Calls to the state changing method that allows the first method to complete will have to wait until it does complete, which will never happen.

SOLUTION

Consider the class diagram in Figure 9.8.

Figure 9.8 shows a class named `Widget` that has two synchronized methods named `foo` and `bar`. There is an exceptional state that `Widget` objects can enter. When a `Widget` object enters that exceptional state, its `isOK` method returns false; otherwise, it returns true. When a widget object enters the exceptional state, a call to its `bar` method may take it out of that state. There is no way to take it out of the exceptional state other than a call to `bar`. Taking a `Widget` object out of its exceptional state is a side effect of the `bar` method's main purpose, so it is not acceptable to call the `bar` method just to take a widget object out of its exceptional state.

A call to a `Widget` object's `foo` method cannot complete if the `Widget` object is in its exceptional state. If this happens, because the `foo` and `bar`

Widget
isOK( ):boolean foo( ) {concurrency=guarded} bar(:int) {concurrency=guarded}

FIGURE 9.8 Unguarded suspension class.

methods are synchronized, subsequent calls to the `Widget` object's `foo` and `bar` methods will not execute until the call to `foo` returns. The call to `foo` will not return until a call to bar takes the `Widget` object out of its exceptional state.

The purpose of the Guarded Suspension pattern is to avoid the deadlock situation that can occur when a thread is about to execute an object's synchronized method and the state of the object prevents the method from completing. If a method call occurs when an object is in a state that prevents the method from executing to completion, the Guarded Suspension pattern suspends the thread until the object is in a state that allows the method to complete. The collaboration diagram in Figure 9.9 illustrates this.

Notice that Figure 9.9 indicates a precondition that must be satisfied before a call to a `Widget` object executes. If a thread tries to call a `Widget` object's `foo` method when the `Widget` object's `isOK` method returns false, the thread will be forced to wait until `isOK` returns true before it is able to execute the `foo` method. While that thread is waiting for `isOK` to return true, other threads are free to call the `bar` method.

CONSEQUENCES

Using the Guarded Suspension pattern allows a thread to cope with an object that is in the wrong state to perform an operation. It copes by wait-

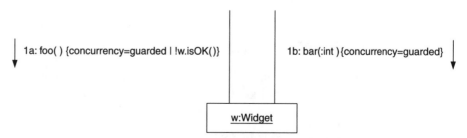

FIGURE 9.9 Guarded Suspension collaboration.

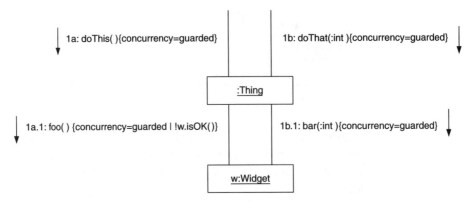

FIGURE 9.10 Guarded Suspension under nested synchronization.

ing, without owning the object's synchronization lock, until the object is in a state that allows it to perform the operation.

Because the Guarded Suspension pattern requires synchronized methods, it is possible for multiple threads to be waiting to execute a call to the same method of the same object. The Guarded Suspension pattern specifically does not deal with selecting which of the waiting threads will be allowed to proceed when the object is in a state that will allow the method to be executed. You can use the Scheduler pattern to accomplish this.

A situation that can make it difficult or impossible to use the Guarded Suspension pattern is nested synchronization. Consider the collaboration diagram in Figure 9.10.

In Figure 9.10, access to the `Widget` object is through the synchronized methods of a `Thing` object. This means that when thread `1a` calls the `Widget` object's `foo` method when the state of the `Widget` object causes its `isOK` method to return false, the thread will wait forever for the `Widget` object's `isOK` method to return true. The reason for this is that the methods of the `Thing` object are synchronized without any preconditions. This gives us the same problem that the Guarded Suspension pattern was intended to solve.

IMPLEMENTATION

The Guarded Suspension pattern is implemented using the `wait` and `notify` methods like this:

```
class Widget {
    synchronized void foo() {
```

```
        while (!isOK()) {
            wait();
        }
        ...
    } // foo

    synchronized void bar (int x) {
        ...
        notify();
    } // bar(int)
} // class Widget
```

The way that it works is that a method such as `foo` must satisfy pre-conditions before it actually begins executing. The very first thing that such a method does is test its preconditions in a while loop. When the pre-conditions are false, it calls the `wait` method.

Every class inherits the `wait` method from the `Object` class. When a thread calls an object's `wait` method, the `wait` method causes the thread to release the synchronization lock it holds on the object. The method then waits until it is notified that it may return. Then, as soon as the thread is able to recapture the lock, the `wait` method returns.

When the `wait` method returns, control returns to the top of the while loop, which tests the preconditions again. The reason for testing the preconditions in a loop is that between the time that the thread first tries to recapture the synchronization lock and the time that it captures it, another thread may have made the preconditions false.

The call to the `wait` method is notified that it should return when another method, such as `bar`, calls the object's `notify` method. Such methods call the `notify` method after they have changed the state of the object in a way that may satisfy a method's preconditions. The `notify` method is another method that all classes inherit from the `Object` class. What the `notify` method does is notify another thread that is waiting for the `wait` method to return that it should return.

If more than one thread is waiting, the `notify` method chooses one arbitrarily. Arbitrary selection works well in most situations. It does not work well for objects that have methods with different preconditions. Consider a situation in which multiple method calls are waiting to have their different preconditions satisfied. Arbitrary selection can result in a situation where the preconditions of one method call are satisfied, but the thread that gets notified is trying to execute a method with different pre-conditions that are not satisfied. In a situation like this it is possible for a method call to never complete because the method is never notified when its preconditions are satisfied.

For classes where arbitrary selection is not a good way to decide which thread to notify, there is an alternative. Their methods can call the notifyAll method. Rather than choosing one thread to notify, the notifyAll method notifies all waiting threads. This avoids the problem of not notifying the right thread. However, it may result in wasted machine cycles as a result of waking up threads waiting to execute method calls whose preconditions are not satisfied.

CODE EXAMPLE

Here is the code that implements the Queue class design discussed under the "Context" heading:

```
public class Queue {
    private Vector data = new Vector();

    /**
     * Put an object on the end of the queue
     * @param obj the object to put at end of queue
     */
    synchronized public void put(Object obj) {
        data.addElement(obj);
        notify();
    } // put(Object)

    /**
     * Get an object from the front of the queue
     * If queue is empty, waits until it is not empty.
     */
    synchronized public Object get() {
        while (data.size() == 0){
            try {
                wait();
            } catch (InterruptedException e) {
            } // try
        } // while
        Object obj = data.elementAt(0);
        data.removeElementAt(0);
        return obj;
    } // get()
} // class Queue
```

Notice that in the preceding listing, the call to the wait method is wrapped in a try statement that catches the InterruptedException that calls to the wait method may throw. Simply ignoring the InterruptedException that the wait method is declared to throw is the simplest thing to do for programs that do not expect the `wait` method to actually throw an `InterruptedException`. See the discussion of the Two-Phase Termination pattern for an explanation of when the `wait` method throws an `InterruptedException` and what you should do about it.

RELATED PATTERNS

Balking   The Balking pattern provides a different strategy for handling method calls to objects that are not in an appropriate state to execute the method calls.

Two-Phase Termination   Because the implementation of the Two-Phase Termination pattern usually involves the throwing and handling of `InterruptedException`, its implementation usually interacts with the Guarded Suspension pattern.

Balking [Lea97]

SYNOPSIS

If an object's method is called when the object is not in an appropriate state to execute that method, have the method return without doing anything.

CONTEXT

Suppose that you are writing a program to control an electronic toilet flusher. Such devices are intended for use in public bathrooms. The flusher has a light sensor mounted on its front. When the light sensor detects an increase in the light level, it assumes that a person has left the toilet and it triggers a flush. The electronic toilet flusher also has a button that can be used to manually trigger a flush. Figure 9.11 shows a class diagram demonstrating classes to model this behavior.

As shown in Figure 9.11, when a LightSensor object or a FlushButton object decides that there should be a flush, it requests the Flusher object to start a flush. It does this by calling the Flusher object's flush method. The flush method starts a flush and then returns once the flush is started. This arrangement raises some concurrency issues that need to be resolved.

You will need to decide what happens when the flush method is called while there is already a flush in progress. You will also need to decide what happens when both the LightSensor object and the FlushButton object call the Flusher object's flush method at the same time.

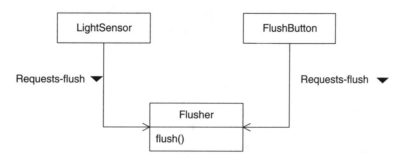

FIGURE 9.11 Flusher classes.

The three most obvious choices for how to handle a call to the `flush` method while there is a flush in progress are:

1. **Start a new flush immediately.** Starting a new flush while a flush is already in progress has the same effect as making the flush in progress last longer than a normal flush. The optimal length of a normal flush has been determined through experience. A longer flush would be a waste of water, so this is not a good option.
2. **Wait until the current flush finishes and immediately start another flush.** This option effectively doubles the length of a flush, so it is a bigger waste of water than the first option.
3. **Do nothing.** This option wastes no water, so it is the best choice.

When there are two concurrent calls to the flush method, allowing one to execute and ignoring the other is also a good strategy. Like option 3, it wastes no water.

Suppose that a call is made to an object's method when the object is not in a state to properly execute the method. If the method handles the situation by returning without performing its normal function, we say that the method has *balked*. UML does not have a standard way of indicating a method call with balking behavior. The technique used in this book to represent a method call that exhibits balking behavior is an arrow that curves back on itself, as shown in Figure 9.12.

FORCES

- An object may be in a state in which it is inappropriate to execute a method call.
- Postponing execution of a method call until the object is in an appropriate state is an inappropriate policy for the problem at hand.
- Calls made to an object's method when the object is not in an appropriate state to execute the method may be safely ignored.

FIGURE 9.12 Flusher collaboration.

FIGURE 9.13 Balking collaboration.

SOLUTION

Figure 9.13 shows objects collaborating in the Balking pattern.

In Figure 9.13, a `Client` object calls the `doIt` method of a `Service` object. The back-curved arrow indicates that the call may balk. If the `Service` object's `doIt` method is called when the `Service` object is in a state that is inappropriate for executing a call to its `doIt` method, then the method returns without having performed its usual functions.

The `doIt` method returns a result, indicated in the diagram as `didIt`, that indicates if the method performed its normal functions or balked.

CONSEQUENCES

- Method calls are not executed if they are made when their object is in an inappropriate state.
- Calling a method that can balk means that the method may not perform its expected functions, but may do nothing instead.

IMPLEMENTATION

If a method can balk, the first thing that it generally does is check the state of the object it belongs to, to determine if it should balk. It may be possible for the object's state to change to an inappropriate state for a balking method to run while that method is running. If this is possible, then an application of the Single Threaded Execution pattern can be used to prevent that inconsistency.

Instead of telling its callers that it balked by passing a return value, it is also reasonable for a method to notify its callers that it balked by throwing an exception. If a method's callers do not need to be interested in whether it balked, the method does not need to return this information.

CODE EXAMPLE

Here is the code for the `Flusher` class discussed under the "Context" heading:

```
public class Flusher {
   private boolean flushInProgress = false;

   /**
    * This method is called to start a flush.
    */
   public void flush() {
      synchronized (this) {
         if (flushInProgress)
            return;
         flushInProgress = true;
      }
      // code to start flush goes here.
      ...
   }

   /**
    * Notify this object that a flush has completed.
    */
   void flushCompleted() {
      flushInProgress = false;
   } // flushCompleted()
} // class Flusher
```

Notice the use of the synchronized statement in the flush method. It is there to ensure that if two calls to the flush method occur at the same time, one of the calls will proceed normally and the other will balk.

Also, notice that the flushCompleted method is not synchronized. This is because there is never a time when setting the flushInProgress variable to false will cause a problem.

RELATED PATTERNS

Double Checked Locking   The Double Checked Locking coding pattern (described in Volume 2) is structurally similar to the Balking pattern. Its intention is different. The Balking pattern avoids executing code when an object is in the wrong state. The Double Checked Locking pattern avoids executing code to avoid unnecessary work.

Guarded Suspension   The Guarded Suspension pattern provides an alternate way to handle method calls to objects that are not in an appropriate state to execute the method call.

Single Threaded Execution   The Balking pattern is often combined with the Single Threaded Execution pattern to coordinate changes to an object's state.

Scheduler [Lea97]

SYNOPSIS

Controls the order in which threads are scheduled to execute single threaded code using an object that explicitly sequences waiting threads. The `Scheduler` pattern provides a mechanism for implementing a scheduling policy. It is independent of any specific scheduling policy.

CONTEXT

Suppose that you are designing software to manage a building's physical security. The security system will support security checkpoints where a person must pass an identification badge through a scanner before passing through the checkpoint. When someone passes an identification badge through a checkpoint scanner, the checkpoint either allows the person to pass through or rejects the badge. Whenever someone passes through a security checkpoint or a badge is rejected, an entry will be printed on a hard-copy log in a central security office. Figure 9.14 shows a collaboration diagram demonstrating the basic collaboration.

Figure 9.14, an interaction diagram, shows `SecurityCheckpoint` objects creating `JournalEntry` objects and passing them to a `Printer` object's `print` method. Simple though it is, there is a problem with this organization. The problem occurs when people go through three or more checkpoints at about the same time. While the printer is printing the first

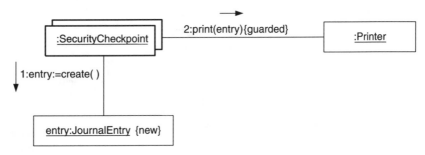

FIGURE 9.14 Security journal collaboration.

of the log entries, the other print calls wait. After the first log entry is printed, there is no guarantee which log entry will be printed next. This means that the log entries may not be printed in the same order as the security checkpoints sent them to the printer.

To ensure that journal entries are printed in the same order as they happen, you could simply put each journal entry in a queue and then print the journal entries in the same order as they arrive in a queue. Though this still leaves open the possibility of three or more journal entries arriving at the same time, the likelihood is greatly reduced. It may take as long as a second to print a journal entry. For the problem to occur, the other two journal entries must both arrive within that time period. Queuing a journal entry may take only about a microsecond. This reduces the likelihood of journal entries printing out of sequence by a factor of 1 million.

You could make the queuing of journal entries to be printed the responsibility of the `Printer` class. However, the queuing of method calls to be executed sequentially is a capability that has a lot of potential reuse if it is implemented as a separate class. The collaboration diagram in Figure 9.15 shows how a printer object could collaborate with another object to queue the execution of calls to its `print` method.

In Figure 9.15, a `SecurityCheckpoint` object calls the `printer` object's `print` method. The `print` method begins by calling the `Scheduler` object's `enter` method. The `enter` method does not return until the `Scheduler` object decides that it should. When the `print` method is finished, it calls the `Scheduler` object's `done` method. Between the time that the `enter` method returns and the `done` method is called, the `Scheduler` object assumes that the resource it is managing is busy. No call to its `enter` method will return while the `Scheduler` object believes that the resource it is managing is busy. This ensures that only one thread at a time executes the portion of the `print` method after its call to the `Scheduler` object's `enter` method until it calls the `Scheduler` object's `done` method.

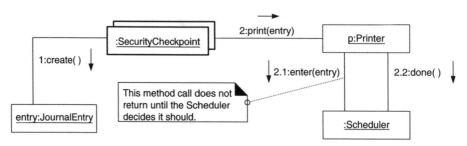

FIGURE 9.15 Security journal with scheduler.

The actual policy that the Scheduler object uses to decide when a call to the enter method returns is encapsulated in the Scheduler object. This allows the policy to change without affecting other objects. In this example, the policy you want when more than one call to the enter method is waiting to return is as follows:

- If the Scheduler object is not waiting for a call to its done method, then a call to its enter method will return immediately. The Scheduler object will then wait for a call to its done method.
- If the Scheduler object is waiting for a call to its done method, then a call to its enter method will wait to return until a call to the Scheduler object's done method. When the Scheduler object's done method is called, if there are any calls to its enter method waiting to return, then one of those enter method calls is chosen to return.
- If multiple calls to a Scheduler object's enter method are waiting to return, then the Scheduler object must select the next enter method call to be allowed to return. It will select the one that was passed a JournalEntry object with the earliest timestamp. If more than one JournalEntry object has the same earliest timestamp, then one of them is chosen arbitrarily.

In order for the Scheduler class to be able to compare the timestamps of JournalEntry objects and still be reusable, the Scheduler class must not refer directly to the JournalEntry class. However, it can refer to the JournalEntry class through an interface and still remain reusable. This is shown in Figure 9.16.

The Scheduler class does not know about the JournalEntry class. It merely knows that it schedules processing for objects that implement the ScheduleOrdering interface. This interface declares the scheduleBefore method that the Scheduler class calls to determine which of two ScheduleOrdering objects it should schedule first. Though the Scheduler class encapsulates a policy governing when processing will be allowed for a ScheduleOrdering object, it delegates the decision of what order they will be allowed to process in to the ScheduleOrdering object.

FORCES

- Multiple threads may need to access a resource at the same time and only one thread at a time may access the resource.
- The program's requirements imply constraints on the order in which threads should access the resource.

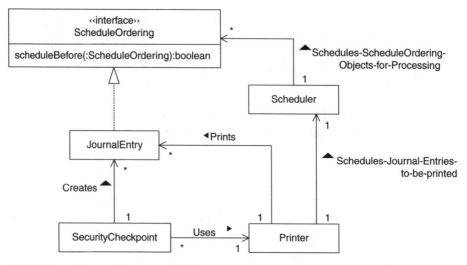

FIGURE 9.16 Journal entry scheduling classes.

SOLUTION

The Scheduler pattern uses an object to explicitly schedule concurrent requests by threads for nonconcurrent processing. Figure 9.17 shows the roles that classes play in the Scheduler pattern.

Here are the descriptions of the roles the classes play in the Scheduler pattern:

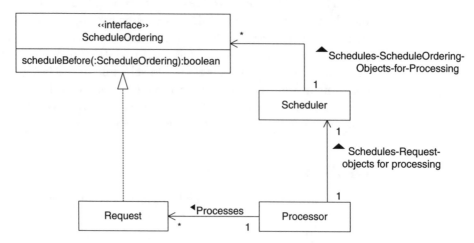

FIGURE 9.17 Scheduler classes.

Request   Classes in this role must implement the interface in the ScheduleOrdering role. Request objects encapsulate a request for a Processor object to do something.

Processor   Instances of classes in this role perform a computation described by a Request object. They may be presented with more than one Request object to process at a time, but they can process only one at a time. A Processor object delegates to a Scheduler object the responsibility for scheduling Request objects for processing, one at a time.

Scheduler   Instances of classes in this role schedule Request objects for processing by a Processor object. To promote reusability, a Scheduler class does not have any knowledge of the Request class that it schedules. Instead, it accesses Request objects through the ScheduleOrdering interface that they implement.

A class in this role is responsible for deciding when the next request will run. It is not responsible for the order in which the requests will run. It delegates that responsibility to a ScheduleOrdering interface.

ScheduleOrdering   Request objects implement an interface that is in this role. Interfaces in this role serve two purposes:

1. By referring to a ScheduleOrdering interface, Processor classes avoid a dependency on a Request class.
2. By calling methods defined by the ScheduleOrdering interface, Scheduler classes are able to delegate the decision of which Request object will be processed next, which increases the reusability of Scheduler classes. The class diagram in Figure 9.17 indicates one such method, named scheduleBefore.

The interaction between a Processor object and a Scheduler object occurs in two stages, as is shown by Figure 9.18.

The interaction in Figure 9.18 begins with a call to a Processor object's doIt method. The very first thing the doIt method does is call the enter method of the Scheduler object associated with the Processor object. If there is no other thread currently executing the rest of the doIt method, then the enter method returns immediately. After the enter method returns, the Scheduler object knows that the resource that it is managing is busy. While its resource is busy, any calls to the Scheduler object's enter method will not return until the resource is not busy and the Scheduler object decides that it is that call's turn to return.

After its enter method returns, a Scheduler object considers the resource it manages to be busy until the Scheduler object's done method

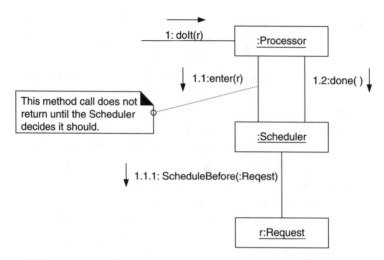

FIGURE 9.18 Scheduler interaction.

is called. When one thread makes a valid call to a `Scheduler` object's `done` method, if any threads are waiting to return from the `Scheduler` object's `enter` method then one of them returns.

If a call to a `Scheduler` object's `enter` method must wait before it returns and there are other calls waiting to return from the `enter` method, then the `Scheduler` object must decide which call will return next. It decides by consulting the `Request` objects that were passed into those calls. It does this indirectly by calling methods declared for that purpose by the `ScheduleOrdering` interface and implemented by the `Request` object.

CONSEQUENCES

- The Scheduler pattern provides a way to explicitly control when threads may execute a piece of code.
- The scheduling policy is encapsulated in its own class and is reusable.
- Using the Scheduler pattern adds significant overhead beyond what is required to make a simple call to a synchronized method.

IMPLEMENTATION

In some applications of the Scheduler pattern, the `Scheduler` class implements a scheduling policy that does not require it to consult `Request` objects to determine the order in which calls to its enter method will return. An example of such a policy is to allow calls to the enter method to return in the order in which they were called. In such cases, there is no need to pass Request objects into the enter method or to have a ScheduleOrdering interface. Another example of such a policy is to not care about the order in which requests are scheduled, but to require at least five minutes between the end of one task and the beginning of another.

CODE EXAMPLE

Here is some of the code that implements the print-scheduling design discussed under the "Context" heading. The first listing is for the Printer class that manages the printing of security checkpoint journal entries.

```
class Printer {
    private Scheduler scheduler = new Scheduler();
    public void print(JournalEntry j) {
        try {
            scheduler.enter(j);
            ...
        } catch (InterruptedException e) {
        } //try
        scheduler.done();
    } // print(JournalEntry)
} // class Printer
```

Each Printer object uses a Scheduler object to schedule concurrent calls to its print method so that they print sequentially in the order of their timestamps. It begins by calling the Scheduler object's enter method, passing it the JournalEntry object to be printed. The call does not return until the Scheduler object decides that it is the JournalEntry object's turn to print.

The print method ends by calling the Scheduler object's done method. A call to the done method tells the Scheduler object that the JournalEntry object has been printed and another JournalEntry object can have its turn to be printed.

Here is the source for the Scheduler class:

```
public class Scheduler {
    private Thread runningThread;
```

The runningThread variable is null when the resource that a Scheduler object manages is not busy. It contains a reference to the thread using the resource when the resource is busy.

```
private ArrayList waitingRequests = new ArrayList();
private ArrayList waitingThreads = new ArrayList();
```

An invariant for this class is that a request and its corresponding thread are in `waitingRequests` and `waitingThreads` only while its call to the `enter` method is waiting to return.

The `enter` method is called before a thread starts using a managed resource. The `enter` method does not return until the managed resource is not busy and this `Scheduler` object decides it is the method call's turn to return.

```
public void enter(ScheduleOrdering s) throws InterruptedException {
    Thread thisThread = Thread.currentThread();

    // When the managed resource is not busy, synchronize on
    // this object to ensure that two concurrent calls to
    // enter do not both return immediately.
    synchronized (this) {
        if (runningThread == null) {
            runningThread = thisThread;
            return;
        } // if
        waitingThreads.add(thisThread);
        waitingRequests.add(s);
    } // synchronized (this)
    synchronized (thisThread) {
        while (thisThread != runningThread) {
            thisThread.wait();
        } // while
    } // synchronized (thisThread)
    synchronized (this) {
        int i = waitingThreads.indexOf(thisThread);
        waitingThreads.remove(i);
        waitingRequests.remove(i);
    } // synchronized (this)
} // enter(ScheduleOrdering)
```

A call to the `done` method indicates that the current thread is finished with the managed resource.

```
synchronized public void done() {
    if (runningThread != Thread.currentThread())
        throw new IllegalStateException("Wrong Thread");
    int waitCount = waitingThreads.size();
    if (waitCount <= 0)
        runningThread = null;
    else if (waitCount == 1) {
        runningThread = (Thread)waitingThreads.get(0);
```

```
            waitingThreads.remove(0);
        } else {
            int next = waitCount - 1;
            ScheduleOrdering nextRequest;
            nextRequest = ScheduleOrdering
                            waitingRequests.get(next);
            for (int i = waitCount-2; i>=0; i--) {
                ScheduleOrdering r;
                r = (ScheduleOrdering)waitingRequests.get(i);
                if (r.scheduleBefore(nextRequest)) {
                    next = i;
                    nextRequest = (ScheduleOrdering)
                                    waitingRequests.get(next);
                } // if
            } // for
            runningThread = (Thread)waitingThreads.get(next);
            synchronized (runningThread) {
                runningThread.notifyAll();
            } // synchronized (runningThread)
        } // if waitCount
    } // done()
} // class Scheduler
```

The done method uses the notifyAll method to wake up a thread, rather than the notify method, because it has no guarantee that there will not be another thread waiting to regain ownership of the lock on the runningThread object. If it used the notify method, and there were additional threads waiting to regain ownership of the runningThread object's lock, then the notify method could fail to wake up the right thread.

RELATED PATTERNS

Read/Write Lock   Implementations of the Read/Write Lock pattern usually use the Scheduler pattern to ensure fairness in scheduling.

Read/Write Lock [Lea97]

SYNOPSIS

Allows concurrent read access to an object but requires exclusive access for write operations.

CONTEXT

Suppose that you are developing software for conducting online auctions. Items will be put up for auction. People will access the online auction to see the current bid for an item. People will then decide whether to make a greater bid for the item. At a predetermined time, the auction will close, and the highest bidder at that time will get the item at the final bid price.

You expect that there will be many more requests to read the current bid for an item than to update it. You could use the Single Threaded Execution pattern to coordinate access to bids. Though this will ensure correct results, it could unnecessarily limit responsiveness. When multiple users want to read a current bid at the same time, Single Threaded Execution requires that only one user at a time be allowed to read the current bid. This unnecessarily forces users who just want to read the current bid to wait for other users who just want to read the current bid.

There is no reason to prevent multiple users from reading the current bid at the same time. Single threaded execution is required only for updates to the current bid. Updates to the current bid must be processed one at a time to ensure that updates that do not increase the value of the current bid are rejected.

The Read/Write Lock pattern avoids unnecessary waiting to read data by allowing concurrent reads of data but allowing only single threaded access to data when it is being updated. Consider the collaboration diagram in Figure 9.19.

Figure 9.19 shows multiple user interface objects calling a bid object's getBid and setBid methods. The getBid method waits until there are no calls to setBid waiting to complete before it returns the current bid. The setBid method waits for any executing calls to getBid or setBid to complete before it updates the current bid. The readWriteLock object encapsulates the logic that coordinates the execution of the getBid and setBid methods to allow it to be reused.

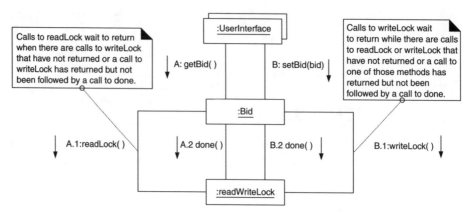

FIGURE 9.19 Bid collaboration.

All calls to a readWriteLock object's readLock method return immediately, unless there are any calls to its writeLock method executing or waiting to execute. If any calls to a readWriteLock object's writeLock method are executing or waiting to execute, then calls to its readLock method wait to return. They wait until all the writeLock calls have completed and there have been corresponding calls to its done method.

Calls to a readWriteLock object's writeLock method return immediately, unless one or more of the following are true:

- A previous call to writeLock is waiting to execute.
- A previous call to readLock or writeLock has finished executing, but there has been no corresponding call to the readWriteLock object's done method.
- There are any executing calls to the readWriteLock object's readLock method.

FORCES

- There is a need for read and write access to an object's state information.
- Any number of read operations may be performed on the object's state information concurrently. However, read operations are only guaranteed to return the correct value if there are no write operations executing at the same time as a read operation.

- Write operations on the object's state information need to be performed one at a time, to ensure their correctness.
- There will be concurrently initiated read operations.
- Allowing concurrently initiated read operations to run concurrently will improve responsiveness and throughput.
- The logic for coordinating read and write operations should be reusable.

SOLUTION

The Read/Write Lock pattern organizes a class so that concurrent calls to methods that fetch and store its instance information are coordinated by an instance of another class. Figure 9.20 shows the roles that classes play in the Read/Write Lock pattern.

A class in the Data role has methods to get and set its instance information. Any number of threads are allowed to concurrently get a Data object's instance information, so long as no thread is setting its instance information at the same time. On the other hand, its set operations must occur one at a time, while there are no get operations being executed. Data objects must coordinate their set and get operations so that they obey those restrictions.

The abstraction that Data objects use to coordinate get operations is a read lock. A Data object's get methods do not fetch any information until they get a read lock. Associated with each Data object is a ReadWriteLock object. Before one of its get methods gets anything, it calls the ReadWriteLock object's readLock method, which issues a read

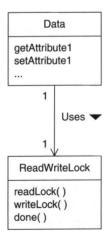

FIGURE 9.20 Read-Write Lock classes.

lock to the current thread. While the thread has a read lock, the get method can be sure that it is safe to get data from the object. This is because the ReadWriteLock object will not issue any write locks while there are any outstanding read locks. If there are any outstanding write locks when the ReadWriteLock object's readLock method is called, it does not return until all the outstanding write locks have been relinquished by calls to the ReadWriteLock object's done method. Otherwise, calls to the ReadWriteLock object's readLock method return immediately.

When a Data object's get method is finished getting data from the object, it calls the ReadWriteLock object's done method. A call to this method causes the current thread to relinquish its read lock.

Similarly, Data objects use a write lock abstraction to coordinate set operations. A Data object's set methods do not store any information until they get a write lock. Before one of a Data object's set methods stores any information, it calls the associated ReadWriteLock object's writeLock method, which issues a write lock to the current thread. While the thread has a write lock, the set method can be sure that it is safe to store data in the object. This is because the ReadWriteLock object issues write locks only when there are no outstanding read locks and no outstanding write locks. If there are any outstanding locks when the ReadWriteLock object's writeLock method is called, it does not return until all of the outstanding locks have been relinquished by calls to the ReadWriteLock object's done method.

The preceding constraints that govern when read and write locks are issued do not address the order in which read and write locks are issued. The order in which read locks are issued does not matter, so long as get operations can be performed concurrently. Since write operations are performed one at a time, the order in which write locks are issued should be the order in which the write locks are requested.

The one remaining ambiguity occurs when there are calls to both of a ReadWriteLock object's readLock and writeLock methods waiting to return and there are no outstanding locks. If get operations are intended to return the most current information, then this situation should result in the writeLock method returning first.

CONSEQUENCES

- The Read/Write Lock pattern coordinates concurrent calls to an object's get and set methods so that calls to the object's set methods do not interfere with each other or with calls to the object's get methods.

- If there are many concurrent calls to an object's get methods, using the Read/Write Lock pattern to coordinate the calls can result in better responsiveness and throughput than using the Single Threaded Execution pattern for that purpose. This is because the Read/Write Lock pattern allows concurrent calls to the object's get methods to execute concurrently.
- If there are relatively few concurrent calls to an object's get methods, using the Read/Write Lock pattern will result in lower throughput than using the Single Threaded Execution pattern. This is because the Read/Write Lock pattern spends more time managing individual calls. When there are concurrent get calls for it to manage, this results in a net improvement.

IMPLEMENTATION

Because read locks and write locks do not contain any information, there is no need to represent them as explicit objects. It is sufficient to just count them.

CODE EXAMPLE

Here is the code that implements the design discussed under the "Context" heading. The first listing is the `Bid` class, which is rather straightforward.

```
public class Bid {
    private int bid = 0;
    private ReadWriteLock lockManager = new ReadWriteLock();
...
    public int getBid() throws InterruptedException{
        lockManager.readLock();
        int bid = this.bid;
        lockManager.done();
        return bid;
    } // getBid()

    public void setBid(int bid) throws InterruptedException {
        lockManager.writeLock();
        if (bid > this.bid) {
            this.bid = bid;
        } // if
        lockManager.done();
    } // setBid(int)
} // class Bid
```

As you can see, the methods of the Bid class simply use a ReadWriteLock object to coordinate concurrent calls. They begin by calling the appropriate lock method before getting or setting any values. When they are finished, they call the ReadWriteLock object's done method to release the lock.

The ReadWriteLock class is more complex. As you read through its listing, you will notice that it focuses on two main things:

1. It carefully tracks state information in a way that will be consistent for all threads.
2. It ensures that all preconditions are met before its lock methods return.

Any other class that is responsible for enforcing a scheduling policy will have these implementation concerns.

```
public class ReadWriteLock {
    private int waitingForReadLock = 0;
    private int outstandingReadLocks = 0;
    private ArrayList waitingForWriteLock = new ArrayList();
    private Thread writeLockedThread;
```

A ReadWriteLock object uses the preceding instance variables to keep track of threads that have requested or been issued a read or write lock. It uses the list referred to by the waitingForWriteLock variable to keep track of threads that are waiting to get a write lock. Using this list, it is able to ensure that write locks are issued in the same order as they are requested.

A ReadWriteLock object uses the waitingForReadLock variable to count the number of threads waiting to get a read lock. Simple counting is sufficient for this because all threads waiting for a read lock will be allowed to get them at the same time. This means that there is no reason to keep track of the order in which threads request read locks.

A ReadWriteLock object uses the outstandingReadLocks variable to count the number of read locks that have been issued but have not yet been relinquished by the threads they were issued to.

A ReadWriteLock object uses the writeLockedThread variable to refer to the thread that currently has a write lock. If no thread currently has a write lock from the ReadWriteLock object, then the value of the writeLockedThread variable is null. By having a variable that refers to the thread that has been issued the write lock, the ReadWriteLock object can tell whether it awakened the thread to receive a write lock or the thread was awakened for another reason.

The `ReadWriteLock` class's `readLock` method follows. It issues a read lock and returns immediately, unless there is an outstanding write lock. All that it does to issue a read lock is increment the `outstandingReadLocks` variable.

```
synchronized public void readLock() throws InterruptedException {
    waitingForReadLock++;
    while (writeLockedThread != null) {
        wait();
    } // while
    waitingForReadLock--;
    outstandingReadLocks++;
} // readLock()
```

A listing of the `writeLock` method follows. The first thing you will notice is that it is longer than the `readLock` method. This is because it manages threads and a data structure. It begins by checking for the case in which there are no outstanding locks. If there are no outstanding locks, it issues a write lock immediately. Otherwise, it adds the current thread to a list that the `done` method uses as a queue. The current thread waits until the `done` method issues it a write lock and then the `writeLock` method finishes by removing the current thread from the list.

```
public void writeLock() throws InterruptedException {
    Thread thisThread;
    synchronized (this) {
        if writeLockedThread==null
        && outstandingReadLocks==0) {
            writeLockedThread = Thread.currentThread();
            return;
        } // if
        thisThread = Thread.currentThread();
        waitingForWriteLock.add(thisThread);
    } // synchronized(this)
    synchronized (thisThread) {
        while (thisThread != writeLockedThread) {
            thisThread.wait();
        } // while
    } // synchronized (thisThread)
    synchronized (this) {
        int i = waitingForWriteLock.indexOf(thisThread);
        waitingForWriteLock.remove(i);
    } // synchronized (this)
} // writeLock
```

The final part of the `ReadWriteLock` class is the `done` method. Threads call a `ReadWriteLock` object's `done` method to relinquish a lock that the `ReadWriteLock` object previously issued to them. The `done` method considers three cases:

1. **There are outstanding read locks, which implies that there is no outstanding write lock.** It relinquishes the read lock by decrementing the `outstandingReadLocks` variable. If there are no more outstanding read locks and threads are waiting to get a write lock, then it issues a write lock to the thread that has been waiting the longest to get a write lock. Then it wakes up the waiting thread.

2. **There is an outstanding write lock.** It causes the current thread to relinquish the write lock. If there are any threads waiting to get the write lock, it transfers the write lock to the thread that has been waiting the longest by having the `writeLockedThread` refer to that thread instead of the current thread. If there are no threads waiting to get a write lock and there are threads waiting to get a read lock, then it grants read locks to all of the threads that are waiting for a read lock.

3. **There are no outstanding locks.** If there are no outstanding locks, then the `done` method has been called at an inappropriate time, so it throws an `IllegalStateException`.

```
synchronized public void done() {
    if (outstandingReadLocks > 0) {
        outstandingReadLocks--;
        if ( outstandingReadLocks==0
            && waitingForWriteLock.size()>0) {
            writeLockedThread = (Thread)
                                waitingForWriteLock.get(0);
            writeLockedThread.notifyAll();
        } // if
    } else if (Thread.currentThread() == writeLockedThread) {
        if ( outstandingReadLocks==0
            && waitingForWriteLock.size()>0) {
            writeLockedThread = (Thread)
                                waitingForWriteLock.get(0);
            writeLockedThread.notifyAll();
        } else {
            writeLockedThread = null;
            if (waitingForReadLock > 0)
                notifyAll();
        } // if
    } else {
        throw new IllegalStateException("Thread does not have lock");
    } // if
```

```
    } // done()
} // class ReadWriteLock
```

One last detail to notice about the done method is that is uses the notifyAll method, rather than the notify method. When it wants to allow read locks to be issued, it calls the ReadWriteLock object's notifyAll method to allow all of the threads waiting to get a read lock to proceed. When it issues the write lock to a thread, it calls that thread's notifyAll method. Calling its notify method will work in most cases. However, in the case in which another thread is waiting to gain the synchronization lock of the thread to be issued the write lock, using the notify method could cause the wrong thread to wake up. Using the notifyAll method guarantees that the write thread will wake up.

RELATED PATTERNS

Single Threaded Execution   The Single Threaded Execution pattern is a good and simpler alternative to the Read/Write Lock pattern when most of the accesses to data are write accesses.

Scheduler   The Read/Write Lock pattern is a specialized form of the Scheduler pattern.

Producer-Consumer

SYNOPSIS

Coordinates the asynchronous production and consumption of information or objects.

CONTEXT

Suppose you are designing a trouble-ticket dispatching system. Customers will enter trouble tickets through web pages. Dispatchers will review the trouble tickets and forward them to the person or organization best suited to resolve the problem.

Any number of people may submit trouble tickets through the web page at any given time. There will usually be multiple dispatchers on duty. When a trouble ticket comes in, if there are any dispatchers who are not busy, the system will immediately give the trouble ticket to one of them. Otherwise, it will place the trouble ticket in a queue where the trouble ticket will wait its turn to be seen by a dispatcher and dispatched. Figure 9.21 shows a class diagram demonstrating a design for classes that implement this behavior.

Figure 9.21 shows a `Client` class whose instances are responsible for getting trouble tickets that have been filled out by users and placed in a `Queue` object. Trouble tickets stay in the `Queue` object until a `Dispatcher` object pulls them out of the `Queue` object.

The `Dispatcher` class is responsible for displaying trouble tickets to a dispatcher and then forwarding them to the destination selected by the dispatcher. When an instance of the `Dispatcher` class is not displaying a trouble ticket or forwarding it, it calls the `Queue` object's `pull` method to get another trouble ticket. If there are no trouble tickets in the `Queue` object, the `pull` method waits until it has a trouble ticket to return.

Figure 9.22 shows a collaboration diagram that demonstrates the interactions just described.

FORCES

■ Objects are produced or received asynchronously of their use or consumption.

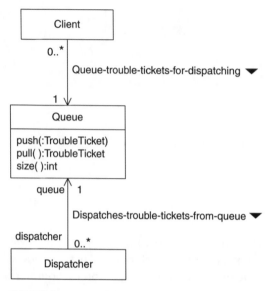

FIGURE 9.21 Trouble-ticket classes.

■ When an object is received or produced, there may not be any object available to use or consume it.

SOLUTION

The class diagram in Figure 9.23 show the roles in which classes participate in the Producer-Consumer pattern.

Here are the descriptions of the roles that classes can play in the Producer-Consumer pattern:

Producer   Instances of classes in this role supply objects that are used by Consumer objects. Instances of Producer classes produce objects asynchronously of the threads that consume them. This means that sometimes a Producer object will produce an object when all of the Consumer objects are busy processing other Consumer objects. Rather than wait for a Consumer object to become available, instances of Producer classes put the objects that they produce in a queue and then continue with whatever they do.

Queue   Instances of classes in this role act as a buffer for objects produced by instances of Producer classes. Instances of Producer classes place the objects that they produce in an instance of a Queue class. The objects remain there until a Consumer object pulls them out of the Queue object.

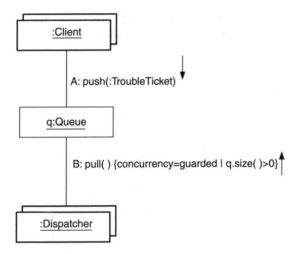

FIGURE 9.22 Trouble-ticket collaboration.

Consumer Instances of Consumer classes use the objects produced by
Producer objects. They get the objects that they use from a Queue
object. If the Queue object is empty, a Producer object that wants to get
an object from it must wait until a consumer object puts an object in
the Queue object.

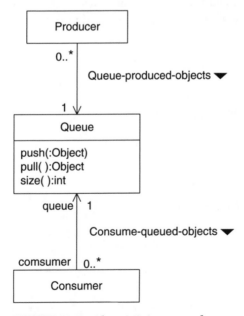

FIGURE 9.23 Producer-Consumer classes.

The collaboration diagram in Figure 9.24 shows the interactions between objects that participate in the Producer-Consumer pattern.

CONSEQUENCES

- Producer objects are able to deliver the objects they produce to a Queue object without having to wait for a Consumer object.
- When there are objects in the Queue object, Consumer objects are able to pull an object out of the queue without waiting. However, when the queue is empty and a Consumer object calls the Queue object's pull method, the pull method does not return until a Producer object puts an object in the queue.

IMPLEMENTATION

Some implementations of the Producer-Consumer pattern limit the queue to a maximum size. In those implementations, a special case to consider is that in which the queue is at its maximum size and a producer thread wants to put an object in the queue. The usual way to handle this is for the queue to use the Guarded Suspension pattern to force the producer thread to wait until a consumer thread removes an object from the queue. When there is room for the object that the producer wants to put in the queue, the producer thread is allowed to finish and proceed with whatever else it does.

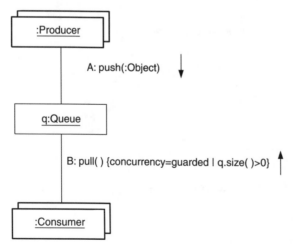

FIGURE 9.24 Producer-Consumer collaboration.

JAVA API USAGE

The core Java API includes the classes `java.io.PipedInputStream` and `java.io.PipedOutputStream`. Together, they implement a variant of the Producer-Consumer pattern called the Pipe pattern. The Pipe pattern involves only one `Producer` object and only one `Consumer` object. The Pipe pattern usually refers to the `Producer` object as a data source and the `Consumer` object as a data sink.

The `java.io.PipedInputStream` and `java.io.PipedOutputStream` classes jointly fill the role of the `Queue` class. They allow one thread to write a stream of bytes to one other thread. The threads perform their writes and reads asynchronously of each other, unless the internal buffer they use is empty or full.

CODE EXAMPLE

The following listings show the code that implements the design discussed under the "Context" heading. The first two listings shown are skeletal listings for the `Client` and `Dispatcher` classes.

```java
public class Client implements Runnable {
    private Queue queue;
    ...
    public void run() {
        TroubleTicket tkt = null;
        ...
        queue.push(tkt);
    } // run()
} // class Client

public class Dispatcher implements Runnable {
    private Queue queue;
    ...
    public void run() {
        TroubleTicket tkt = queue.pull();
        ...
    } // run()
} // class Dispatcher
```

The only things the `Client` and `Dispatcher` classes do that are interesting with respect to the Producer-Consumer pattern is to put objects into the queue and take them out.

The final listing is for the `Queue` class.

```java
public class Queue {
    private ArrayList data = new ArrayList();

    /**
     * Put an object on the end of the queue
     * @param obj the object to put at end of queue
     */
    synchronized public void push(TroubleTicket tkt) {
        data.add(tkt);
        notify();
    } // push(TroubleTicket)
    /**
     * Get a TroubleTicket from the front of the queue
     * If queue is empty, wait until it is not empty.
     */
    synchronized public TroubleTicket pull() {
        while (data.size() == 0){
            try {
                wait();
            } catch (InterruptedException e) {
            } // try
        } // while
        TroubleTicket tkt = (TroubleTicket)data.get(0);
        data.remove(0);
        return tkt;
    } // pull()

    /**
     * Return the number of trouble tickets in this queue.
     */
    public int size() {
        return data.size();
    } // size()
} // class Queue
```

RELATED PATTERNS

Guarded Suspension   The Producer-Consumer pattern uses the Guarded Suspension pattern to manage the situation of a Consumer object wanting to get an object from an empty queue.

Pipe   The Pipe pattern is a special case of the Producer-Consumer pattern that involves only one Producer object and only one Consumer object. The Pipe pattern usually refers to the Producer object as a data source and the Consumer object as a data sink.

Scheduler The Producer-Consumer pattern can be viewed as a special form of the Scheduler pattern that has scheduling policy with two notable features:

1. The scheduling policy is based on the availability of a resource.
2. The scheduler assigns the resource to a thread but does not need to regain control of the resource when the thread is done so it can reassign the resource to another thread.

Two-Phase Termination [Grand98]

SYNOPSIS

Provides for the orderly shutdown of a thread or process through the setting of a latch. The thread or process checks the value of the latch at strategic points in its execution.

CONTEXT

Suppose that you are responsible for writing a server that provides middle-tier logic for a stock-trading workstation. A client connects to the server. The client then indicates that it is interested in certain stocks. The server sends the current price of those stocks to the client. When the server receives information that shares of a stock have been traded, it reports the trade to clients who are interested in the stock.

Part of the internal mechanism the server uses to provide this service is to create a thread for each client. This thread is responsible for delivering information about stock trades to the client that it serves.

Aside from its core functions, there are administrative commands that the server must respond to. One of these commands forces the disconnection of a client. When the server is asked to disconnect a client, from an internal point of view this means shutting down the thread that is servicing that client and then releasing the related set of resources that the thread is using.

Another administrative command that the server must respond to is a command to shut down the entire server.

Both commands are similar in what they do. The main difference is in their scope. One command shuts down a single thread. The other command shuts down an entire process. In both cases, the implementation techniques are similar. Figure 9.25 shows a collaboration diagram that demonstrates how a server thread could be organized to shut down cleanly on request.

Figure 9.25 begins with a call to a `Session` object's `run` method. The `run` method first calls the `Session` object's `initialize` method. It then repeatedly calls the `Portfolio` object's `sendTransactionsToClient`

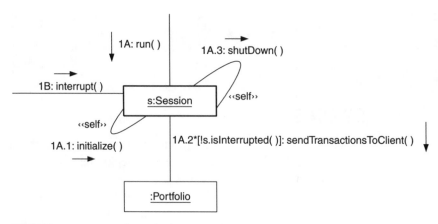

FIGURE 9.25 Server thread shutdown.

method. It keeps calling that method as long as the Session object's isInterrupted method returns false. The Session object's isInterrupted method returns false until the Session object's interrupt method is called.

The normal sequence of events that shuts down a session begins with a different thread than the one that called the run method. This other thread calls the Session object's interrupt method. The next time that the Session object calls its isInterrupted method, it returns true. The run method then stops calling the Portfolio object's sendTransactionsToClient method. It then calls the Session object's shutDown method, which performs any necessary cleanup operations.

The technique for shutting down a process in an orderly manner is similar to the technique for threads. When a command is received to shut down an entire process, it sets a latch that causes every thread in the process to shut down.

FORCES

- A thread or process is designed to run indefinitely.
- There could be unfortunate results if a thread or process is forcibly shut down without first having the chance to clean up after itself.
- When a thread or process is asked to shut down, it is acceptable for the thread or process to take a reasonable amount of time to clean up before shutting down.

SOLUTION

Shut down a thread or a process by asking the thread or process to terminate. Then expect it to comply with the request by first performing any necessary cleanup and then terminating.

Figure 9.26 shows a class diagram for a class that you might use to coordinate the shutdown of a process. Such a class is used to allow a process to receive a request to shut down and then clean up after itself before shutting down. Each of the process's threads call the isShutdownRequested method at strategic points in their execution. If it returns true, the thread cleans up and shuts down. When all the application threads have died, the process exits.

Shutting down an individual thread involves using a thread-specific latch. Every Java thread has one because it is part of the Thread class. It is set to true by calling the thread's interrupt method. It is queried by calling the thread's isInterrupted method.

CONSEQUENCES

■ Using the Two-Phase Termination pattern allows processes and threads to clean up after themselves before they terminate.
■ Using the Two-Phase Termination pattern can delay the termination of a process or thread for an unpredictable amount of time.

IMPLEMENTATION

After a process or thread has been requested to shut down, it can be difficult or impossible to determine if the process or thread will actually terminate until it does. For this reason, if there is any uncertainty that the thread or process will terminate after it has been requested to do so, after a predetermined amount of time the thread or process should be forcibly terminated.

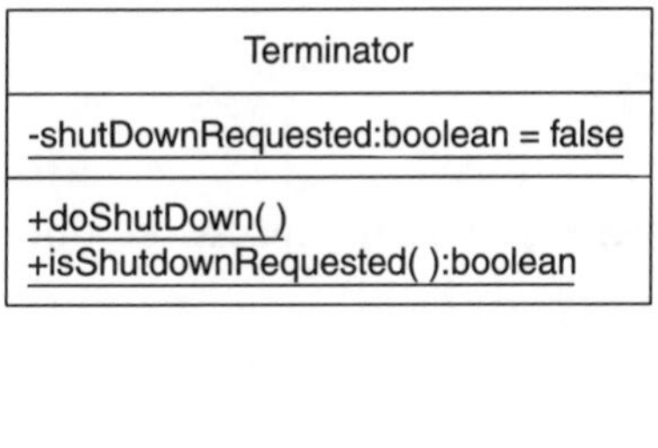

Terminator
-shutDownRequested:boolean = false
+doShutDown( ) +isShutdownRequested( ):boolean

FIGURE 9.26 Process shutdown.

You can forcibly terminate a thread by calling its stop method. The mechanism for forcibly terminating a process varies with the operating system.

Methods that set a termination latch to true do not need to be synchronized. Flag setting is idempotent. One or more threads can perform the operation, concurrently or not, and the result is still that the termination latch is set to true.

JAVA API USAGE

The core Java API does not make use of the Two-Phase Termination pattern. However, it does have features to support the Two-Phase Termination pattern.

To support the two-phase termination of threads, the Thread class provides the interrupt method to request a thread's termination. The Thread class also provides the isInterrupted method to allow a thread to find out if its termination has been requested.

There are some methods, such as sleep, that are known to put a thread in a wait state. There is an assumption that if a thread is asked to shut down while waiting for one of those methods to return, the thread will detect the request for its termination and comply as soon as the waiting method returns. To help insure the timeliness of a thread's shutdown, some methods that cause a thread to wait for something throw an InterruptedException if a thread is waiting for one of those methods to return when its interrupt method is called. The methods that can throw an InterruptedException include Thread.sleep, Thread.join and Object.wait. There are a number of others.

To support the shutdown of a process, when a thread dies, if there are no threads still alive that are not daemon threads, then the process shuts down.

Note that Java does not provide any direct way of detecting or catching signals or interrupts from an operating system that cause a process to shut down.

CODE EXAMPLE

Here is the code that implements the design discussed under the "Context" heading:

```
public class Session implements Runnable {
    private Thread myThread;
    private Portfolio portfolio;
    private Socket mySocket;
...
    public Session(Socket s) {
        myThread = new Thread(this);
        mySocket = s;
        ...
    } // constructor()

    public void run() {
        initialize();
        while (!myThread.interrupted()) {
            portfolio.sendTransactionsToClient(mySocket);
        } // while
        shutDown();
    } // run()

    /**
     * Request that this session terminate.
     */
    public void interrupt() {
        myThread.interrupt();
    } // interrupt()

    /**
     * Initialize this object.
     */
    private void initialize() {
    ...
    } // initialize()

    /**
     * perform cleanup for this object.
     */
    private void shutDown() {
    ...
    } // shutDown()
...
} // class Session
```

B I B L I O G R A P H Y

[ASU86] Alfred V. Aho, Ravi Seti, and Jeffery D. Ullman. *Compilers, Principles, Techniques and Tools*. Reading, Mass.: Addison-Wesley, 1997.

[Appleton97] Brad Appleton. "Patterns and Software: Essential Concepts and Terminology." *Object Magazine Online* 2(5). http://www.sigs.com/omo; http://www.enteract.com/~bradapp/docs/patterns-intro.html. May 1997.

[Bentley] Jon Louis Bentley. *Programming Pearls*. New York: ACM, 1986.

[BMRSS96] Frank Buschmann, Regine Meunier, Hans Rohnert, Peter Sommerlad, and Michael Stal. *A System of Patterns*. Chichester, U.K.: John Wiley & Sons, 1996.

[GoF95] Erich Gamma, Richard Helm, Ralph Johnson, and John Vlissides. *Design Patterns: Elements of Reusable Object-Oriented Software*. Reading, Mass.: Addison-Wesley, 1995.

[Grand98] The present volume.

[Larman98] Craig Larman. *Applying UML and Patterns*. Upper Saddle River, N.J.: Prentice Hall PTR, 1998.

[Lea97] Doug Lea. *Concurrent Programming in Java.* Reading, Mass.: Addison-Wesley, 1997.

[Woolf97] Bobby Woolf. "Null Object," in R. Martin, D. Riehle, and F. Buschmann (eds.), "Pattern Languages of Program Design 3." Reading, Mass.: Addison-Wesley, 1997, pp. 5–18.

A P P E N D I X

The CD-ROM

The CD-ROM contains the complete code for the examples that appear in the book, as well as evaluation copies of some software you might find useful:

- *Rational Rose 98* from Rational, Inc., is the most popular case tool. It is a leading visual modeling tool that allows developers to define and communicate a software architecture.
- *System Architect* from Popkin Software is the only case tool that covers the entire software life cycle within one tool. It integrates industry-leading support for all major areas of modeling, including object-oriented modeling with UML, relational data modeling, business process modeling, and structured analysis and design. This tool handles sharing of data within a work group particularly well.
- *Together/J Whiteboard Edition* from Object International is the first platform-independent UML modeler for enterprisewide software development that delivers simultaneous Round-trip Engineering for Java. Versions with Sun's VM for Windows 95/NT and Microsoft's VM for Windows 95/NT are included on the CD-ROM.

- *OptimizeIt 2.0 Professional* from Intuitive Systems is a comprehensive Java profiling tool that allows developers to understand and solve performance issues in their Java programs. You need to download a registration key before installing this software package.

The files for the figures in this book are located at the author's Web site at http://www.mindspring.com/~mgrand in .vsd format. Check the site for updates to the book as well.

User Assistance and Information

The software accompanying this book is being provided as is without warranty or support of any kind. Should you require basic installation assistance, or if your media is defective, please call our product support number at (212) 850-6194 weekdays between 9 A.M. and 4 P.M. Eastern Standard Time. Or, we can be reached via e-mail at: wprtusw@wiley.com.

To place additional orders or to request information about other Wiley products, please call (800) 879-4539.

You may contact the author of this book, Mark Grand, through his Web site at http://www.mindspring.com/~mgrand.

I N D E X

CUSTOMER NOTE: IF THIS BOOK IS ACCOMPANIED BY SOFTWARE, PLEASE READ THE FOLLOWING BEFORE OPENING THE PACKAGE.

To use this CD-ROM, your system must meet the following requirements:

Platform/Processor/Operating System. To use the Java examples, you must have a Java Virtual Machine installed on your machine. The demonstration applications included on the CD require a machine running Windows 95/NT or better with a Pentium processor.

RAM. The demo applications included on the CD require 8MB RAM minimum. Refer to the documentation for the specific application for exact RAM and hard drive space required.

Peripherals. CD-ROM drive. Internet browser installed required for navigation through the CD.